WORK, ORGANISATION AND LABOUR IN DUTCH SOCIETY

WORK, ORGANISATION AND LABOUR IN DUTCH SOCIETY

A State of the Art of the Research

Edited by

Gerard Evers
Tilburg University

Bert van Hees
SISWO Netherlands Universities Institute for Coordination of Research in Social Sciences

and

Joop Schippers
University of Utrecht

SPRINGER-SCIENCE+BUSINESS MEDIA, B.V.

A C.I.P. Catalogue record for this book is available from the Library of Congress.

ISBN 978-94-010-6013-4 ISBN 978-94-011-4794-1 (eBook)
DOI 10.1007/978-94-011-4794-1

Printed on acid-free paper

The book has been commissioned by the Netherlands' Universities
Institute for Coordination of Research in Social Sciences (SISWO)
Plantage Muidergracht 4, 1018 TV Amsterdam
Phone: 31(0)20-5270627, Fax: 31(0)20-6229430
e-mail: siswo@siswo.uva.nl http://www.siswo.uva.nl

PREFACE

Research on labour market, labour relations, quality of work, human resources management, organisation of work and related topics has always been an important element in the activities of SISWO. The Netherlands' Universities Institute for Coordination of Research in Social Sciences (SISWO), is a national agency that initiates and supports, both scientifically and organisationally, research endeavours on a great variety of themes. This is done by organising discussion groups, congresses and conferences, expert meetings, newsletters and publications.

For the field of labour and organisation, WESWA, the Netherlands' Universities Working Committee on Social Science Research of Labour and Organisation, is the inter-university network that, in close cooperation with SISWO, unites experts from Dutch universities.

WESWA and SISWO are convinced that an overview of the Dutch state of the art, in English, will be welcomed by an international audience.

This state of the art work on research into labour and organisation in The Netherlands was edited by Gerard Evers, Bert van Hees and Joop Schippers. I do hope that this book will receive the attention both within and outside our country that it deserves.

Dr. Johan G.M. Sterk, Director, SISWO

CONTENTS

INTRODUCING DUTCH ORGANISATION AND LABOUR RESEARCH

Gerard Evers, Bert van Hees and Joop Schippers

This book on Dutch Labour and Organisation Research covers six main fields:
- the labour market;
- industrial or labour relations;
- the quality of work and working life;
- human resources management;
- work and organisation; and
- gender studies.

In this introduction we first give the profile of the network of universitary researchers from which this book originates. In Section 2 we sketch the main disciplines involved in Labour and Organisation studies. Section 3 contains summaries of the six articles in this book. Finally, in Section 4, we reflect on a few major trends or developments in these fields.

1. THE WESWA NETWORK

WESWA stands for the Netherlands Universities Working Committee on Social Science, Labour and Organisation Research. The committee acts as a representative body of research experts from the Dutch universities. Its activities are supported by the Netherlands Universities Institute for Coordination of Research in Social Sciences (SISWO). The committee has evolved from a research evaluation committee on Labour and Organisation research proposals within the National Organisation of Sciences (NWO) to a congress committee for bi-annual congresses, after the National Organisation of Sciences stopped using broad range expert committees for evaluating research proposals. The location of the WESWA congress alternates between the universities.

The WESWA network comprises researchers from various disciplinary backgrounds: sociologists, management scientists, economists, psychologists, personnel and public administration scientists, and others. A number of researchers from private research and consultancy bureaus, institutes and firms are also affiliated.

Major fields and themes of the WESWA are industrial relations, labour market, personnel management, human resources management, organisation studies and networks, production structures and design (including logistics), quality of work and working life, gender studies, unpaid labour (informal and voluntary work), the position of labour in society (institution labour, policies towards labour e.g. education, structure of organisations, role in decision making), technical and organisational innovation.

While the field of organisation and labour studies in the Netherlands is extraordinarily diverse, elements of organisation and labour play a role in a number of disciplines, such as general economics, sociology, psychology, labour economics, the sociology of labour, organisational economics, the psychology of labour and organisation and are also found in pedagogy (training, management development), political sciences, technical sciences (ergonomics), etc. There are a number of research groups and schools which have a multidisciplinary basis: in management and policy sciences, public administration, organisation sciences, labour and social security/ welfare, etc. Finally, there are multidisciplinary research programmes on subjects such as gender or ethnicity, in which the subjects labour and organisation are found.

There is a lively network of publications, discussions and journals. Publications in the Dutch language reach a more specific audience of users and policy makers, public or media than the international publications. This makes for quicker communication, which is important in policy-related fields such as Labour and Organisation. A second reason for Dutch language journals to flourish is that translation has its costs and disadvantages, especially in less formal and more historical approaches. Certain fields of research are more internationally oriented, such as, for instance, the business economics subdiscipline, finance.

2. DISCIPLINES AND FIELDS IN LABOUR AND ORGANISATION STUDIES

If we make a rough distinction between organisation studies and labour studies, we can circumscribe these as follows.

Organisation studies covers, in principle, all organisational processes, elements of which are division of labour, structure, culture, process, behaviour, administration, information and decision making, management, environment, logistics, accounting, marketing, and strategy. It covers a great number of disciplines: sociology, economics, personnel sciences, management sciences and administrative sciences, public administration, psychology, anthropology, and political science.

Three major disciplines in organisation studies are the sociology of organisation, management science and organisational or business economics. We give a short overview of these here and we also add a few remarks on other organisational disciplines.

Labour studies covers research into labour markets, work (unpaid and paid, work and care, household and non-household work, etc.), labour relations, the institutionalisation and political position of labour in society. This overlaps somewhat with organisation studies, for example in the area of work and the management of work. The human resources management discipline can be seen as a sort of 'in between discipline'. Labour studies are carried out from various disciplinary bases. Its major disciplines include: labour economics, the sociology of labour, labour relations.[1] We give an overview of these and include the 'in between discipline' of HRM.

2.1. *Sociology of organisations*

Lammers, Mijs and Van Noort (1997) give an encompassing overview of both national and international research, starting with classical authors such as Weber, Marx and Tönnies and ending with the present decade. They define the sociology of organisations on the basis of six characteristics (pp. 476-7):

1. a fairly strong accent on the organisation as a whole and the interactions between organisation and society;
2. focus on the actual functioning of the organisation;
3. organisations have what is called 'a life of their own';
4. the propensity to 'de-mask', to de-mystify, common or dominant conceptions;
5. research is oriented to problems, defined by the researcher, who has the right to decide which problems are worth investigating. This is in contrast to applied research which does not have this freedom;
6. organisations are a combination of a parties and a social cultural system-model—they have a so-called 'double character' (p. 554).

Organisation sociology is seen as focusing on four major problems:
- *accountability*: the degree to which it is possible to find out whether a decision has been taken and the degree to which one can relate this decision to norms linked to its content and norms linked to the way it was taken;
- *social acceptability*:[2] the degree to which one can live acceptably in a situation;
- *administrability*: the degree to which one can let the organisation function according to certain goals;
- *controllability*: the degree to which one can give and enact guidelines for constructing, functioning and developing of organisations.

The work by Lammers et al. is at the core of Dutch organisational sociology, which can be characterised by as a 'diaspora', in that most organisation sociologists work in multidisciplinary faculties or research groups.

One approach to organisational design is worth special mention here, because it is related to both organisational sociology and management science: the so-called Dutch modern sociotechnical (MST) approach. In the Dutch academic world, and also internationally, MST has come to be recognised as a valuable contribution in redesigning organisational structures in the architecture of the division of labour (Lammers et al.: 651). Within MST, the division of labour and the coordination of tasks are called the production and administrative structure, respectively. A third structure, the information structure, covers the registration, processing and exchange of decision-making information. Re-design or design is, in the first instance, a re-design of the production structure. This is followed by the design of the administrative structure. When designing the production structure, one works from the external to the internal, i.e. by first analysing the strategic environment and then coming to conclusions about which products or services are to be put on the market. On the basis of this, a decision can be reached about which strategic work units are to be formed. Thereafter, the production structure can be designed from the top downwards and eventually to the lowest level of the task groups, placing tasks showing the greatest interdependency in the same unit. The administrative structure, on the other hand, is designed from the bottom upwards. The ambitions of Dutch MST have grown and nowadays, they not only cover a sociotechnical design theory, but also a methodology of design and a specific approach to organisational change. The programme is called 'integral organisational renewal'.

2.2. Management science and business administration

A well-known textbook on management and organisation is that written by Keuning and Eppink (1987, 1996). The book covers three core managerial problems:

- external attunement, in which the manager is seen as strategist and planner;
- internal attunement in which the manager is seen as leader and steersman;
- structuring in which the manager is seen as constructor of the organisation.

The first problem relates to theories or approaches to environment and strategy. The second and third problem relate to structure theory, the theory of growth and development of organisations, contingency theory, revisionism, communication- and information theory, human relations and scientific management. There are three theories which are of general importance when thinking about management: those of management process, decision making and systems theory.

A number of themes were dominant in management science and business administration research projects in the period up to the mid nineties (the numbers refer to the numbers of universitary projects between 1992 and 1996):

1. decision making (information systems, management of information resources, accounting, auditing, optimisation, knowledge based systems) (7);
2. financial and economic management (2);
3. marketing (innovation management) (2);
4. networks and innovation (strategy, international business) (4);
5. primary process (work and organisation, innovation of production systems, logistic control) (4);
6. organisational change (control, design, renewal, management technology and policy, governance, operations research, continuity) (8).

Within the field, there are also a number of interdisciplinary approaches.

2.3. Business economics

Business economics covers a broad area: the structure and behaviour of, and within, organisations, in interaction with their environment (Van Witteloostuijn 1995). There are six subdisciplines within business economics: accounting, finance, marketing, logistics, information and organisation. The subdiscipline 'organisation' is quite heterogeneous in nature and covers topics such as industrial economics, personnel management, strategic management, organisational behaviour, etc. Research groups in this subdiscipline are, likewise, heterogeneous.

Within the WESWA, the work on personnel and strategic management and on organisational behaviour is of particular interest. In these areas, there is a clear accent on the introduction and implementation of new ideas on the theory of the firm. As an example, we mention the book by Douma and Schreuder (1991). In this introductory textbook on the economics of organisation, several models or theories of the firm are discussed. Both the behavioural and the economic approaches, such as transaction costs and agency, are elaborated. The book shows how disciplines such as economics and behavioural sciences and psychology and sociology are intertwined when it comes to the analysis of organisations.

2.4. Organisation studies in other disciplines: political science, industrial economics, public administration, psychology and anthropology

Below is a list of some of the areas in which the work of these disciplines relates to labour and organisation studies.

- Political scientists have been studying processes such as globalisation, the restructuring of multinationals, internationalisation and their implications for the management of work and workers, (e.g. W. Ruigrok and R. van Tulder in their *The Logic of International Restructuring*, 1995).
- Industrial economists have focused on the performance of firms and the role of the state and other social actors. They have argued, for example, that mergers are driven not only by considerations of efficiency and monopoly, but also by imitative and defensive routines (Schenk 1996). Work has also been done on the performance of big European firms in different governance contexts (German, Anglo–Saxon, Latin), using as performance criteria: net added value, productivity and employment levels (De Jong 1996).
- The science of public policy and administration is well instituted at eleven Dutch universities. Some major research themes are: policy research, limits to planning and administration, administering complex networks,

local and regional government, public management and organisations, departments, de-regulation, privatisation, and the informatisation of public administration (Kickert 1996).

- In the psychology of organisation and labour there are two major universitary research institutes: the Research Institute for Psychology and Health and the Kurt Lewin Institute. The first has a research area on work, stress and health, which encompasses the study of organisational change and the effects of work practices and job content on stress risks, absenteeism and withdrawal by employees. Topics include: burnout, mid-career problems, crisis management, teams in organisations, leadership, managerial intuition and decision making, task evaluation, and absenteeism management. The second institute has published on: leadership, interpersonal conflict, health and safety at work, information and communication technology, quality of work, assessment and selection, organisational decision making, teams, influence and power, organisational culture, stress, absenteeism, burnout, participative management, innovative behaviour, risk management, negotiation, motivation, stereotypes, and group performance.
- In the anthropology of organisations the focus is on the cultures, identities and meanings of organisation members and groupings, configurations of structure, culture, and power within and outside organisations, etc. Everyday experiences are a starting point of analysis (Koot 1995).

2.5. HRM studies

The field of human resources management studies in the Netherlands has been in well-shaped existence since the last decade. Within different disciplines such as labour and organisation psychology, sociology, business economics and labour law, researchers have understood the necessity to combine their efforts and concepts in order to obtain better answers for both fundamental as well as empirical and applied questions on the themes of organisational design and efficiency and individual performance and well-being. The field of HRM has its historical roots in the United States, where the main concepts —labelled the 'Michigan' models and 'Harvard' models—have emerged. Several authors outside the United States have adapted these preliminary models in order to correct for the biases that can be found in the typical US approach. The role of institutions such as government, trade unions, social security, and the culture of bargaining and negotiating on wages and other labour conditions is different in many countries, so typical US-based examples do not have a general (worldwide) validity. Also, the emphasis on HRM as a typical managerial discipline that leaves employee interests as a residual has been criticised. Hence, the scientific field of human resources management sciences can be depicted as a huge umbrella under which many different approaches and schools flourish.

Next to this, there is the question of the scientific basis, as such. In some cases, HRM has manifested itself as a kind of ethic, when normative and prescriptive arguments dominate the debate. Fortunately, there are many contributions that do rely on the proper scientific basis of testing concepts and theories.

In the field of research, in human resources management sciences, there are some 6 well-developed academic groups and several para-academic circles such as large consultancy firms and contract-research institutions. The research agenda for these groups can be described as various. In certain cases, the accent is clearly put on work councils, participation and labour relations. Some research is also done on the connection between organisational strategy and HRM. Larger research projects involve internal labour mobility, governance structures, and strategic renumeration. Connected areas are payment for overtime work, the effects of the length of the working day, the perception of income differentials within the organisation, flexible manpower planning and retirement schemes, and decision making with respect to working times.

2.6. Labour economics

Most research in labour economics in the Netherlands fits into the Anglo–Saxon tradition. Except for some special items, discussed below, Dutch labour market economists follow the steps of their American and British colleagues. Most publications can be found in journals (as opposed to books) and are primarily designated for the 'world market'. The 'local Dutch market' is primarily concerned with policy related research. As Wielers and Schippers discuss in their chapter, the focus in labour market research has shifted from macro- to microeconomics, with many economists cooperating with econometricists or using econometric techniques themselves. As will be discussed below, the greater attention given to microeconomics has also resulted in greater attention being given to organisational issues. Different research groups concentrate on different fields of interests. Together, all labour economists working in the Netherlands cover almost the complete field of labour economics. For those who read Dutch, the broad variety of themes under discussion is clearly illustrated by the series of reports published by the Organisation for Strategic Labour Market Research (OSA). Almost all labour economists have contributed to this series in the recent past and the topics discussed vary from general analyses of supply and demand in the labour market as a whole as well as in specific branches of industry, to analyses of wage rate differentials, job mobility and the way workers and employers search for new jobs and workers, respectively. Not only economists, but also other social scientists such as sociologists have contributed to this series. This is especially true where it concerns issues regarding the company level or issues concerning the combination of paid work and care tasks. Sociologists who do not claim to be specialised in labour sociology also often devote much attention to labour-related issues (e.g. Ultee et al. 1992), as these issues themselves are often closely related to topics such as educational attainment, stratification and the division of income and wealth. Labour economists researching within the human capital tradition have, in particular, benefited strongly from the insights brought forward by sociologists.

2.7. Sociology of labour

Van Hoof (1990) states that since the 60s a sociology of labour has developed, focusing on the labour market, labour relations and the professions. It pays a lot of attention to processes of distribution, control and interest representation within different arenas around labour in society. The control of the work situation has become its dominant subject (Mok 1990, Van Hoof 1987). The labour market is seen as being heavily influenced by rules, institutions and power processes whereby individual and collective actions have unintended consequences. Van Hoof (1990) points to the predominance of work in informal and/or unpaid contexts as against formal or official contexts, and sees the sociology of labour extending to all these contexts. He notes that the analysis of gender has given a new thrust to the discipline.

Van Hoof (1994) states that even though forms of class inequality have changed, the concept of work remains closely related to those of class and social inequality. Note that there is a tradition of inequality research in the Netherlands (see e.g. Ultee et al. 1992).

2.8. Labour relations

Labour relations are widely studied in the Netherlands. The textbook written by Nagelkerke and De Nijs (1994) gives as topics: the actors in labour relations and their contacts; the system of industrial relations in the private and the public sector; the way contracts and industrial conflicts are negotiated; the functioning of the labour market, co-determination in the company, personnel policy; labour relations and European integration. The book also discusses some theoretical approaches to labour relations: one based on Dunlop, one on Marxism and a pluralist one.

As can be seen in the article on labour relations research in this book, workplace industrial relations have gained prominence as a distinct subject. Worth special mention is the study by De Swaan (1988) on healthcare, education and welfare in Europe and the United States in the modern era, which is insightful, because it covers in a comparative study, using a dependencies- and collective action perspective, the development of social security, that is so vitally linked to labour relations. It is also an excellent exemplar of a historical–sociological approach, about which much is published in the *Amsterdams Sociologisch Tijdschrift* (Amsterdam Sociological Journal).

3. SUMMARIES OF THE ARTICLES

3.1. Labour market

In Chapter 2, Wielers and Schippers discuss the development and state of the art in Dutch labour market research. Their main interest is in the paradigms used in contributions from economics and sociology. Wielers and Schippers conclude that in the eighties the neoclassical principles quickly gained in adherence at the cost of the older theories. Nowadays, it is hard to find reflections on the assumptions of the sociological paradigm in labour market research, although the strong empirical orientation of the present labour market research may be seen as an inheritance from that time. Keynesian macroeconomics has also almost completely disappeared from Dutch research. Both paradigms have been superseded by neoclassical theory, which is the leading theory, not only in research, but also in policymaking. Normative neoclassical theory assumes that the uninhibited invisible hand establishes the most efficient outcomes.

Labour market research effort in the Netherlands is steered, to a large extent, by current labour market policy problems. The problems on the research agenda correspond closely to the social problems, as perceived by policy makers. However, it is hard to evaluate whether a problem is the focus of attention simply because researchers or policy makers have defined it as a problem. This is due to the symbiosis in problem definition, research programming and the policy theory of labour market researchers and labour market policy makers, that has developed during the last fifteen years. For the near future, Wielers and Schippers do not see any rival paradigm as being able to provide an acceptable explanation of the anomalies in neoclassical theory. By far the strongest criticism of neoclassical economic theory comes from neoclassical economists, rather than from critics external to the paradigm.

3.2. Industrial or labour relations

Chapter 3 gives an overview of Dutch research in the nineties, placed within major developments in the Netherlands. Research on five issues is presented: the system of industrial relations, change in trade unions, collective bargaining, co-determination within the company, and workplace industrial relations.

The system has seen a transformation from (neo-)corporatism to a consultation economy. The merits of the Dutch model are seen partly in the efficiency effect of rules and structures (the positive effect on employment; the negative effect on wage increases and wage differentials) and partly in the flexible consensus making necessary for the reform of the welfare state.

Generally, most research is policy-driven. Theoretical approaches are taken as seems fitting to the problems at hand; there is no theoretical integration which results in diversity or even balkanisation of theoretical approaches. There are no attempts to develop a multidisciplinary framework. Economic reasoning and approaches have become significant. Several institutions, and the system of industrial relations as a whole, have been evaluated, particularly in terms of macroperformance. However, the discussion has suffered from ideological overtones.

In company industrial relations, the performance idea is becoming more important, although research on this is mainly from a management perspective. Integration in company industrial relations research comes expressly from modern sociotechnics researchers who wish to integrate industrial relations with workplace re-design.

Public and semi-public industrial relations have received little attention and, similarly, the topic of employers and government as actors.

3.3. The quality of work

In Chapter 4, Oeij, Fruytier and Van den Broek describe recent developments in the area of quality of work. First, the concept of quality is outlined. Several definitions are given and compared. It appears that a proper combination of subjective and objective factors measuring the quality of work should be used. Next, the discussions are placed within the social context of the Netherlands. The general socio-economic developments during the last decades and also governmental policies have influenced the way the concept of work and its quality is perceived. The road to flexibilisation, employability and de-regulation has its effects on workers in different ways: core workers have a heavy work-load; temporary workers, uncertain positions and low-skilled work. The authors then make an inventory and analysis of four themes that are manifest in the debate on the quality of working life: the employment and division of labour; organisational change; the development of functions, and the issue of health and well-being. This inventory is based on recent articles in Dutch journals, and the contributions are classified according to whether the research was theoretical, descriptive, action-oriented or focused on evaluation. It appears that there is a clear accent on topics such as health and well-being. At the same, time there is a conspicuous lack in (governmental) policies on employment of a relationship with the quality of work. Very limited attention is given to the evaluation of such policies. The authors observe that explanatory research into the link between quality of work at the one hand and organisational development and change at the other hand is almost non-existent.

3.4. HRM

In Chapter 5, Looise and Paauwe offer a broad overview of the evolving paradigms and research issues in Dutch research. After a description of historical developments in HRM before and after the 1980's, with special reference to the role of works councils and industrial relations, an overview of Dutch research is presented. It appears that there are quite a number of different research topics which can be discussed. Furthermore, the field of human resource studies is highly driven by practice, with only little theoretical background. Practitioner-oriented issues dominate, in an instrumental and short-term based context. The authors then discuss the possibilities of deriving an appropriate paradigm for HRM. Several possible types and perspectives are presented and discussed: the behavioural perspective, cybernetic models, agency and transaction-cost theories, the resource based theory of the firm, power and dependence models and institutional theory. The authors underline that it is important to include perspectives from all stakeholders in the paradigm or theoretical model. In other words, HRM is more than just a management discipline aimed at maximising performance from the point of view of economic rationality. Hence, a strong plea is made for taking the resource-based theory of the firm as a starting point for the future research agenda. The unique synthesis between strategic demands and characteristics on the one hand, and the aspirations of the workforce on the other hand is seen as a major advantage of this paradigm.

3.5. Work and organisation studies

A number of trends in work and organisation studies from the seventies, to the nineties, inclusive, are outlined by Van der Zwaan in Chapter 6.

The trends in the last decade were:

- a drift towards applied research and management science;
- more attention to micro-systems (teamwork, group dynamics and group performance);
- a greater use of process approaches;
- a greater use of new management concepts related to alternatives to the classical Taylor-based, high-division-of-labour concept, and
- increased attention to qualitative methodology.

There are a number of popular research objects in the more applied research projects in this field. These can be grouped into two major streams:

- organisational development, change, commitment and trust, learning and participation;
- self managing teams, microsystems, production redesign, product innovation and new production concepts.

There are a number of theoretical concepts connected to these streams: rational choice, participatory regulation, organisational learning, transaction-cost economics, sociotechnics and: HRM, flexibility and mobility, employment relationship, internal labour market, segmentation and the quality of working life.

3.6. Gender

In the final chapter, Benschop, Brouns and De Bruijn discuss the development of the way gender is included (was excluded) from studies on labour and organisation. They see an increasing attention in the Netherlands to women's and gender issues during the last two decades. While the actual position of women was the central issue in early studies, the focus has shifted during recent years towards the relations between organisations and gender issues. Four lines of approach can be distinguished. The first two focus on the unequal positions of men and women in organisations, firstly by stressing the importance of factors within the labour market, and, secondly, by concentrating on factors outside the labour market. The third line of approach studies the (re)production of gender and its relation to organisation structures and cultures. Finally, the fourth line includes studies that address the involvement of gender in the definition, organisation and evaluation of work itself. The authors conclude that the variation in epistemology, theoretical perspectives, scope and research of these lines of approach give a more complete picture of the field of gender in work and organisation. Asking the right questions with respect to gender issues, however, is not only beneficial to understanding these issues, but also contributes to a better understanding of the way we think about 'a worker' or 'the organisation' and may help future society to deal with increasing diversity and pluralism.

4. REFLECTIONS ON THE DUTCH SCENE

In this section we will comment on three topics concerning Dutch research. First, we observe fragmentation in the research field and counter tendencies, not only through multidisciplinary approaches, but in other directions, too. Next, we will discuss some trends in different fields, highlighting those in labour market studies. We conclude with a remark on research methods.

4.1. Fragmentation, multidisciplinarity and integration

First of all, it is clear that the domain of labour and organisation studies in the Netherlands is fragmented. This is probably not specifically a Dutch feature. Many disciplines have put effort into addressing appropriate topics from their own perspective. Within different disciplines—for instance, labour economics, labour law, the organisation of work, labour sociology and labour psychology—there is little communication and collaboration across boundaries. Each discipline has its own vocabulary and there is a high degree of incommensurability in basic notions and theoretical problems. Concepts such as 'organisational change', 'work systems' and 'labour relations'—just to mention a few—can therefore have quite a distinct meaning in the different disciplines. A consequence of this fragmentation is that, within each separate discipline, it is hard to get enough 'critical mass' for a thorough and fully fledged labour and organisation research programme.

During recent decades, in the Netherlands, the need has been stressed for a more comprehensive and integral way of conceptualising and organising labour and organisation research. In many research departments, we see specialists from different disciplines working together on key topics such as organisational design, renumeration, job evaluation, etc. The last decade has also shown a tremendous rise in multidisciplinary departments for university training and research. Management sciences, organisational sciences, human-resources sciences, social-security sciences, and so on. Nowadays, all of them are rooted in university research and teaching.

The multidisciplinary research groups were founded to address a wide range of management issues in public and private organisations in a more comprehensive way than is possible by means of the 'traditional' monodisciplinary approaches. The development of more comprehensive paradigms has benefited from the important and basic contribution made by Kuhn (1962). It was he who described 'the structure of scientific revolutions' and who introduced the concept of 'paradigms', defined as 'universally recognised scientific achievements that for a time provide model problems and solutions to a community of practitioners'. Contrary to Popper's view on falsification and critical rationalism, Kuhn argued for the importance of changing the paradigms to define the nature of reality in new ways. By loosening some of the restrictive parameters of classical, monodisciplinary research, the possibility opens up of building new theories and models to incorporate different concepts or angles. For instance, in human-resources management sciences, it is noted that the classical contributions from labour economists, organisational psychologists and labour sociologists do not offer sufficient solutions for the complex human-resources management issues within organisations. The explanatory power of these monodisciplines is limited. However, in many cases, the new paradigms are not yet completely recognised and worked out, so the label 'pre-paradigmatic' would be more appropriate.

The claim of the new multi-disciplinary approaches that they are more fruitful and better suited, to provide answers for management problems is not proven in depth, and their claim of bringing about a scientific 'revolution' is debatable. For instance, it will be clear that any multi-disciplinary approach should be based on a sound knowledge of the possibilities and constraints of the relevant mono-disciplines. Multi-disciplinarity still faces the 'normal' scientific criteria when it comes to theory building and empirical statistical testing.

While the integration of approaches and disciplines through multidisciplines has been one road to integration, it has its limits. Integration between mono- and multidisciplines has been hampered by the fact that the latter are more of an applied nature and thus the wedge between fundamental and applied science has been institutionalised, to some extent.

It is not only through multidisciplines that integration has come about. There are other developments worth mentioning:

- some approaches and disciplines have gained prominence across fields; take, for example, the spread of transaction-cost analysis in labour relations or organisational analysis and the popularity of neo-classical thinking (see the article on labour market research, Chapter 2);
- a discipline can enlargen the range of its problems and enter neighbouring fields; see, for instance, labour economics (see section 4.2.1, below) and the economic analysis of institutions in labour relations;
- of importance has been the foundation of graduate schools, some of which have firmly established the position of multidisciplinary and interdisciplinary research;
- there are examples of successful cooperation between researchers from different disciplines in commissioned research projects;
- fields such as gender studies have, to some extent, become an interface. The sharing of a common interest or theme has brought together different research programmes, theoretical problems and different disciplines.

4.2. Trends in different fields

Of interest, now, is the question of interaction and overlap between the different fields. We will briefly review the fields and answer the question of whether basic theoretical problems found in some fields are also encountered in others, such as, for example, coordination, distribution (inequality), cohesion, performance, meaning or sense making.

In gender studies, much attention is given to major concepts such as markets, institutions, cohesion and distribution and, increasingly, to meanings (identity, diversity of identities). The core of the gender research on labour and organisation has focused on inequality, the role of institutions and on images and meanings.

When the gender studies programme comes to include all types of segmentation and inequality, not only the one based on gender, it may enhance a stream of research that combines a spectre of personal attributes, group composition and population characteristics, and social processes. Although the concept of diversity management, encompassing multiculturality, gender, race, age, etc. is gaining importance — though remarkably hardly any attention is given to the issue of diversity in many of the other fields — it is the fields of gender, labour market, demographical and cross-cultural research, in particular, that seem to have the opportunities to contribute to its development. Especially interesting will be the confrontation between corporate and organisational culture theory and studies of diversity, because they depart from different angles, the one from ideas of an integrated culture enhancing performance and the other from the idea of diversity doing the same (Van Doorne-Huiskes 1997).

Markets, institutions and process are at the core of labour relations research. The coordination mechanisms that can be discerned are: market, hierarchy (central planning), solidarity (norms and values), negotiation, mutual coordination (power) (De Haan et al. 1994) and spontaneous cooperation (Weesie and Raub 1993). Employment relationships are closely linked with coordination and governance problems. Industrial relations research increasingly shows links with measures of company- and system performance. Inequality and cohesion are studied; the first as an outcome of negotiations, and the second as a precondition of the Dutch model. Processes of meaning and sense making (the rationalisation and the constructivistic paradigm) are not, as in gender, a major line of research.

Research into the quality of work shows a shift in focus towards new individual rights (health, stress, well-being), while the attention paid to autonomy and self-determination appears to be waning. In quality of work hardly any attention is paid to distribution problems and cohesion (solidarity being an element of cohesion). Performance is focused on the level of individual problems within a psychologistic perspective. The study of well-being, health, etc. carries with it the possibility of being related to the study of sense-making and meaning.

In the field of human resources management sciences the focus is on both organisational strategy and individual behaviour. HRM is sometimes seen as a management tool (the optimalisation of the production factor, labour), sometimes the focus is broader, also incorporating other stakeholders (open system: the resource-based approach). As, by nature, it has a multi-disciplinary approach, HRM gives a lot of attention to questions, such as the meaning of work, the effects of employment and work policies on individual well-being and social cohesion, both at the organisational and individual level.

Little attention is given to the problems of inequality and distribution, which comes as a surprise, as the negotiations and outcomes of stakeholders are supposed to have some prominence. Attention to sense making and meaning is also relatively lacking in HRM, despite the fact that attention is directed towards the motivation and commitments of stakeholders and the meaning of work. The subject of defining self- and common interests of, and between, parties has apparently still to be entertained in HRM.

In work and organisation research we do find some attention being given to cohesion (work teams, organisational learning), but hardly any to distribution issues (inequality). Process and change models and contractual relationships are gaining in importance, but this does not lead to more attention being given to (structural) negotiation, power and conflict models, and perhaps this also holds for HRM studies.

The construction of meaning and sense making does not seem to figure prominently. The issue of organisational culture seems to be taken up by psychologists and anthropologists, in particular, who also work with the concept of identities.

It is remarkable that the issue of inter-organisational networks and alliances has been taken up more extensively by management and business economics, than by work and organisational sociologists. The fact that research into organisational culture and interorganisational networks follows such disciplinary lines is an indication of the fragmentation of the field.

As we can see, in various fields, the potential has been created for a platform between major streams of research. Also in labour market research there is clearly a potential for creating a broader platform, though for somewhat different reasons. We will turn to this next.

The research on labour markets stand outs because of a number of tendencies:
- growing attention for organisational studies among labour economists;
- growing attention for labour relations (following the public discussion with respect to 'the Dutch delta model');
- an increasing interest in multi- and interdisciplinary research.

We will now consider these more extensively.

4.2.1. Labour market research as an interface

The first of these three tendencies has developed over an extended period. Following labour market studies in the seventies and eighties on individual behaviour, more and more researchers have come to the conclusion that adequate research involving the demand side of the labour market requires entering the 'black box' of the organisation. While, for example, labour supply can easily be studied using data on individuals, the analysis of labour demand should either be studied at the macro level (though usually such studies do not contribute to a real explanation: they only show relations, without being able to 'prove' causality), or within the context of an organisation. Stressing the organisational context gives room for issues such as cooperation or non-cooperation, power or lack of it and formal and informal rules and regulations. Among the subjects studied are the re-integration of the partly disabled (see e.g. Klosse et al. 1998), affirmative action (Remery 1998), the position of elderly workers (Von Bergh 1997; Henkens 1998) and work–family policies (Den Dulk et al. 1998). In the meantime, there has also been a growing understanding of the fact that the context in which decisions are made also matters on the supply side. Growing interest in household decision making, issues with respect to the combination of paid labour and informal care can be seen as examples of this view (see, e.g., with respect to child care: Van Dijk 1994 and Schippers et al. 1998, and with respect to taxes: Grift 1998; and Vlasblom 1998). As Wielers and Schippers discuss in their chapter in this volume, the systematic way in which neoclassical theory has 'conquered' different fields of interest has contributed significantly to this development. It is remarkable, however, that Van der Zwaan in Chapter 6, looking at it from the work and organisation studies field, does not perceive a stronger connection between labour market and organisational research.

The successful performance of the Dutch economy, characterised by limited wage growth agreed upon between unions and employers over a series of years, growing employment, increasing exports and reduced government budget deficits, has led to extensive discussions, both in the Netherlands and abroad, about the causes and factors contributing to this success (see Chapter 3). Central questions in these discussions relate to the unique characteristics of Dutch socio-economic order and the possibilities for transferring 'the Dutch miracle' to other economies, to the interaction between institutions and employers and unions, and to the conditions needed to bring about a continuance of the successful performance of the Dutch economy (see, e.g., Hessel et al. 1998). The fields participating in these discussions are labour economics, public economics, industrial organisation, and, of course, plain macroeconomics. Economists should not be considered monopolists with regard to the issues at stake, as researchers in the fields of law, sociology, history and public administration also participate heavily in discussions about the Dutch delta model. These discussions have brought new impulses to the field of labour relations studies in the Netherlands (see Chapter 3).

This brings us to the third tendency, the increasing focus on multidisciplinary research with respect to labour in the Netherlands. During the eighties, it became clear that individual behaviour in the labour market cannot be as easily explained in terms of prices and income as, for instance, supply and demand in financial markets. The labour market can be considered a unique market to the extent that individuals are, by definition, personally involved when they make decisions on whether, and how, to offer their labour. Usually, these decisions not only involve the decision maker him/ herself, but also the family of which s/he is a part. While selling shares, or buying a new videoplayer involves 'only money', accepting a job also implies that a husband or wife is not at home to take care of the children, to do the laundry or to go shopping, that s/he comes home tired or excited, becomes friends with colleagues, has to work late, and so on. A worker is therefore involved in the labour market with the whole of his person. As a result, decision making with respect to that market will involve a much broader range of factors than those usually included in economic analyses.

The idea that it might be fruitful for labour economists to cooperate with researchers from other disciplines was supported in the institutional field by the foundation of graduate schools such as the Interuniversity Centre for

Social Theory and Methodology (ICS) and the School for Social Policy and Welfare State Research (AWSB). Not only have these schools become strong competitors in the field of labour market research, but they have also firmly established the position of multidisciplinary and interdisciplinary research. Other examples of successful cooperation between researchers originating from different disciplines can be found in studies by the Netherlands Interdisciplinary Demographic Institute (NIDI) (e.g. Beets et al. 1997), the Organisation for Strategic Labour Market Studies (OSA) and the Social and Cultural Planning Bureau (SCP).

Of course, this does not imply that monodisciplinary labour market research is obsolete and no longer relevant. It certainly is relevant, but current policy issues often pose questions that go beyond the scope of traditional labour economics. The case of labour market flexibility offers a striking and clear example. Introduced by supply-side economists, the discussion on labour market flexibility in the Netherlands was soon taken over by jurists on labour law and researchers involved with organisational studies. Very soon, the discussion framework was broadened to include issues regarding 'employability' and the reconciliation of labour and care tasks, which also brought sociologists, psychologists and demographers into the arena (see, e.g., Faber et al. 1997).

4.3. A remark on research designs and methods

We conclude by pointing to the saliency of research designs and methods in labour and organisation studies. There is an increasing need for research data, because many of the concepts outlined above need empirical verification, which can only be achieved when accurate and sufficient data are available. There is also a need to compare the outcomes of measurements based on different research methods (e.g. triangulation).

Traditionally, there is a difference between research methods and designs in economics and other social sciences. In economic sciences there are many econometric techniques, often used on secondary data, mostly on a macro level (but at a micro level as well). Social sciences have both quantitative and qualitative research methods. Nowadays, the attention within economics is also on laboratory experiments (experimental economics), simulation studies and case studies. The research methods in both types of sciences are likely to converge at certain points (Van Ees and Garretsen 1991).

We expect that it will be most fruitful to combine different research designs. One can think of collecting of large scale data on macro, meso and micro level (surveys), of panel studies on individual employees and firms, of case research with qualitative data, controlled experiments with individuals and managers (decision makers) on topics, such as bounded rationality, risk perception, simulation, etc.

We started this chapter with some remarks on WESWA. The reflections that have been outlined in this chapter stress the importance of an institutional carrier to enhance scientific integration and progress in the field of labour and organisation studies. When it is a matter of crossing disciplinary boundaries, integrating research methods, and where empirical research should also contain proper recommendations for policies, there is a clear need for a platform where ideas and results can be interchanged. WESWA has the capacity to act as such a platform into the coming decade.

NOTES

1 Law is also a major discipline, but is not covered here.

2 This concept is related to utility.

REFERENCES

Beets, G.C.N. et al., 1996. *Social causes and effects of delayed parenthood: preliminary evidence from the Netherlands, Report written on behalf of the Commission of the European Union*, Den Haag/Utrecht, 67 pp.

Bergh, M. von, 1997. *Loopbanen van oudere werknemers* (Careers of older employees), Amsterdam, Thesis Publishers.

Dijk, L. van, 1994. *Choices in child care*, Amsterdam, Thesis Publishers.

Doorne-Huiskes, J. van, et al., 1997. *Nieuwe research programma* (New organisational forms and employees in the future, Outline of the research programme), Research paper nr. 1, June 1997. See especially project nr. 3: *Nieuwe organisatievormen en leiderschapsstijl* (New organisational forms and style of leadership).

Douma, S. and H. Schreuder, 1991. *Economic approaches to organisations*, New York, Prentice Hall.

Dulk, L. den, et al., 1998. *Work-family arrangements in Europe*, Amsterdam, Thesis Publishers, forthcoming.

Ees, H. van en J.H. Garretsen, 1991. De kristallen bol der economen, in: *Economisch Statistische Berichten*, 7-8-1991, pp. 788-791.

Faber, G. en J.J. Schippers, 1997. *Flexibilisering van arbeid* (Flexibilisation of labour), Bussum, Coutinho.

Grift, Y.K., 1998. *Female labour supply. The influence of taxes and social premiums*, Utrecht, E.G. de Haan.

Jong, Ph.R. de and P.J. Vos, 1997. *Flexibiliteit van de arbeid. Op zoek naar zekerheid* (Flexibility of labour. Searching for security), Amsterdam.

Henkens, K., 1998. *Older workers in transition. Studies on the early retirement decision in the Netherlands*, Utrecht/Den Haag.

Hessel, B., J.J. Schippers and J.J. Siegers (eds.), 1998. *Market efficiency versus equity*, Amsterdam, Thesis Publishers.

Hoof, J.J.B.M. van, 1987. *De arbeidsmarkt als arena* (The labour market as an arena), Amsterdam.

Hoof, J.J.B.M. van, 1990. *Vernieuwing en restauratie. Ontwikkelingen in het arbeidsbestel en in de arbeidssociologie* (Renewal and restoration. Developments in the system of labour and the sociology of labour) Amsterdam.

Hoof, J.J.B.M. van, 1994. *Arbeid, klasse en sociale ongelijkheid* (Labour, class and social inequality), Leiden.

Jong, H.W. de, 1996. 'Rijnlandse ondernemingen presteren beter' (Rhineland companies perform better), in: *ESB* (Economic Statistical Reports) pp. 228-232.

Keuning, D. and D.J. Eppink, 1987, 1996. *Management en organisatie. Theorie en praktijk* (Management and organisation. Theory and practice), Leiden/Antwerpen.

Kickert, W.J.M., 1996. 'Beleids- en bestuurswetenschappen in Nederland' (Policy and public management sciences in the Netherlands), in: *Bestuurswetenschappen* (Administrative sciences): 1: 34-61.

Klosse, S. et al., 1998. *Rehabilitation of partially disabled people. An international perspective*, Amsterdam, Thesis Publishers.

Koot, W.C.J., 1995. *De complexiteit van het alledaagse. Een antropologisch perspectief op organisaties* (The complexity of the ordinary. An anthropological perspective on organisations).

Lammers, C.J., A.A. Mijs and W.J. Van Noort, 1997. *Organisaties vergelijkenderwijs. Ontwikkeling en relevantie van het sociologisch denken over organisaties* (Comparative organisation studies. Outcomes and relevance of the sociology of organisations), Utrecht.

Mok, A.L., 1990. *In het zweet uws aanschijns* (In the sweat of thy face), Leiden/Antwerpen.

Nagelkerke, A.G. and W.F. De Nijs, 1994. *Regels rond arbeid. Arbeidsverhoudingen in Nederland en op het niveau van de Europese gemeenschap* (Rules around labour. Labour relations in the Netherlands and at the level of the European community), Leiden.

Remery, C., 1998. *Effecten van emancipatiegericht personeelsbeleid* (Effects of emancipation-centered personnel policy), Dissertation EUR, Rotterdam.

Ruigrok, W. and R. van Tulder, 1995. *The logic of international restructuring*, London.

Schenk, H., 1996. 'Bandwagon mergers, international competitiveness and government policy', in: *Empirica, Journal of Applied Economics and Economic Policy*, p. 255-278.

Schippers, J.J., J.J. Siegers and J. de Jong-Gierveld (eds.), 1998. *Child care and female labour supply in the Netherlands*, Amsterdam, Thesis Publishers.

Swaan, A. de, 1989. *In care of the state. Health care, education and welfare in Europe and the USA in the modern era.* Amsterdam, Bert Bakker.

Toren, J.P. van den, 1996. *Achter gesloten deuren? Cao-overleg in de jaren negentig* (Translated, see Nagelkerke, De Nijs), Dissertatie Rijksuniversiteit Leiden, Amsterdam, Welboom.

Ultee, W., W. Arts, H. Flap, 1992. *Sociologie. Vragen, uitspraken, bevindingen* (Sociology. Questions, statements, findings) Groningen.

Visser, J. and A. Hemerijck, 1997. *A Dutch miracle; job growth, welfare reform and corporatism in the Netherlands*, Amsterdam, Amsterdam University Press.

Vlasblom, J.D., 1998. *Differences in labour supply and income of women in the Netherlands and the Federal Republic of Germany. A comparative analyses of the effect of taxes and social premiums*, Utrecht.

VSNU, 1997. *Quality assessment of research. Management science and business administration*, Utrecht, VSNU (Association of Universities in the Netherlands).

Weesie, J. and W. Raub, 1993. *The management of matches. Decentralised mechanisms for cooperative relations with applications to organisations and households.* September, ISCORE-paper, University of Utrecht.

Williamson, O.E., 1991. 'Comparative Economic Organisation: The analysis of discrete structural alternatives', in: *Administrative Science Quaterly* 36: 269-296.

Witteloostuijn, A. van, 1995. *Een verkenning van het Nederlandse onderzoek in de bedrijfswetenschappen* (An exploration into the Dutch research in business sciences) Universiteit van Maastricht, Faculteit economie, paper.

AUTHORS

Dr. G.H.M. Evers
Tilburg University, Dept. Personnel management
P.O. box 90153, 5000 LE TILBURG
tel: 013-4662371, fax: 013-4662370
e-mail: G.H.M.EVERS@KUB.NL

Dr. G.B. van Hees
SISWO (internet SISWO: http://www.siswo.uva.nl)
tel. 020-5270600/27, fax: 020-6229430
e-mail: hees@siswo.uva.nl

Dr. J.J. Schippers
University of Utrecht, Faculty of Economics/CIAV
Kromme Nieuwegracht 22, 3512 HH Utrecht
tel. +31 (0)30 2537116/7100, fax. +31 (0)30 2537131
e-mail: j.schippers@pobox.ruu.nl

LABOUR MARKET RESEARCH: The supremacy of neoclassical economic theory

Rudi Wielers and Joop Schippers

1. INTRODUCTION

In this chapter we describe the state of the art in Dutch labour market research. Our main interest is in the paradigm (Kuhn 1970) used in contributions from economics and sociology. A paradigm consists of elementary theories, a methodology and a view on the cumulation of research, which scientists test and develop within their own field. It offers a cognitive framework for the recognition of a problem and for the appreciation of the results of empirical research. A paradigm may also extend beyond scientific research to influence laymen and policy makers.

In this paper, we describe present labour market research as a stage in paradigm development. In its initial stage, a paradigm is recognised as providing answers to acute problems. It then becomes a cognitive framework for scientific practice, until, finally, it is unable to provide any further answers. At that stage, it is likely to be superseded by a rival paradigm. The development of paradigms is determined by problems inherent in research and by current labour market policy problems. The core and development of the relevant paradigms are sketched in chronological order. Our description of Dutch labour market research starts in the seventies.

2. THE SOCIOLOGICAL PARADIGM

Twenty-five years ago, most labour market researchers were committed to what we will call the sociological paradigm. These were sociologists, who, in their theories about labour market behaviour, elaborated on more general sociological theories of action, such as role theory and attitude theory.

Researchers working on this labour market research paradigm viewed the labour market either as a so-called wage market or as an allocation market—a distinction developed by Lulofs (1960) in his influential book on the American labour market. Lulofs argued that the process of wage formation had become separated to such an extent from that of job searching, that these processes could be treated as independent objects of research. Sociologists focused on the allocation process.

Allocation was to be explained from behaviour determined by complex preferences. A worker was attracted to a job, not only because of its monetary benefits, but also because of other conveniences (sometimes called collectively, the psychic income) such as status, approval by colleagues or intrinsic work satisfaction. Since each worker valued specific conveniences in her/his own way, the conveniences of a job could not be determined beforehand, but had to be established by carrying out empirical research. In research practice, price incentives were not considered to be an important determinant of allocation. Researchers shared the feeling that workers were not very sensitive to wage differentials.

The aim was for the research to contribute to the solution of problems of modern society. As the outstanding problems at that time were manpower shortages at the docks and in a number of manufacturing industries, it would be logical, to suppose that a descriptive knowledge of the complex preferences of these workers would be the basis for tailor-made solutions. A considerable part of the research was financed by employers, who indeed needed the knowledge to solve their manpower problems.

The methodology was inductive. New theories were developed elaborating on the results of empirical research. It was hoped that a further cumulation of research results would pave the way for an empirically well-founded model of the labour market. To a certain extent, research results did indeed accumulate.

In a first phase, workers in different organisations and sectors were the main focus of interest. The aim of this research was the description of opinions, attitudes and the behaviour of different groups of workers. These were thought to differ according to their occupations, and the educational credentials necessary to gain access to them. Thus, workers belonged to a large number of non-competing groups (as already distinguished by Cairnes 1874; Taussig 1929), some of which constituted the first objects of empirical research. Large-scale survey research was done amongst the (potential) workers in the metal- and textile industries (especially, IJzerman 1959) and at the docks in Amsterdam (Ter Hoeven 1963; Van Berkel 1965).

In a second phase, the focus was broadened to include the allocation process in the labour market (Hamaker 1976) and the conditions for the institutionalisation of labour market processes (Van Voorden 1975). Results of the previous research were elaborated upon in this later research.

The paradigm was in clear opposition to the neoclassical model of the labour market. Dutch sociologists joined 'American' labour economists, such as Dunlop, Lester, Kerr and Reynolds, in their criticism of neoclassical economic theory. Their main criticism was that the neoclassical model is not realistic in its assumptions. Thus it was argued that it was not competitive market forces, but trade unions and employers' organisations that determined wage rates. Wage rates, sometimes called the 'norms of the transaction' (Van Doorn 1961), were negotiated in collective agreements, and this precluded competition. This was better so, since, in a modern society, competition on the labour market was imperfect because labour had become very heterogeneous. Relevant research had to take segmentation of the modern labour market as a basic assumption. From the point of view of 'American' labour economists and Dutch labour market sociologists, the neoclassical model referred to a past era, during which labour was not yet specialised and trade unions did not exist. The ordered modern society, however, had a different structure, and the neoclassical model could not provide satisfactory answers to its problems.

At the end of the seventies, the sociological paradigm itself came under severe criticism (especially Van Hoof 1977). This criticism was partly caused by problems in the paradigm. It proved hard to construct a general model from partial research results, since it appeared that an enormous amount of data were necessary to feed it. To a certain extent, this kind of problem was inherent in the paradigm, and it may be argued that the problem of the elaboration and refinement of different models of allocation would, in any case, have been put on the research agenda for the decade to come. Nevertheless, there were other, even more serious, problems for the paradigm.

One was the problem of the generation of inequality in the labour market. Attention to this problem was stimulated by the development of dual labour market theory in the United States. Formerly, inequality had been interpreted as resulting from differences in jobs, education, gender, age and parental status. These wage differentials were corrected by fiscal policies, to achieve politically acceptable inequality. According to dual labour market theory, the source of inequality was the structure of the labour market itself. Good jobs that paid well and offered good promotional opportunities were in the primary segment. It was argued that, in particular, it was well-educated white males, who were allocated to these jobs and that discrimination was an important reason why women and ethnic minorities were denied access to them. As a consequence, women and minorities had to accept the far less attractive jobs in the secondary segment.

The concept of a dual labour market was not very novel for Dutch labour market sociologists, whose paradigm included non-competing groups and segmentation, as core assumptions. As they were unfamiliar with the distribution of wages, and, having argued time and again that wage incentives were not important in the labour market, they found it hard to shift the focus of their argumentation to the labour market as a generator of inequality.

Probably even more important for the development of the paradigm was the development of the labour market itself. During the seventies, the Dutch labour market developed from a tight to a loose market, and, as a consequence, lasting unemployment was emerging as a new phenomenon. In addition, so-called qualitative discrepancies had appeared in that, for example, the educational credentials supplied did not correspond to the skills demanded or expected by the employer. As a consequence, not only did the number of unemployed increase, but also the number of vacancies (though at a slower rate). Therefore, despite their strong policy orientation, it appeared that labour market sociologists had neither the theories nor the instruments to cope with these new problems.

3. THE LABOUR MARKET IN MACRO-ECONOMIC THEORY

In the seventies, sociology and economics were involved with different labour market research programmes. The separation of the allocation and the wage formation processes was the basis of this division of labour. Each of the disciplines specialised and the results were felt to be supplementary to understanding the work of labour markets. As we have argued above, sociologists specialised in the allocation process, which was perceived as a micro-level phenomenon. Economists, on the other hand, specialised in prices, on the wage market, and this was perceived as a macro-level phenomenon. This emphasis on the macro-level was in accordance with the then accepted economic theory.

Mainstream economics had been strongly orientated towards macroeconomics since the end of World War II. Following Keynes and Tinbergen, an active government was thought to be a necessary precondition for stable economic growth. It was thought that a market could generate too small an aggregate demand, and that this would disrupt economic activity, as it had done in the great crisis of the thirties. The reason why markets did not clear was that wages were rigid in a downward direction and decisions on labour supply and expenditure could not (always) be made simultaneously. This precluded the establishment of a new market clearing equilibrium in the labour market, and also on the product markets. To prevent economic catastrophes, aggregate demand should be maintained at acceptable levels. However, economists and government were also afraid of wage increases that were too large. This was perceived to be the main cause of inflation. Policy had to be wise, to avoid the scylla of a too low aggregate demand and the charybdis of inflation.

For such a policy to be effacious, it was necessary to develop institutions that contributed to a balanced wage growth. Wages were to be negotiated by trade unions and employers' organisations. They had the responsible task of establishing balanced wage growth. To supervise whether responsibility was taken, negotiations were placed under the vigilant eye of government appointed experts. Economists focused on the development of the wages in these institutions, and paid special attention to the role of trade unions in the wage formation process. Promising young economists, such as Pen (1950), De Galan (1957) and Albeda (1957) focused on precisely this subject in their dissertation research. These economists also often participated as experts in the corporate institutions.

Economists contributed in another way to policy, namely by computing future developments. Tinbergen was the great predecessor. He stood not only at the cradle of the development of econometric models, but also advocated the establishment of institutional arrangements to apply them fruitfully. Tinbergen's vision was that economic life could and should be planned. This idea of planning, however, was gradually abandoned, to be replaced by ordering, which became the parole. Institutions and policies had to preclude the undesired effects of unrestrained market forces. Scientifically based computations were the means for detecting future discrepancies. Having computed discrepancies, the government and the other relevant parties should develop policies, that would lead to balanced economic growth.

In the handbooks, all theories evaluated as relevant for labour market research were represented, and, although clearly based on different assumptions, they were, nevertheless, presented in juxtaposition, to emphasise their supplementary character. Thus, in the handbooks, the exposition of the neo-classical micro-economic model of the labour market is followed by an exposition of the development of the labour market institutions. This approach to the labour market can be found in both the textbooks (e.g. that of Delfgaauw 1977), and also in the only Dutch textbook on labour economics, (De Galan and Miltenburg, 2nd print, 1981). This approach must be understood on the basis of the assumption shared with the sociologists that the neoclassical model was no longer realistic, since wages were established through negotiation procedures between unions and employers' organisations. This underscored the importance of the economist's task in carefully monitoring the process of wage negotiations.

The economists were not only interested in wage negotiation, but also in its consequences for income distribution, the development of which was the focus of their attention. Many economists shared the idea that large income differences would inhibit economic development and frustrate the price mechanism. They argued that rich people bought goods that probably had greater utility for poor people, who could not afford them. Institutional factors, such as collective agreements and trade unions, were assumed to determine income distribution. For that reason, economists did not conceptualise income differences as being caused by market forces. Consequentially, when dual labour market theory was developed, the economists had to join the sociologists in not having clear answers to its provocative questions.

More important for the development of macro-economic labour market theory, however, was the problem of the Phillips curve, thus the simultaneous process of (growing) unemployment and inflation. Macro-economic theory predicted that too small an aggregate demand would increase unemployment, but should have no or hardly any inflationary effect. A large aggregate demand could cause inflation, but would also lead to a decrease in unemployment. However, the simultaneous processes of increasing unemployment and inflation in the seventies required an explanation that could not be found in the accepted paradigm. This contributed to the feeling that macro-economics did not offer adequate theories and instruments to solve the then current economic problems.

4. THE REDISCOVERY OF NEOCLASSICAL ECONOMICS

During the seventies unemployment had slowly but steadily increased. It proved to be increasingly difficult to counter growing unemployment with Keynesian instruments of increasing aggregate demand. The effects of policies to create additional employment proved to be limited, but costs were huge. The issue was less what the government should do to counter unemployment, but more whether the government could do anything at all.

As already mentioned, not only did unemployment increase, but the number of vacancies increased at the same time. It was felt that there was an increasing discrepancy between the qualifications demanded and those supplied by the labour market. Employers complained of a lack of skills and high wage costs for young school-leavers. This stimulated the debate and research on the link between the educational system and the labour market. An important conclusion reached was that educational qualifications could be applied much more flexibly than had been assumed within the sociological paradigm of the labour market. This cast doubt on the assumption that qualifications were the main cause of the segmentation of the labour market. The problems of unemployment and the qualitative discrepancies led to a substantial increase in labour market research, that henceforth has hardly decreased.

It was against this background of growing unemployment and deficient macro-economic and sociological theories of the labour market, that the neoclassical economic theories were rediscovered. The neoclassical theory was attractive for a number of reasons. It offered an adequate explanation for the simultaneous processes of increasing unemployment and inflation (Phelps 1970). Furthermore, it appeared that the neoclassical corpus contained mutually consistent and powerful theories about the important issues of quantitative and qualitative discrepancies and about distribution in the labour market. As a normative theory, it could be applied to advise policies, and it was discovered that neoclassical micro-economics contained a consistent and advanced methodology. In this section we elaborate on these reasons.

The problem of increasing unemployment could only be countered by wage restraints. Keynesian instruments, such as the enlargement of aggregate demand and the creation of additional jobs, had proven to be very costly and not very effective. By practising wage restraint, a new equilibrium in the labour market could be established, and this would contribute to new economic growth and healthy public finances. The lesson to be learnt was that the government should be moderate in its ambitions; that it should not try to change the equilibrium in the labour market, but only to enhance the beneficial effects of the price mechanism. Accordingly, the advice was to dismantle the labour market institutions, since these inhibited market forces.

The problem of educational discrepancies in the labour market could fruitfully be analysed by elaborating on human capital theory, which was developed in the sixties. At first, this theory had mainly been applied for computing the optimal societal investments in its education system: an effort that failed. However, next to this macro-economic interpretation, a micro-economic interpretation had been elaborated (Becker 1964). Becker's theory assumes that individuals invest in education up to the point at which the cost of the additional investment is equal to its marginal revenue. The (generally) higher wages of better educated workers reflect their higher productivity, facilitated by skills acquired through education. This interpretation of human capital theory offered instruments for analysing the costs and benefits of schooling in the educational system and of firm-specific schooling. It provided instruments for dealing with heterogeneity in educational qualifications, within a neoclassical framework. The value of Becker's elaboration of human capital theory for empirical research was demonstrated by Mincer (1974). This framework provided an approach to the qualitative discrepancies in the labour market. According to human capital theory, students based their decisions about making additional investments in education on information concerning the demand side of the labour market. Wage rates and unemployment figures were important factors in this decision-making process. Accordingly, the price mechanism could and should provide the solution to these discrepancies.

At the same time, though, Becker's elaboration of human capital theory had come under debate (e.g. Blaug 1976), especially because of its assumption that a better education was synonymous with higher productivity. It was argued that information problems preclude such a straightforward assumption. To a certain extent, Spence's screening theory (Spence 1974), that education does not determine, but only indicates productivity, offered an answer. A number of alternative theories were developed—the so-called credentialist theories—that have in common the statement that the number of years in the educational system is largely independent of productivity. Taubman and Wales (1974) argued that differences in educational attainment reflected genetic differences in talent that were sorted in the educational system. Collins (1979), who was very influential in Dutch sociology, argued that, although educational credentials in modern society primarily legitimised wage differentials, they were certainly not determinants of them. It was this debate that stimulated the interest in human capital theory and its rivals.

Furthermore, neoclassical economists showed that they had a well-developed corpus of theories and methods by which to analyse both allocation and income distribution in the labour market. Cain (1976) wrote a sharp criticism of the segmented labour market theories. He argued that their explanation for this segmentation was often incomplete, and that neoclassical theories were able to explain many of the phenomena described. For example, Becker (1957) had developed a neoclassical theory of discrimination twenty years prior to this, arguing that, in a free market, wage discrimination could only last if exogeneous causes perpetuated wage inequality. Mincer and Polachek (1975) had shown that standard statistical analyses helped to make the wage discrimination differential visible. Holding constant for the productive characteristics (such as education and experience), they could show that there were huge wage differentials between males and females. The contradiction between the prediction that wage discrimination could not be perpetuated in a free market, and the research result that revealed of a huge unexplained wage differential, triggered a lot of research, both in the United States and in the Netherlands (for an overview, see Schippers 1987).

Neoclassical economists were also able to deal with the criticism of unrealistic assumptions. The solution was proposed by Friedman at the beginning of the fifties (Friedman 1953). He turned the criticism upside down, arguing that the issue of realistic assumptions was not a serious problem and that, on the contrary, the model should be evaluated on the basis of its informational value to the hypotheses deduced. Support for this argument was found in Popper's falsificationist philosophy of science, that was clearly a step beyond the positivism that had inspired the requirement of realistic assumptions. From then onwards, it has been argued that assumptions such as the transparency of the market are intendedly unrealistic to keep the model simple by reducing the number of assumptions. The greater the information value of a model, the more hypotheses can be deduced from fewer assumptions.

Friedman's argument thus protected the core of the neoclassical model against the criticism of unrealistic assumptions. It also laid out a methodology, pointing out that the neoclassical model with its unrealistic assumptions, was incomplete by definition. From then onwards, neoclassical economists have stated that it is their aim to increase the realism of the model by increasing its predictive power. This was to be achieved by adding new assumptions to the model taken from new theories, the implications of which should be tested empirically. This procedure was fully in accordance with falsificationist epistemology.

Research results accumulate by applying such a methodology. After some time, however, the newly developed theories need to be evaluated to determine whether they contribute to the explanation of empirical phenomena. The first critical evaluations of important theories and their status in empirical research started to appear at the end of the seventies, (especially in the *Journal of Economic Literature*—Blaug 1980). These reviews are crowning pieces of advanced methodology, that far surpass the criticism that their assumptions lack realism.

Dutch labour market research has been strongly affected by this new acquaintance with neoclassical theory. The renewed interest in neoclassical economics stimulated an interest in the labour market behaviour of the different actors. It was now assumed that if price incentives were strong enough, actors would react to them, so price incentives became the core of the behavioural assumptions from which hypotheses about allocation were deduced. In addition, from now on, allocation and wages were conceptualised as outcomes of the same labour market processes. Wages were no longer perceived as being determined by institutionalised wage negotiations. According to the neoclassical argument, it was useless to distinguish between a wage and an allocation market. The emphasis now focused on the argument that the outcomes of negotiation processes were strongly dependent on supply and demand in the labour market. Negotiators had to take account of market forces, and the more they did so, the better the results would be. Attempts by trade unions to resist market forces were viewed with suspicion. These were thought to probably favour worker-members (the 'insiders') at the cost of the unorganised unemployed (the 'outsiders').

This criticism of trade unions was part of a more general criticism of welfare-state institutions. The neoclassical paradigm prescribed that the number of institutions should be restricted to a minimum, since these institutions inhibit the process of price determination by market forces. The argument is that institutions distort the signalling effect of prices, thereby leading to over- or underconsumption, both of which are socially undesirable phenomena. Furthermore, the people who govern such institutions will tend to behave like 'monopolists', interested more in the promotion of their own interests rather than the common good (see especially Friedman 1962). Accordingly, the programme was to dismantle the welfare-state institutions, thereby releasing the price mechanism in the labour market.

5. THE PRESENT STATE OF THE NEOCLASSICAL MODEL

In the eighties, neoclassical principles quickly gained in adherence, at the cost of the older theories. Nowadays it is hard to find reflections on the assumptions of the sociological paradigm in labour market research. The strong empirical orientation of present labour market research is perhaps an inheritance from the eighties. Keynesian macro-economics has also almost completely disappeared from Dutch research, though rigidities in wage formation processes have been, and still are, a focus of attention. However, both paradigms have been superseded by neoclassical theory.

In this section, we shall describe the present state of labour market research, by presenting the hard core of the theory, then describing the research practices and finally the relationship between research and policy.

The theoretical starting point of neoclassical economics is methodological individualism, which implies that analysis focuses primarily on individual actors. The presence of collective actors, such as representative organisations of workers and employers, is recognised, but their behaviour is conceptualised as being determined by individual actors, who have preferences and follow these in their behaviour, which is assumed to maximise utility. In their choice of alternatives, the individual actors are sensitive to price incentives, and are able to gather and process information about prices quickly. These behavioural assumptions are common to all neoclassical theories.

Neoclassical labour market theory, though, is more specific, in that it distinguishes two kinds of actors. On the one side of the market, there are workers, who, in their individual choices, trade off wages against leisure time. Employers, on the demand side, are assumed to recruit workers until the productivity of the last recruited employee is equal to the wage of that worker.

Labour supply theory is well developed too. Its basic assumption of a trade-off between wage rate and leisure time has been elaborated into complex utility functions. Leading from this, assumptions specify the earning capacity and value of leisure time for different people. Human capital theory has inspired many of the assumptions added later concerning differences in earning capacities. Killingsworth (1983), Siegers (1985) and Grift and Siegers (1992) present overviews of supply models.

Less developed is the theory on demand side behaviour, based on the theory of marginal productivity, i.e. that an employer recruits new employees until the productivity of the last worker equals the wage of that worker. This theory of labour demand has been contested, especially as far as the direct link between labour productivity and wage is concerned, and its empirical status came under profound discussion, when labour economist Lester (1946) reported that marginal productivity considerations were almost absent in recruitment practices (cf. Machlup 1968). In response, the theory was protected, but, since then, there has been repeated criticism that it lacks empirical substance (e.g. Thurow 1975; Medoff and Abraham 1980; Blaug 1980). We will return to this issue later, answering the question of why marginal productivity theory was maintained, despite such strong criticism over a period of time.

In the neoclassical model, individual actors enter relationships with other actors. The core of their interaction is exchange that furthers the well-being of both actors. The aggregate of all relevant relationships between the individuals concerned is the market. It has been proved that when rational utility maximising behaviour is in force, the market generates its own equilibrium, which includes both an allocation and a price. An uninhibited price mechanism clears the market and establishes a pareto-optimal equilibrium, thereby creating an optimal situation for each individual actor, i.e. nobody can be better off without someone else being worse off.

However, when the price mechanism is inhibited, the equilibrium is sub-optimal. The causes of such inhibition are, for example, government regulation and intervention and trade union negotiation power. Such inhibition often has unintended negative side-effects, whereby people become disadvantaged by trying to evade the regulation or arrangement, and advantaged in trying to maintain their position by implicating the political force. However, it might be the case that regulation, rather than inhibiting, actually enhances the price mechanism. This is not the first intuition, however, and the onus of proof lies with the person who advocates regulation. As there is no general rule, as to when government intervention should be preferred instead of the price mechanism, evidence for the proof has to be gathered and presented, casewise.

The above assumptions are the core of the neoclassical model of the labour market, which is a popular model in the different contexts of both research and policy making.

In research practice, the theory is developed by adding assumptions to the core model and deducing their effects on the equilibrium. The assumptions added should not contradict that of utility maximisation. The simpler they are and the easier they are to formalise, the greater is the appreciation of the assumptions added.

The relationship between theory and empirical research may take different forms. The most valuable empirical work is the submission of hypotheses deduced from a theoretical model to an empirical test. Such tests verify the empirical relationships predicted by the model. More often, though, the relationship between theory and empirical research is less close, because the notion of equilibrium in empirical research is often pushed into the background, since it is assumed that market imperfections, such as information problems, preclude the establishment of an equilibrium in the short run. For this reason, empirical research often consists of the establishment of a relationship between wage rate as the dependent variable, and a number of personal characteristics and jobs as independent variables. In such research, the neoclassical theoretical corpus mainly serves as a heuristic.

Empirical research practice is increasingly characterised by the application of advanced statistical methods to so-called micro-data—data from, and about a large number of individual actors. The development of new micro-technology has stimulated the application of statistics, as this reduces the costs of computing time. Nevertheless, there is also a strong incentive in the paradigm to subject the simple, abstract theories to empirical tests. The assumption of methodological individualism corresponds to the structure of the data sets containing a record per person. Empirical research on the demand side of the labour market is more difficult, if only because of the structure of these data sets.

The research programme broadens by selecting theories. Economists, just as philosophers of science, do not agree about the rules that should be applied in the selection process. In fact, the practice is consistent with the principle of revealed preferences, that it is those theories that have been popular in research practice for some time that are incorporated into the paradigm.

Such a newly incorporated theory probably satisfies two conditions. One is that an empirical phenomenon is explained more specifically (and therefore better) than it was previously, and the second is that its behavioural assumptions conform with utility maximisation. A theory disappears after some time when it does not satisfy these two conditions anymore. An example is the disappearance from the literature of the implicit contract theory (see, in particular, Azariades 1975), developed in the mid-seventies. According to this theory, wages are rigid because of an informally concluded agreement between employer and worker. This informal contract implies that the worker will not ask large wage increases during periods of cyclical boom but will not suffer from wage decreases in periods of slump. In its origins, the theory promised to provide the micro-foundation for Keynesian policies, but later it proved not to be robust enough to withstand a critical review (Rosen 1985). Consequently it has not been elaborated on in articles. More often, however, a theory is not withdrawn, following critical funerial oration, rather it falls victim to silence in journals and books.

Some theories survive by want of a better theory, even though they are very much criticised. A clear example is the theory of marginal productivity, mentioned earlier. This theory has resisted many a critical review, since it is an important link between labour market theory, general equilibrium theory and growth theory. General equilibrium theory is the theoretical foundation of the claim that under strictly defined assumptions an inhibited price mechanism produces efficient equilibria in all markets simultaneously and is therefore a core theory in the neoclassical paradigm.

Neoclassical theory is the foremost theory, not only in research, but also in policy making. Normative neoclassical theory assumes that the uninhibited invisible hand establishes the most efficient outcomes. It therefore prescribes that government policies should be minimal, consisting of the removal of any obstacles that inhibit the price mechanism from doing its work. Accordingly, a wise government should take account of the effects on the price mechanism before actually intervening.

Current labour market policy problems steer to a large extent labour market research effort in the Netherlands. The problems on the research agenda closely correspond to the social problems as perceived by the policy makers. It is hard to evaluate whether a problem is a focus of attention simply because researchers or policy makers have defined it as a problem. This is due to the symbiosis developed during the last fifteen years, in problem definition, research programmes and the policy theory of labour market researchers and labour market policy makers.

6. NORMAL SCIENCE AND ANOMALIES

By far the greatest part of Dutch labour market research can be characterised as 'normal science'. This is especially the case with the large number of descriptive studies written to inform labour market policy makers. Applications of new statistical techniques is also considered as normal science. An example of such a technique in the eighties was survival analysis, applied especially to establish determinants for the lengths of unemployment. In general, such descriptive work is not driven very much by theory, in fact, theory serves primarily as a heuristic in such studies. Somewhat more theory-driven are attempts to develop instruments to measure important theoretical concepts. Interesting recent examples are the attempts to measure the costs of recruitment and dismissal (Hassink and Van Ours 1994, 1995), and productivity (Gelderblom et al. 1994). Of direct influence on the development of the paradigm is the further specification of theory. An important specification in the eighties was Hartog's elaboration of the hedonic theory of allocation in the labour market (Hartog 1986, 1988).

Of primary importance for the paradigm are its anomalies. These refer to conditions that contradict or, at least, are hard to explain by the accepted theory. Anomalies are weak spots that make the paradigm vulnerable. A weak paradigm has a number of anomalies, that are starting-points for external criticism. In a strong paradigm, the adherents of the model themselves look for such anomalies, to stimulate theory development.

Overviewing the field, we think that for the neoclassical model two important anomalies can be distinguished. The first is the existence and persistence of unemployment. Despite decreasing governmental intervention in the eighties, unemployment has not disappeared. Why?

The traditional answer of neoclassical analysis is that the price mechanism is inhibited by labour market institutions. The specific argument is that minimum wages and social security regulation preclude market clearance. Full employment can only be established by abandoning minimum wage regulation and reducing social security benefits. Empirical support for this analysis is found in the United States. There, the decrease in unemployment in the eighties has often been attributed to the lowering of minimum wage, unemployment and other social benefits.

However, this analysis is questioned by a number of neoclassical economists. The results of empirical research raise doubts that the abandonment of the minimum wage and the lowering of social security benefits contribute to a substantial decrease in unemployment. Card and Krueger (1994), for example, have argued, on the basis of empirical research, that lower minimum wages have not contributed to more employment, and these results have stimulated debate in the Netherlands (Teulings 1994, 1995a; Breedveld 1995). Empirical research appears to show that, in general, the labour market behaviour of the Dutch unemployed is not very sensitive to monetary incentives (Groot, Mekkelholt and Theeuwes 1994).

The second anomaly is the existence and perpetuation of non-productive wage differentials. By this we do not mean the persistence of wage discrimination, since this may be argued to be caused by latent differences in supply characteristics. However, non-productive wage differentials, caused by the demand side of the labour market, are even more important as anomalies. The existence of such differentials implies that different employers are prepared to pay different wages for the same worker. Such non-productive wage differentials have been found in statistics for both the United States and the Netherlands for different firm sizes (larger firms pay better) and for different economic sectors (Brown and Medoff 1989; Krueger and Summers 1988; Hartog et al. 1994; Teulings 1995b). An interesting result from comparing such wage differentials is that they are found to be greater in the United States than in the Netherlands. This result enhances the anomaly, since the American labour market is characterised by fewer institutions (and therefore much more decentralised wage negotiations) and far greater worker mobility and should therefore have fewer of these types of differentials.

It is a paradox that the anomalies for neoclassical labour market theory have become enhanced since the criticisms of the American labour economists and the Dutch labour market sociologists. The existence of non-productive wage differentials between firms of unequal size, and between different sectors, was well-known and was often positioned against neoclassical economics (Lester 1946; for the Netherlands: Van Voorden 1975). The persistence of unemployment, however, is a relatively new phenomenon, although it may be argued that this problem is much less acute in the more market orientated economy of the United States than in the more corporative economies of Western Europe.

7. MARKET FAILURE AND EQUILIBRIUM

The question for the future development of research is whether, within the paradigm, solutions for the anomalies can be found, or whether a rival paradigm is able to provide a positive explanation for the anomalies. As a tentative answer, we do not see any rival paradigm that is able to provide an acceptable explanation for either of the anomalies. By far the strongest criticism of neoclassical economic theory comes from neoclassical economists, not from critics external to the paradigm. As the framework of a paradigm is always fallible, this is an indication that the theory is powerful. Nevertheless, this also indicates that there is doubt about fundamental assumptions and this influences labour market research.

In standard neoclassical analysis, an uninhibited price mechanism produces optimal results on any market, including the labour market. If a market clearing equilibrium is not established, the paradigm gives guidance in looking for reasons why the price mechanism is inhibited from acting effectively. This protects the core assumptions, because, since the basic assumptions of the neoclassical theory are not very realistic, it is easy to find an institution that hampers the price mechanism. Alternatively, it is argued that there is a time lag, caused by the fact that the actors need time to gather and process information about the state of the market. The implication is that a clearing equilibrium may never be established, even though market forces work towards this. Both arguments—the hampered price mechanism and the clearance time-lag—protect the standard neoclassical model.

In recent years, however, theories of market failure have attracted attention. It has been shown that there are good explanations for the absence of a market clearing equilibrium, and thus for market failure. Natural monopolies, economies of scale, collective goods, external effects and information asymmetries may all cause market failure.

Information asymmetries are a particular source of clearance problems in the labour market. Such asymmetries refer to problems of hidden characteristics (often called the problem of adverse selection) and of hidden decisions (also known as moral hazard). The basic idea is that a worker's characteristics or decisions may be of great importance for productivity, and, for that reason, an employer is interested in them. However, they are not directly measurable and the worker has an interest in not providing this information, since this may decrease his wage. A clear example, is the worker's strategy concerning his level of effort. It is reasonable to assume that a worker will not report to his employer that he has been shirking. If his output is low, he will attribute this to hardly measurable contingency factors. When the effort and output of the worker are hard to measure, the employer faces a hidden decision problem.

The consequences of information asymmetries for the labour market have been elaborated in the so-called efficiency wage theories (Akerlof and Yellen 1986). The common core of these theories is that employers have a good reason to pay a better wage than the market clearing rate because of information problems. In the best-known of these models, the reason is that a wage premium makes dismissal a credible threat (Shapiro and Stiglitz 1984). Having been dismissed from a well-paid job, it will be hard for a worker to find an equally attractive job, and so he will exert effort to ensure that he is not dismissed. The better wage is conceptualised not only as a motivation incentive, but also as an incentive to stay in the job, or as a signal from the employer to the worker that he wants to build up a trust relationship (Akerlof 1984). However, as the market does not clear, a consequence of such wage premiums is involuntary unemployment.

Specific investments in human capital are another cause of market clearance problems. Specific investments in human capital increase the worker's wages. A worker who has specific knowledge about the production process can credibly threaten to leave his employer in order to get a better wage. The employer has an interest in binding this employee, and will give in to the threat by paying a better wage. Such a relationship has large transaction costs, and these hamper the price mechanism. Although transaction cost arguments may not provide a full explanation, they do add significantly to the explanation of internal labour markets. Within the framework of market failure, the establishment of a market-clearing equilibrium is the exception, rather than the rule (Clower 1965; Hansen 1970). As a consequence, the theory of general equilibrium loses significance. What remains are separate theories, which share the assumptions of rational, well-informed, utility maximising behaviour. These may be turned into a new paradigm, in which not the equilibrium but the actual behaviour is the focus of theoretical attention (cf. Kreps 1990; Milgrom and Roberts 1992). Elements of such a paradigm may be found especially in game theory, but also in parts of price theory and in the developed radical, marxist and sociological theories (Rebitzer 1993; Swedberg 1992). Such a paradigm will enlarge the domain of labour market research. It will not be restricted to 'external' market problems, but will also address problems of work organisation (or 'agency').

In such a field, the governance of employment relationships will be the main focus of interest for theory. Neoclassically trained authors such as Milgrom and Roberts (1992) and Lazear (1995) explicitly assume the possibility of opportunistic behaviour in the employment relationship, and thus recognise the importance of governance structures for employment relationships. In the Netherlands, it is mostly sociologists who use elements from this relatively new branch of economic organisation theory in their analysis of labour market problems (see Korver 1989; Wielers 1991; Glebbeek 1993; Ten Have 1993). Consequently, the boundary between markets and organisations may be expected to fade.

Such an approach has consequences for government policies. If the market does not clear, institutions will have to be designed to contribute to market clearing, and, in fact, a change in the appreciation of institutions can now, once again, be readily observed. Many of the institutions developed in the post-war period that have survived the sharp criticism of neoclassical economics are now being re-evaluated as parts of the so-called 'poldermodel'. Corporate institutions are now glorified, and there is national pride in this new 'export product'. Trade unions and employers' organisations are loudly praised for having practised wage restraint, thus laying the foundation for the considerable job growth. Appreciating the importance of wage restraint, it is now argued that the government should retain instruments to influence the development of the wage rates. Policies should steer the market mechanism, such that the desired outcomes are obtained. This new policy theory is clearly different from the neoclassical one which takes the view that institutions hamper the market. The new policy theory is that citizens should receive the right incentives. Thus, they should get material rewards for socially good behaviour, and be made to pay the costs of socially undesired behaviour.

The new approach to institutions is elaborated in the economic analysis of law (Hondius et al. 1991), according to which it is mainly because of transaction costs (Williamson 1975, 1985) that institutions need to exist at all. This contributes to their inclusion within policies, as opposed to other institutions which may now be exposed as inefficient, since they cause transaction costs and appear to serve only one goal, that of effecting benefits for a small number of parties in the market.

We do not expect the change of paradigm, described above, to shake Dutch labour market research. For one reason, labour market research has a strong empirical orientation. In such a context, it is not necessary to explicate the theoretical argument about market clearance. In practice, behavioural assumptions and neoclassical methodology are adopted, without explicit reference to equilibrium assumptions.

We do not find strong doubts about the paradigm in the more theoretically oriented debates either. This is due not only to the absence of a rival paradigm, but also to the fact that the core of the neoclassical paradigm is protected and thus does not come under debate. Other assumptions may come under debate, preferably after researchers who are strongly committed to the neoclassical paradigm have presented the results of empirical research. However, labour market researchers, and especially the economists among them, seldom discuss the paradigm. At the most, now and again they write a review article presenting their view on the state of the art (e.g. Hartog and Theeuwes 1990). For these reasons, it is to be expected that the repertoire of theories applied will change almost unobserved.

8. BALANCE

Do we know more, and do we understand better than IJzerman, Lulofs and De Galan did? As with so many other questions about progress, the question about progress in Dutch labour market research is hard to answer.

The older literature is characterised by very rich descriptions and theories. This was extended by adding new descriptions and theories. The claim was that, in the end, on the basis of empirical research, a complete model of the labour market could be elaborated. This programme was part of the vision of a welfare state under construction. The model should and could prevent catastrophes, such as the crisis of the thirties, by foreseeing discrepancies and advising on policies.

In comparison to this older programme, on the one hand ambitions have become smaller. In recent years, a sorting process has led to a decrease in the number of theories accepted. Theories now have to satisfy other requirements. Analytically, they must be internally and mutually consistent at the level of individual behaviour. Theories are tested more often and explored less frequently. Large data sets are used to describe and test them, and advanced statistical methods are successfully applied to analyse them. Anomalies have proved to be fruitful starting points for research. One might conclude that great ambitions have lost ground to modest and laborious craftsmanship.

At the same time, however, labour market research is still linked to policy, but in another way. Whereas the older researchers advised on policies by drawing on their knowledge of theories and research results, now the theory itself has become the basis of policies, in that the theory provides their foundation and thus their legitimation. Even the criticism of the policies is in the language of neoclassical economic theory and therein lies the power and the supremacy of neoclassical economic labour market theory.

REFERENCES

Albeda, W., 1957. *De rol van de vakbeweging in de moderne maatschappij* (The role of trade unions in modern society), Hoorn, Edeca.

Akerlof, G.A., 1984. 'Labor contracts as partial gift exchange', *Quarterly Journal of Economics* 97: 543-569.

Akerlof, G.A. and J.L. Yellen, eds., 1986. *Efficiency wage models of the labor market*, New York NY, Cambridge University Press.

Azariades, C., 1975. 'Implicit contracts and underemployment equilibria', *Journal of Political Economy* 83: 1183-1202.

Becker, G.S., 1957. *The economics of discrimination*, Chicago, University of Chicago Press.

Becker, G.S., 1964. *Human capital*, New York, Colombia University Press.

Berkel, P. van, 1965. *Spanningen op de arbeidsmarkt. Institutionele en sociaal-psychologische componenten in de structuur van een stedelijke arbeidsmarkt* (Tensions in the labour market. Institutional and social-psychological elements in the structure of an urban labour market), Meppel, Boom.

Blaug, M., 1976. 'Human capital theory. A slightly jaundiced view', *Journal of Economic Literature* 14: 827-855.

Blaug, M., 1980. *The methodology of economics. Or how economists explain*, 2nd ed., Cambridge, Cambridge University Press, 1992.

Breedveld, C., 1995. 'Minimumloon vernietigt banen' (Minimum wage destroys jobs), *Economisch-Statistische Berichten* 80: 15-16, (4-1-1995).

Brown, C. and J. Medoff, 1989. 'The employer size-wage effect', *Journal of Political Economy* 97: 1027-1059.

Buiter, J.H., 1968. *Modern salariaat in wording. Van arbeidersklasse naar werknemersstand* (Modern salariat in the making. From working class to emplyee estate), Rotterdam, Universitaire Pers.

Cain, G.C., 1976. 'The challenge of segmented labor market theories to orthodox theory. A survey', *Journal of Economic Literature* 14: 1215-1257.

Cairnes, J.E., 1874. *Some leading principles of political economy newly expounded*, London.

Card, D. and A.B. Krueger, 1994. 'Minimum wages and employment: a case study of the fast food industry in New Jersey and Pennsylvania', *American Economic Review* 84: 772-793.

Clower, R., 1965. 'The Keynesian counterrevolution: a theoretical appraisal' in: F. Hahn and F.P.R. Brechling (eds.), *The theory of interest rates*, London, MacMillan.

Collins, R., 1979. *The credential society. A historical sociology of education and stratification*, New York, Academic Press.

Delfgaauw, G.Th.J., 1977. *Inleiding tot de economische wetenschap. Deel I. Theorie van het proces der prijsvorming* (Introduction into the science of economics. Volume 1. Theory of prices), Wassenaar, Delwel.

Doorn, J.A.A. van, 1961. *Arbeidsmarkt en arbeidsbestel. Brugpijlers tussen sociologie en economie* (Labour market and institutional arrangements. Bridging pillars between sociology and economics), Assen, Van Gorcum.

Friedman, M., 1953. *Essays in positive economics*, Chicago, University of Chicago Press.

Friedman, M., 1962. *Capitalism and Freedom*, Chicago, University of Chicago Press.

Galan, C. de, 1957. *De invloed van de vakvereniging op loonshoogte en werkgelegenheid. Een macro-economische beschrijving van vraagstukken van groepsvorming* (The effect of the trade union on wage rates and employment. A macro-economic description of issues concerning group formation), Leiden, Stenfert Kroese.

Galan, C. de and A.J.M. van Miltenburg, 1985. *Economie van de arbeid* (Economics of labour), Alphen aan de Rijn, Samsom (2e dr.; oorspr. 1981).

Gelderblom, A., N.B.J.G. 't Hoen and J. de Koning, 1994. *Beloning en produktiviteit* (Wages and productivity), Den Haag, OSA.

Glebbeek, A.C., 1993. *Perspectieven op loopbanen* (Perspectives on careers), Assen, Van Gorcum.

Grift, Y.K. and J.J. Siegers, 1992. 'Het arbeidsaanbod door individuen en huishoudens in Nederland. Wat heeft vijftien jaar onderzoek opgeleverd?' (Supply of labour by individuals and households in the Netherlands. What has been the yield of fifteen years of research?) *Maandschrift Economie* 56: 248-270.

Groot, W., E. Mekkelholt and J. Theeuwes, 1994. *Allocatie en beloningsverschillen* (Allocation and wage differentials), Den Haag, OSA.

Haagsma, R., 1995. *Microeconomic models of gender discrimination in labour markets with asymmetric information*, Dissertatie, Amsterdam, Universiteit van Amsterdam.

Hamaker, H.G., 1976. *Arbeidsmarkt en personeelsvoorziening* (Labour market and personnel recruitment), Alphen aan de Rijn, Samsom.

Hansen, B., 1970. *A survey of general equilibrium systems*, New York.

Hartog, J., 1986. 'Earning functions: beyond human capital', *Applied Economics* 11: 97-110.

Hartog, J., 1988. 'Een hedonische interpretatie van allocatie en beloning' (A hedonic interpretation of allocation and rewards), *Tijdschrift voor Arbeidsvraagstukken* 4(3): 47-52.

Hartog, J. and J.J.M. Theeuwes, 1990. 'Arbeidseconomie' (Labour economics) in: L. van der Geest (red.), *Economische theorie. De stand van zaken* (Economic theory. The state of the art), Schoonhoven, Academic Service, pp. 211-231.

Hartog, J., R. van Opstal and C.N. Teulings, 1994. 'Loonvorming in Nederland en de Verenigde Staten' ("The wage formation process in the Netherlands and in the United States"), *Economisch-Statistische Berichten* 79: 528-533, (8-6-1994).

Hassink, W. and J. van Ours, 1994. *Werkgelegenheid in verandering. Een analyse op bedrijfsniveau* (Employment in change. An analysis on the firm level), Den Haag, OSA.

Hassink, W. and J. van Ours, 1995. *Aanpassing van werkgelegenheid. Een nadere analyse op bedrijfsniveau* (Adaptation of employment. A further analysis on the firm level), Den Haag, OSA.

Have, K. ten, 1993. *Markt, organisatie en personeel in de industrie* (Market, organisation and personnel in the manufacturing sector), Tilburg, Tilburg University Press.

Hoeven, P.J.A. ter, 1963. *Havenarbeiders van Rotterdam en Amsterdam. Sociologische analyse van een arbeidsmarkt* (Workers in the harbours of Rotterdam and Amsterdam. A sociological analysis of a labour market), Leiden, Stenfert Kroese.

Hondius, E.H., J.J. Schippers and J.J. Siegers (red.), 1991. *Rechtseconomie en recht* (Economics of law and law), Zwolle, Tjeenk Willink.

Hoof, J.J. van, 1977. 'Arbeidsmarktonderzoek op een keerpunt' (Labour market research on a turning point), *Sociologische Gids* 24: 5-33.

IJzerman, Th.J., 1959. *Beroepsaanzien en arbeidsvoldoening met betrekking tot de arbeidsvoorziening in de Twents-Achterhoekse textielindustrie* (Occupational prestige and workers' satisfaction with regard to personnel recruitment in the textile industry), Leiden, Stenfert Kroese.

Killingsworth, M.R., 1983. *Labor supply*, Cambridge, Cambridge University Press.

Korver, T., 1989. *A matter of discretion. An essay on the U.S. labour market*, De Lier, Academisch Boeken Centrum.

Kreps, D.M., 1990. *A course in microeconomic analysis*, New York, Harvester Wheatsheaf.

Krueger, A.B. and L.H. Summers, 1988. 'Efficiency wages and the inter-industry wage structure', *Econometrica* 56(2): 259-293.

Kuhn, T.S., 1970. *The structure of scientific revolutions*, Chicago, University of Chicago Press.

Lazear, E.P., 1995. *Personnel economics*, Cambridge, MA, MIT-Press.

Lester, R.A., 1946. 'Shortcomings of marginal analysis for wage-employment problems', *American Economic Review* 36: 63-82.

Lulofs, J.G., 1960. *De Amerikaanse arbeidsmarkt* (The American labour market), Meppel, Boom.

Machlup, F., 1968. 'Theories of the firm: marginalist, behavioral, managerial' *American Economic Review* 57: 1-33.

Medoff, J.L. and K.G. Abraham, 1980. 'Experience, performance and earnings', *Quarterly Journal of Economics* 94: 703-736.

Milgrom, P. and J. Roberts, 1992. *Economics, organisation and management*, Englewood Cliffs NJ, Prentice Hall.

Mincer, J., 1974. *Schooling, experience and earnings*, New York, NBER.

Mincer, J. and S.W. Polachek, 1974. 'Family investments in human capital. Earnings of women' *Journal of Political Economy*: S76-s108.
Pen, J., 1950. *De loonvorming in de moderne volkshuishouding. Theorie der collectieve loononderhandelingen* (Wage formation in the modern economy. The theory of collective wage negotiations), Leiden, Stenfert Kroese.
Phelps, E.S. (ed.), 1970. *Microeconomic foundations of employment and inflation theory*, London, MacMillan.
Rebitzer, James B., 1993. 'Radical political economy and the economics of labor markets', *Journal of Economic Literature* 31: 1394-1434.
Rosen, S., 1985. 'Implicit contracts', *Journal of Economic Literature* 23: 1144-1175.
Schippers, J.J., 1987. *Beloningsverschillen tussen mannen en vrouwen* (Wage differentials between men and women), Groningen, Wolters-Noordhoff.
Shapiro, C. and J.E. Stiglitz, 1984. 'Equilibrium unemployment as a worker discipline device', *American Economic Review* 74: 433-444.
Siegers, J.J., 1985. *Arbeidsaanbod en kindertal. Een micro-economische analyse* (Labour supply and fertility), Groningen, Dissertation RUG.
Spence, A.M., 1974. *Market signaling. Informational transfer in hiring and related screening processes*, Cambridge, Harvard University Press.
Swedberg, R., 1992. *Sociology and Economics*, Princeton, NJ, Princeton University Press.
Taubman, P. and T. Wales, 1974. *Higher education and earnings. College as an investment and a screening device*, New York, National Bureau of Economic Research.
Taussig, F.W., 1912. *Principles of economics,* New York, MacMillan.
Teulings, C.N., 1994. 'Hoger minimumloon: meer werkgelegenheid' (Higher minimum wage: more employment), *Economisch-Statistische Berichten* 79: 1112, (7-12-1994).
Teulings, C.N., 1995a. 'Naschrift' (Rejoinder), *Economisch-Statistische Berichten* 80: 16-17, (4-1-1995).
Teulings, C.N., 1995b. 'Efficiënte loonvorming door sociale partners' (Efficient wage formation in collective negotiations), *Economisch-Statistische Berichten* 80: 460-464, (17-5-1995).
Thurow, L.C., 1975. *Generating inequality. Mechanisms of distribution in the U.S. economy*, New York, Basic Books.
Voorden, W. van, 1975. *Institutionalisering en arbeidsmarktbeleid* (Institutionalisation and labour market policy), Alphen aan de Rijn, Samsom.
Wielers, R., 1991. *Selectie en allocatie op de arbeidsmarkt. Een uitwerking voor de informele en geïnstitutionaliseerde kinderopvang* (Selection and allocation in the labour market. An elaboration for informal and institutionalised child care labour markets), Amsterdam, Thesis.
Williamson, O.E., 1975. *Markets and hierarchies. Analysis and antitrust implications*, New York, Free Press.
Williamson, O.E., 1985. *The economic institutions of capitalism*, New York, Free Press.

AUTHORS

Dr. J.J. Schippers
University of Utrecht, Faculty of Economics/CIAV
Kromme Nieuwegracht 22, 3512 HH Utrecht
tel. +31 (0)30 2537116/7100, fax. +31 (0)30 2537131
e-mail: j.schippers@pobox.ruu.nl

Dr. R.J.J. Wielers
Erasmus University of Rotterdam, Faculty of Management sciences
P.O. box 1738, 3000 DR Rotterdam
e-mail: r.wielers@fac.fbk.eur.nl

LABOUR RELATIONS RESEARCH: Changing perspectives

Ad Nagelkerke and Willem de Nijs

1. INTRODUCTION

Rewarding and organising work are two basic, intrinsically connected, elements that come to the fore in industrial and labour relations. Both have given rise to struggles between capital and labour, employers and workers and their respective collective representatives; both have led to different processes and institutions, including those ensuing from state involvement. In essence, from the very beginning of labour relations, the autonomy of capital or labour has been contested, regarding wages and work-related issues, both internally within companies and outside. These processes are at the very heart of the study of industrial and labour relations, which is the main subject of our contribution.

In this chapter, an overview is given of the labour and industrial relations studies undertaken by Dutch scientists during the nineties. Given the large number of studies, we were compelled to make a selection. For this, the following criteria were used:

The research:

- had to be published in the nineties by a Dutch author;
- had to be grounded on theoretical concepts and/or on empirical data;
- had to be focused on a subject considered to be at the heart of the study of labour relations;
- had to have used a multidisciplinary labour relations approach, though, in some cases, this condition was relaxed so as not to exclude relevant research.

Among the studies left out were policy reports of the principal actors (trade unions, employers' organisations, and government agencies); studies by foreign authors analysing developments in the Netherlands; many pure disciplinary studies (economics, sociology, law, psychology); and studies by Dutch authors on foreign labour relations issues, except where these were comparative studies. Despite this radical selection process, a great deal of interesting research remained. A descriptive model was applied to determine whether or not a study could be considered to belong to what we may consider as the nucleus of the field of labour relations.

Reynaerts (1986: 16) developed an analytical scheme to structure this field of study. First, he drew a distinction between *integral* and *partial* analyses. Integral analysis concerns studies of labour relations as a whole, as systems at different levels, internationally, nationally, sectorally, or company-specific. Theoretical studies aimed at developing a conceptual framework were also included in this research category. Partial analyses are directed at well-defined parts of labour relations. Here, Reynaerts made a further subdivision into three groups. The first includes studies of *the interacting actors*, such as a group or organisational formation of workers and employers, the behaviour of employers at company level, and government policies in industrial relations. The second class of partial studies consists of research dealing with *processes of interaction.* These include, consultation, bargaining, and conflict, as well as the joint formation of institutions to channel those processes. The last category consists of studies on the *results of the processes of interaction*, such as formal and informal rules emerging from negotiations as well as labour laws and government policies which may be considered as outcomes of the system of industrial relations.

This classification indicates the comprehensiveness of the study of labour relations. It also makes clear that it is beyond our reach to discuss all the labour relations studies that appeared in the nineties. The selection we have made is based, firstly, on the authors' own, thus arbitrary, judgement about the relevance of certain publications for the research domain in question, and secondly, on the scientific attention those studies have attracted. The major headings under which those studies are given attention correspond by and large to established classifications of Dutch industrial relations study as well as to Reynaerts' scheme; that is, the integral Dutch system of labour relations (Section 2), trade unions (Section 3), collective bargaining (Section 4), co-determination of workers in the company (Section 5), and new workplace industrial relations (Section 6). Some conclusions and judgements have been included in the final, and seventh section. Each section has been given a different structure based upon the characteristics of the area under study as well as upon the extent and qualities of the research undertaken.

Nevertheless, some traditional subjects of labour relations have been excluded. Labour conflict is an issue that has generated little research (e.g. Van der Meer 1996; Akkermans et al. 1995). This also holds for contributions to industrial relations theory. In our opinion, only Coenen and Leisink (1990) and Huiskamp (1992, Section 6), are worth mentioning in this respect. In addition, an important issue such as the influence of changing technology upon the labour input in a company and its further qualitative ramifications (cf. Veersma 1992; Meeus 1994) is, nevertheless, outside the scope of this chapter.

Finally, the reader is asked to bear in mind that, in this chapter, the expressions industrial relations and labour relations are used alternatively, often, but not always, coinciding with expressions such as socio-economic or social and economic systems.

2. THE SYSTEM OF INDUSTRIAL RELATIONS

Even when taking account of several recent changes, the Dutch system of industrial relations may be labelled as rather centralistic. The government is still a mighty player within the system, not only as a legislator but also as a collective party with vital interests in the outcomes of wage settlements, and one that acts accordingly. Through consultation and persuasion, even by threatening the other parties that it will intervene in the wage process, the government tries to direct the other parties and get its piece of the cake as well. Centralism is also indicated by employers' associations and trade unions which still hold important meetings at the central level in an attempt to set the scene for collective bargaining at lower levels. Nonetheless, the industrial relations system has clearly been undergoing a process of transformation in the last ten to fifteen years. This was and still is a process of re-institutionalisation fostered by several factors, both internal and external to the system of industrial relations, and characterised by a steady decentralisation of bargaining structures, deregulation of labour law, a weakening of the trade union movement, and increasing flexibilisation of working time, employment and, in some cases, wages. In the nineties, the changes have proceeded so far, mainly through political activity, that Dutch corporatism seemed to have passed away, but, surprisingly, shortly after its denouncement had reached a high level, the system started to resurrect. However, the concept of 'corporatism' had now become outmoded, most probably because it was felt that the system of industrial and labour relations had been thoroughly modernised. It has become common practice now to speak about the 'consultation economy'.

On these grounds, the volume of research dealt with here can be divided into two parts. The first consists of research on the system of industrial relations in change: making inquiries into the causes of that change and, sometimes, exploring the opportunities to counteract or balance, politically and socio-economically, the forces which drive the system to change. The goal of the second, smaller part of the research which appeared largely in the second part of this decade, was to search for, sometimes comparatively, the basics of the Dutch system that have come to be so advantageous economically.

With the latter, the influence of economic thinking as well as economic science itself has become important in Dutch industrial relations research. A fine illustration is the attention the Central Planning Office, which always stuck to mainstream economic modelling, gave to social structure and social developments in an influential prospective study (CPB 1992). Another example is the industrial economists' attention to 'performance' and 'corporate governance' which stimulated interest in labour issues, for instance, by conducting comparative studies of the so called Anglo–Saxon and Rhineland model of social and economic ordering (see De Jong 1996). In the sweeping discussions on the blessings of the market, and, in its wake, the performance qualities of existing social institutions, other economists working in the mainstream tradition also took up the study of industrial relations aspects (e.g. Van Praag and Hop 1994; Hartog et al. 1994; Gradus 1994, and others). Because the structure and outcomes of wage bargaining were central to most of these contributions, they will be treated briefly in the section on collective bargaining. In the present section, some key publications illustrating both kinds of research will be discussed.

Finally, the focus will be exclusively on the private sector, taken as a system with different levels. It is unfortunate that, in the Netherlands, industrial relations within the (semi)public sector is given such poor attention scientifically (exceptions are: Van Voorden 1989; Becking 1996; for the semipublic sector see: Plessen 1996).[1] Another lacuna in Dutch industrial relations research is the lack of publications studying company industrial relations or workplace industrial relations. Only a few historical publications (for instance, Stoop 1993; Schrover 1993) and some sociological research on new production concepts (Fruytier 1994; Huiskamp 1992; see also Section 6) have appeared on the subject.

2.1. Analysing the changing system

Undoubtedly, the most influential publication dealing with the changing Dutch system of industrial relations was written by Reynaerts in 1985. He coined the qualification 'tilting industrial relations', to refer to a transition of the system in which the economy would be more dominant than ever. Reynaerts foresaw a Dutch system less coerced by government, with greater flexibility, less social protection, greater income inequalities, and decentralised decision making (Reynaerts 1985: 8). His analysis was the starting point for several studies and conferences in later years (for instance, De Gier 1991). As such, the eighties could be seen as a transition period, a period between two different kinds of institutional systems. Due to the character of that interval, it could happen, as Trommel (1995) has illustrated, that the utilisation of early retirement provisions by elderly workers would run into enormous proportions; a 'robust' development.[2]

Different aspects of the transformation of the Dutch labour system, including its causes, have been dealt with by Visser (1992a), Nagelkerke (1992), Van Voorden et al. (1993), Buitendam et al. (1990), Klamer (1990), Albeda and Derksen (1994), Van den Toren (1996), and many others. The same holds for the related subject of corporatism, a major research tradition in political science (cf. Streeck and Schmitter 1992; Esping-Anderson 1990; Crouch 1993). For instance, Hemerijck (1993), starting from a historical, cross-national perspective of political institutions, and going back to the roots of the system in seventeenth-century United Netherlands, revealed the historically important effect of *consocialism* — that is the political structure based on sharing parliamentary power among minority parties — and *pillarisation* — the vertical division of society and institutions along religious/ideological lines (Van Dijk and Punch 1993: 172) — on Dutch corporatism. Consocialism and pillarisation were important not only because of their emergence and further development, but also for the effects of their demise in the seventies and eighties of this century. The 'recent immobility' of the Dutch corporatist system, Hemerijck claimed, has illuminated the fundamental paradox of corporatism: 'where state actors engage in corporatist regulation, they essentially choose to make government dependent on organised interests, by integrating them into public policy-making, so as to seek in return greater control over the regulatory process and its outcomes' (Hemerijck 1993: 353). However, when the support from societal circles began to wane, government became imprisoned in an institutional setting that increasingly malfunctioned. According to Hemerijck, the problem was that the political practice of corporatism had historically been based on a contingent foundation, only successful as long as it could lean on the combination of a pillarised society and consocialism in politics. When depillarisation set in, the transient conditions under which Dutch corporatism had come to life ceased to exist and corporatism itself became 'immobile'. As in the past, there might well be a contingent future for the Dutch social and economic order. Such an elaboration was, however, outside the scope of Hemerijck's inquiry.

The early nineties was a critical period for the Dutch institutional system of industrial relations. A number of economists and politicians questioned the merits of long existing institutions, such as the collective agreement, the trade union, the extension of collective agreements, the minimum wage, and so on. Within a few years, several legislative revisions passed parliament, most of them having to do with social security.[3] The labour system came under scrutiny, that is, a balance sheet of strengths and weaknesses of the institutional pattern was drawn up by researchers. This endeavour led the Foundation of Labour, a consultative body of central unions and employers' organisations, to set out guidelines for how industrial relations should be developed in the years to come (SvdA 1993). With this agreement, both unions and employers affirmed a policy line based on wage moderation which was set up in the early eighties.

Another national consultative body, the influential tripartite Social and Economic Council (SER), linked its deliberations on the 'consultation economy' to the convergence criteria of the coming European Monetary Union (SER 1992). The Council's report, reflecting at the same time a self-evaluation of its dominant role in labour relations, stated unanimously that the Dutch model needed new legitimacy. This could be done by revitalising the consultation system, first and foremost by making a clear division of competences between government and social parties. Public and private realms should henceforth be clearly demarcated, the report said, stressing that the government should take up the primary role of guaranteeing basic rights. The social organisations, and, more important, the individuals themselves, should be given broad discretion to take important decisions in many areas of societal life. The council further urged the introduction of more market elements in several areas of industrial relations and strict deregulation of the labour market. These measures would, the council claimed, increase the system's capacity to innovate socially as well as to respond to external challenges. They would make Dutch economy highly competitive while at the same time retaining the valuable elements of Dutch consultation. 'Tripartite institutional arrangements' based on voluntary restrictions of each actor could be feasible instruments to achieve these aims, the Council concluded.

The Council's publication has been important in putting together trends and actualities, desires and necessities, analysing them in the light of the big economic and political changes in the recent past and those ahead of us, as well as sketching the outlines of a decentralised but still coordinated system of industrial relations. Thanks to the report and other publications, the diagnosis of the Dutch system of industrial relations was clear and, thus, the question of how to proceed towards an efficient and legitimate social and economic model could appear vividly on the research screen. For instance, in 1993, the Dutch industrial relations association celebrated its twenty-fifth anniversary with a conference on the 'future of the consultation economy'. In the accompanying book (Hofstra and Nobelen 1993), Albeda claimed that Dutch (neo)corporatist philosophy had gone through an adjustment process to neo-liberal ideas. Coordination of policies between social parties as well as within the parties themselves would, he thought, no longer be a real option. Since each social organisation now had to act on its own strength, it would be more useful for them to establish forms of exchange of ideas and information that might occasionally give birth to those institutional arrangements the SER had suggested. A serious threat to this model, Albeda asserted, was the low union density in the Netherlands (Albeda 1993: 30). In reaction, the leaders of both sides of industry and the Minister of Labour agreed, by and large, with Albeda's analysis. Of course, the employers' representative, Rinnooy Kan, was more hesitant than the others, but he convincingly backed up concertation at the central level, as his successor Blankert would also do.

2.2. The performance of the system

In 1995, Van Waarden published an article on the adjacent territory of institutional change that would produce a significant effect on industrial relations discussion; a reason to take brief notice of his ideas (Van Waarden 1995).

Van Waarden questioned the supposed economic need for deregulation because he felt the efficiency enhancing effects of existing rules and structures were greatly underestimated. His starting point was the ongoing practice in Holland and elsewhere of abandoning various kinds of rules and structures. The theory justifying these measures included arguments, such as: the economy is performing poorly or is threatened by international developments because competition is being restrained and there are too many rules, leading to a frustration of initiatives and rising costs. This view, Van Waarden claimed, is, however, a myth, certainly in the Dutch case. The Dutch economy is doing very well and Dutch companies have an overall strong position in international competition. That is mainly due to Dutch 'cooperative competition' or 'organised capitalism', which order and moderate competition without eliminating it. To stimulate people, an economy needs both incentives to take initiatives and measures to reduce uncertainties; taking away uncertainties may make initiatives worthwhile, Van Waarden argued. Market institutions have to fulfil both needs, though the balance between the two differs greatly between countries. Certain economic institutions are basically needed everywhere, Van Waarden asserted, and therefore are present in every economy: monetary institutions, well-defined property rights, and adequate contract legislation. On top of these basics, a whole variety of different institutions may emerge. For instance, in the Anglo–Saxon economies, incentives are strongly emphasised and given form through legislation, a preference which is also responsible for the severe American anti-trust laws. Other countries are more organised or coordinated, more inclined to reduce uncertainties. In Van Waarden's view, though, this certainly does not mean that organised forms of capitalism are inferior to decentralised systems in terms of economic growth, economic efficiency, the creation of employment, and so on. It might well be the opposite. For that reason, he examined specific Dutch institutions and their scores on economic performance, showing a number of important economic advantages of these institutions as they function on different levels in the economy, in addition to the important socio-political functions institutions usually perform (cf. Van Hoof 1995). Generally, these effects are totally neglected in mainstream economic research on social and economic institutions.

Regarding the industrial relations system, Van Waarden's conclusions may be summarised by two sentences from a later, comparative study on socio-economic coordination (Van Waarden 1997: 31): 'Concertation, and the agreements and regulations produced by it, reduce uncertainties and transaction costs and correct for market failures. Moreover, there are many indications that sectors and countries that are typically concerted economies have performed better than the ideal-typical market economies'.

Van Waarden's article contributed, as already mentioned, to an ongoing debate on the Dutch labour system in journals, magazines, government documents, and newspapers (see also Section 4 for the contributions of economists). To a great extent, this debate was a duel between mainstream economic views, on the one hand, and socio-economic and political approaches on the other (e.g. *Socialisme & Democratie* 4, 1996; *Economisch Statistische Berichten* 4121, 1997; *Zeggenschap* 3, 1997). This debate is, in fact, still going on, though clearly more peacefully since empirically based arguments have been brought in, that is, the recognition that the economy has been performing excellently in recent years. Whereas in the first half of the nineties industrial relations research often implied a sort of apology of the labour system, now a growing number of publications stress, if not cherish, the importance of the characteristics of that system, in particular consultation and consensus. The system itself was often referred to as the 'poldermodel', expressing, so it seemed, its uniqueness as well as its successful adjustment to external forces.

Visser and Hemerijck have recently published a major contribution to the debate just mentioned, entitled *A Dutch Miracle*, which is clearly within the tradition of industrial relations. This book, which avoids the expression 'poldermodel' until the last page, discusses the successful recovery of the Dutch economy since the disastrous economic situation in the early eighties in terms of economic growth, investments, and, in particular, job creation. Even when accounting for some minuses, such as the still low net participation rate in full time equivalents and the extensive creation of part-time work of relatively low quality, it is obvious that the Dutch economy has done a comparatively good job. How could this happen? the authors asked, taking into consideration that The Netherlands, like other European countries, was confronted with a number of fundamental challenges to its welfare system, such as the intensification of international competition, transformation of work and work organisations, and demographic changes.

Visser and Hemerijck tried to provide an answer, as well as one to the question of what lessons, if any, may be drawn for other countries' socio-economic policies. Therefore, the authors developed a model of policy learning containing three dimensions of change, cultural, structural, and instrumental. Their analysis led them to conclude, first, that the economic malaise in the early eighties acted as a 'triggering device' for policy changes. Second and most important, they found that the actors within the institutional framework are of utmost importance for economic recovery because they are able to learn from problems and apply solutions through the consensual consultation system. Corporatism is generally not a stifling mechanism, the authors contend, as the Dutch experience has proved. By exerting influence on one another, the collectivities within the institutional setting have been able successfully to flexibilise existing rules and structures, without disrupting social coherence.

Finally, despite the transiency of the Dutch corporatist system and the fact that systems may differ profoundly, the authors indicated some reasons for other countries to take the recent Dutch experiences seriously. The most important one is that, considering the tremendous challenges confronting European welfare states, societal consensus is the most crucial precondition for successful reform.

One may question the angle of the learning process that the authors have chosen. Organisations like the trade unions are thought to adapt their policies on the basis of what may be called macro-economic reasoning. Painfully, they seem to be confronted with the mighty logic of the market. Moderation of wages was seen as the proper answer to the challenges with which the Dutch economy was confronted. However, were the choices made by the unions so straightforward? For instance, why, in the light of the processes of individualisation and decentralisation, did they not learn to look after the very interests of the groups they represented? Why did the union movement take the road to rendering service to the socio-economic elite? As such, the study bears some culture-specific features, in contrast to what the authors claim.

3. TRADE UNIONS AND TRADE UNIONS CHANGE

The majority of the scientific research on the actors in the system of industrial relations in the Netherlands has focused on the trade unions, and, in particular, on its enfeeblement. In its wake, the causes of change, the responses of the organisations to counteract the threats to them and, of course, the prospects of this industrial institution itself have been addressed in the research. Few studies on employers and their organisations have been done during this period (e.g. Van Voorden 1990).[4] The same holds, as has been said, for the government as a social actor.

Confining ourselves to trade unions, it is clear that most scientific research has been done on the issue of trade union change. Of course, other issues have been studied as well, such as the relation of unions to the works council (see Section 5); the (specific) role of unions in labour conflicts or problem issues (e.g. Van der Meer 1996; Rojer 1996b); the view of trade union members on certain issues (Kerkhof 1997); the role of the union *vis-à-vis* specific developments (e.g. flexibility: Ter Steeg 1994; training: Van den Hurk 1995). There has been an unremitting stream of articles and (historical) monographs on specific sectoral/occupational/local unions or working conditions including company histories, all featuring the rich variety of labour situations, struggles, serving workers' interest, and ways of life (cf. Stoop 1993; Leisink and Leisink 1994; Tijdens and Goedhard 1996; and further, Van Hooff 1996; Van Doremalen 1996; Van Eijl 1997; Stenvert 1992).

While we do not underestimate the significance of all these publications for the development of trade unions and the wider system, we have to refrain from further elaboration. The same holds for publications on the economic significance of trade unions, which will be dealt with in the following section. We will focus, as said, on scientific publications about union change, which, in general, differ from each other with respect to (1) the approach used, (2) the causes given emphasis, and (3) the point of view with respect to the trade union.

Under the influence of Jelle Visser and Bert Klandermans, a research tradition has developed that is particularly occupied with membership issues and organisational developments, most often comparatively (for instance Visser 1987/1990, 1991, 1994; Rojer and Visser 1993; De Bruin and Klandermans 1995; Van Rij 1994; Van Rij and Van den Putte 1992; Daalder and Van Rij 1996; Van den Berg 1995, 1996; cf. also Warning, 1992). It is thought that developments in membership and union density can be taken as an apt and fruitful point of departure for further intensive research on matters of labour relations, and certainly indispensable when making comparisons in time and space (Visser and Ebbinghaus 1996: 21). On the basis of membership figures from 1985, therefore, Rojer and Visser (1992) attempted to discover the causes of the persistent differences in intersectoral and intra-sectoral union organisation. By using demographic labour market data, industrial production structures, and specific institutional patterns, and integrating them into an explanatory scheme, they found that demographic factors, such as the share of women's participation in occupations, give the best explanation for union density differences.

Within this group of researchers, a gradual change of focus may be observed: from organisational factors influencing membership towards the individual as a participant in a network of colleagues making decisions about whether or not to join the union. Yet, in later research, the importance of organisational factors is still kept in mind.

The research on union membership and union development converges in two publications: Klandermans and Visser et al. 1995 and Visser et al. 1996. Most of the authors mentioned above contributed to these volumes.

Klandermans and Visser used an eclectic approach in which rational theory, frustration theory, and interaction/network theory are combined. They explain the decline of union membership by pointing to the growing consumer-like attitude of union members towards their interest organisation, a development already indicated by Van Ham, Paauwe, and Williams in 1985. Union membership has become increasingly dependent on the services that unions offer to individuals; at the same time, the function of the union as a social movement has weakened dramatically. Yet, Klandermans and Visser posit that a trade union will never be able to function exclusively as a kind of service institute for individuals. Unions will remain organisations with collective purposes, they argue, and, when it comes to serious labour–management conflicts, they must be able to appeal to the workers as a collectivity.

Another work on structural trade union matters was written by Coenen et al. It is a comprehensive publication aimed at contributing to the future course of the Dutch trade union organisation. As the guiding perspective for the contributions, the authors have chosen the theoretical ideas of the German social scientist Beck, who introduced the concept of 'Risk society'. This concept points to a transitional society through which we are steadily moving, where the production of wealth is increasingly accompanied by risks that can no longer be kept under control by traditional regulatory means. These problems may endanger the world of work. Traditional securities will diminish or at least become unequally distributed. Trade unions will come under great pressure and will be forced to change in order to survive. The direction of this change, Coenen and Van Berkel argued, will be a renewal or modernisation of the social movement function of the organisation.

The two books discussed above differ in their attitude towards the trade union organisation (cf. Leisink 1996: 80). Coenen et al. have a view of a trade union as, in essence, broad and encompassing, a character that must be retained when the organisation becomes modernised. Klandermans and

Visser et al. consider unions to be pragmatic organisations that have to adapt rigorously in response to changing industrial characteristics.

During this decade Dutch researchers have published an increasing number of comparative studies in English (Van Ruysseveldt et al. 1995; Van Ruysseveldt and Visser 1996; Leisink et al. 1996). Again, trade unions and in particular union change, are often the central subjects. Moreover, we may come across factors of union change other than those emphasised in the previously mentioned publications.

Here, too, Visser's contribution has been considerable. In a chapter on European unions in transition, this author examined the overall decline in unionisation in Europe. Using an explanatory matrix combining a constructivist/determinist dimension of union organisation with an actor/network dimension of membership decision, and elaborating subsequently on factors attached to both dimensions, he came to the following conclusions (Visser 1994: 80-108). First, probably the most alarming aspect of union decline is the low popularity of unions among young people (Visser 1994: 101). Establishing contact with this group by providing specific services to them and using a business-like approach is only the first step. Further, the future of trade unions in Europe is thought to depend heavily on the endurance of the German model with its extensive bargaining coverage, coordinated multi-employer negotiations, powerful employers' organisations, detailed, though decentralising agreements, and wide-ranging employee representation at the company level independent of both union and employer. Finally, Visser claimed: 'Unions' power and legitimacy will continue to erode unless they find a way of promoting a feasible and creative policy of full employment'. More than ever, unions have to take notice of the development of the wide-ranging flexibility of work and the growing diversity of interests. Against this background, Visser saw as a major challenge to trade unionism the opening of a new policy perspective on European-wide solidarity that may prevent an impoverishment of social conditions.

Union structure is still relatively centralistic, professionalised, and sectorally organised in the Netherlands. To investigate changes in this structure, Looise compared the trade union with a company, and trade union changes with corporate strategy changes, assuming that changes in market characteristics on the basis of techo-economic developments would lead to changing corporate strategies. This analogy links the fate of union structure to developing market-production characteristics and the question that then arises is how will that structure evolve. To answer that question, Looise used an ideal typical classification, borrowed from Bolwijn and Kumpe (1991), of company strategies as they have come up through changing market conditions from the 1960s onwards. So, in the 1960s, efficiency was the main target that organisationally expressed itself in specialisation and hierarchy; in the 1970s, quality became important, leading to more communication and cooperation; the 1980s brought flexibility, giving an incentive to integration and decentralisation within the organisation; the 1990s, finally, were thought to make innovation the primary objective, which would increase the importance of participation and democracy in the organisation.

Following authors like Teulings (1987) and Paauwe et al. (1985, 1988) Looise asserted that the Dutch trade union organisation is gradually changing into a flexible organisation, following at some distance the techno-economic logic of production organisations (for a comparable view see Korevaar 1990). This means further decentralisation, flexibilisation of production and staff, formation of joint ventures or mergers, and concentration on core business. Moreover, in management terms, unions have to put on the market a clear and attractive product. Small, autonomous business units must be set up along with short communication lines. Looise agreed with Paauwe (1992) who suggested constructing a cluster organisation, roughly on the basis of occupational groups, with different geographical levels for each group. To avoid too much fixation on partial interests, Paauwe proposed creating a number of structures for coordination. Looise, however, thought that for reasons of efficiency it might be better to enlarge the autonomy of the union's business units. The proposals of both Looise and Paauwe are likely to lead to union and federation activities on a decentral level becoming more integrated, although, as Looise argued, these changes of interest representation will be hard to carry out without a more thorough transformation of the total union structure.

Finally, from a different angle, Nagelkerke and Koijen (1996) have also taken up the question of union change. Unions and union development are considered to be products of different forces, notably techno-economic and socio-political developments. Initially, techno-economic developments determine the economic position of the worker. The question of whether or not workers and their fellow workers will be able to organise themselves depends on the nature of the techno-economic conditions, on the one hand, and the permissive character of socio-political culture and institutions on the other. The step towards institutional power of workers' organisations is thought to depend greatly on a specific socio-political culture. However, it is important to note that trade union organisations may themselves exert influence on the formation of the institutional pattern, while also having a certain freedom to choose the organisational form that fits them best.

On the basis of a number of specific developments in the past ten to fifteen years, the authors have set up a matrix with two entries, the level at which the main rules are made and the character of the rules. They drew up four feasible models of future Dutch unionism: a market perspective, a local perspective, an occupational or dual perspective, and a pluriform (multiform) perspective. In contrast to Schilstra and Smit (see Section 5), the authors came to see a multiform (pluriform) union model as the most likely form. In this model, modern unions are genuine labour-market organisations, caring for well-defined individual and group interests in an efficient manner and supporting their members in maintaining their employability. Still, like Klandermans and Visser, the authors expected this multiform union to retain certain broader collectivist aspirations, since, in order to prevent rigorous competition among worker-members, a coordination of labour claims may be unavoidable. In this respect, the *raison d'être* of a union remains that it is an institution that attempts, as far as possible, to reduce insecurity for groups of workers.

4. COLLECTIVE BARGAINING AND THE TERMS OF EMPLOYMENT

Since the end of World War II, the issue of collective bargaining in Holland has been closely linked to the system as a whole. Government has been a wage setting party for a long time, and after it abandoned its restrictive wage policy around 1970, it remained coercive for many years. From 1982 onwards, however, the government was finally ready to give up its dominant role in macro-economic wage formation, leaving the social parties to take full responsibility for the bargaining processes on different levels. Strongly inspired by prevailing economic theories, this change of attitude, by which the market became the sole efficient coordinator, contributed a lot to shifts already occurring within the system of industrial relations, which were mainly caused by changing forms of competition and the rapid advances in information technology. From then onwards, collective bargaining in the Netherlands was given an impetus to 'decentralise' and 'differentiate' while the collective agreement became more than ever the 'mirror' (Van Voorden 1987) of multiform industrial relations. In fact, as Vos and Buitelaar (1996: 72) aptly made clear, collective bargaining as a 'rule-making machinery' has proved to be better at dealing with the changes in the technological, economic and social realm than has socio-economic legislation. However, this does not preclude the possibility that, in the future, labour terms will increasingly be agreed upon without the trade unions having a say in the matter.

For analytical purposes, we may divide the process of collective bargaining into three parts: (1) the structure, (2) the outcomes and effects and (3) the process. However, we have to realise that many studies focus on subjects which cannot simply be confined to a single category. For instance, Rojer (1993) has investigated the relationship between the Dutch plural union representation and the bargaining process, thus dealing with the structure and outcomes of collective bargaining simultaneously. Smit and Miltenburg, similarly, have taken up the relationship between the trade union and the work councils in wage formation (1997; see Section 5). In comparing the system of collective bargaining in Great Britain, France and Germany, Huiskamp (1995) has made a broader inquiry, exposing a shift towards a layered bargaining structure, which allows for more flexible collective agreements. The same holds for Nagelkerke and De Nijs (1998) who have pointed to the nation-specific responses to the flexibilisation trend (cf. also Van Peijpe 1990). In brief, various elements of the process of collective bargaining are dealt with in most of the research.

4.1. The bargaining structure

Scientific work on the collective bargaining structure as such has been rather limited in the current decade. An example of research on integral bargaining is that by Van Heertum and Wilthagen, who have questioned the effects of the central agreements in the Foundation of Labour on negotiations at lower bargaining levels. They found that wage bargaining has only been moderately affected, but that the signalling function of these central frameworks is, nevertheless, important. In particular, the basic agreements under which problems of work and wages and their interrelations are considered and put in a desirable societal perspective, have a significant influence on the content of sectoral and company bargaining. Seen from a historical perspective, the broader significance of the Foundation of Labour has been the research topic of Van Bottenburg (1995). A conclusion of this study is that, due to decentralising industrial relations, declining ideological positions and more clear-cut competences, the Foundation has experienced a revival since 1982. More than before, the Foundation has acted as a platform upon which employers and trade unions can reach agreements on many important issues.

The phenomenon of decentralisation has also attracted scientific attention recently. although the issue had already been covered at great length in the eighties. For instance, Huiskamp had already monitored the changes in Dutch bargaining in the early eighties. He continued, in the nineties, by investigating to what extent the industry-wide agreements were able to establish differentiation and taylor-made packages (Huiskamp 1996). Here, Huiskamp noted that the presence of a sectoral frame may diminish the hesitation, or even the reluctance, of the parties at company level to negotiate.

Nagelkerke (1992, 1994) illustrated the extent of the process of decentralisation by considering changes in norms, rules and structures in the whole bargaining process, all the way from the national to the decentral level, including political interference. It was stipulated that structural changes towards decentralisation lag behind normative decentralisation and, to a lesser extent, regulative decentralisation. A growing possibility to bargain freely on lower levels has, until now, left the formal bargaining structure largely intact (cf. Van den Toren 1996).

A subject that has been given thorough attention is the legal extension of sectoral contracts to companies in the sector which are not members of a contracting employers' organisation, based on a 1937 law. Around 1991, the Ministry of Labour explicitly cast doubt on the advantages of this mechanism, which applied to about 10 per cent of the working population.[5] The Minister was supported by economists, who stated that the extension instrument was impeding competition, leading to higher wage costs and loss of potential employment. In the debate that followed, researchers put forward arguments in favour of the view that extension does indeed lead to higher wages, in particular in those companies which are subject to extension (see, for instance Zalm 1992; Lever and Marquering 1995).[6] Others, however, argued that extension has wage-moderating effects, more industrial peace and probably favourable effects on employment. Abolition of the extension would, in this view, induce more workers to become members of the unions, leading most probably to upward movements of wage levels (Van Voorden 1991; Van Kooten and Stolk 1992; Leemreize 1992; Teulings 1995).

As said earlier, the debate broadened when around 1994/1995 the economy began to flourish and the consultation model came to be applauded as economically very satisfactory. Studies emphasising the comparatively good performance of the Dutch system of industrial relations (Hartog et al. 1994; Teulings 1996a; MSZW 1996; Roorda and Vogels 1997; Paping and Stegeman 1997; Vogels 1997; Freeman et al. 1997) played an important role in the discussion about whether or not to abandon or modify certain institutions, although these studies were also questioned (MEZ 1997; McKensie 1997). In particular, the comparatively favourable increase in employment due to long years of wage moderation was thought to be the pleasant fruit of extensive Dutch consultation. As a consequence, collective bargaining institutions, such as the collective agreement, the extension of contracts and the minimum wage, disappeared from the policy agenda as they came to be seen as important for a well-functioning economy. It also meant a change in interest from the bargaining structure to the outcomes and effects of collective bargaining, quite in accordance with the increased influence of academic economists in the research on industrial relations issues. Although some scientists already had a good record in this respect, Dutch economic research, as in the Anglo–Saxon tradition of labour economics, entered the economically most interesting area of industrial relations in the nineties, that is, the impact of unions and collective bargaining on employment, wage differences and other economic variables.

4.2. Outcomes and effects of collective bargaining

Much scientific work has been carried out on a diversity of bargaining outcomes, often commissioned by the government. A random list shows studies on wage differentiation across countries (Hofman et al. 1992); occupational flexibility (Glasbergen 1994); early retirement (Trommel 1995; Delsen 1992; Henkens 1997); employment conditions under a non-collective regulation regime (Leisink and Spaninks 1994); the effect of sectoral contract extension on small companies (Elsendoorn and Van der Hoeven 1996); the economic dynamics between wage formation and employment (Van Soest and Kalwij 1996); differentiation and decentralisation in the public sector (Becking 1996); flexible contracts and wages (Beke 1996; Faber and Schippers 1997; Jaspers et al. 1998); sectoral collective bargaining (Van der Burgh 1996), and so on. Furthermore, flexibility of labour has become a main topic in studies of all types and perspectives: policy-oriented (De Jong and Van Bolhuis 1997);

as a menu for possible employee relations (Kruif 1996); as a development with several pros and cons (De Haan et al. 1994); comparatively, across European countries (Delsen 1997); and grasping the significance of flexibility in collective bargaining practices (Dankbaar et al. 1998).

In the last-mentioned publication, the authors concluded that the advantages of flexibility are highly dependent on the competition regime to which a sector or company is exposed. Sometimes, competition might well be served by a combination of flexibility and labour security. Flexibility and the accompanying deregulation may well enhance a company's performance, but, at the same time, may impede investments in human capital. The authors argued that the freerider positions of those companies that do not invest in personnel result in a so-called prisoner's dilemma, which means that the individual decisions of the parties concerned will not lead to an optimal solution for all. For the companies that do invest, increased mobility may result in insufficient return on their investments. In the authors' opinion, the only solution to the problems this dilemma might produce, is a strong reliance on concluding collective agreements at the national and the sectoral level, possibly combined with the extension of sectoral contracts.

A publication indicating the increasing differentiation in conditions of employment deals with social security in collective agreements. Boos and Van Oorschot (1998) found a quantitative increase in collective arrangements concerning disablement and sickness issues during the eighties and early nineties. Usually, these arrangements were meant to compensate for the legal decline in disablement-related benefits. In the nineties, these kinds of arrangements increased further but, given the strong legal tightening of the entry conditions of social security provisions, the degree of protection diminished only slightly and, moreover, became more differentiated. In this respect, the authors further observed that whereas the company agreements generally offer better social protection than sectoral agreements do, the agreements of small companies showed a relatively unfavourable score on matters of sickness and disablement arrangements.

Speaking about the effects of Dutch collective bargaining, we are again forced to refer to the debate about the economic performance of the system as a whole. Economic performance has increasingly come to dominate the agenda of labour economists, although labour sociologists have also showna great deal of interest. This relatively new 'tradition' stemmed from a combination of the debate on corporatism led by Schmitter, Streeck,

Katzenstein, Sharp and others, on the one hand, and economists such as Bruno and Sachs, Calmfors and Drifill, Soskice and others, on the other.

Economists such as Teulings and Hartog (1994, 1995, 1996), Groot (1994), Theeuwes (1994) and Van Riel (1995) became interested in the outcomes of the Dutch consultation model, in particular in comparison to other bargaining regimes. They attempted to establish empirically the influence of the 'corporatist', still less decentralised, Dutch bargaining structure on a number of economic indicators. For instance, Teulings has made clear that corporatist institutions are contributing a lot to solving the so-called 'hold--up' problem (the mutual imprisonment of employer and employees in market relations) through disconnecting wage negotiations from issues at the work place. Further, in contrast to Calmfors and Drifill's main conclusion, Teulings (1996b: 31-42) has found that countries with corporatist coordination are experiencing considerably fewer higher wage settlements and smaller wage differentials than countries with decentralised bargaining institutions such as Canada and the United States. It seems, therefore, that the market mechanism is less able to check the insiders' monopoly power of unions in decentralised systems than the (corporatist) institutions do in relatively centralised systems.

These and other studies (e.g. Lever 1993 and 1995; Van den Wijngaert 1994) as well as the broad discussions which have taken place in several journals, constitute important sections of a close inspection process of the Dutch institutional labour pattern. A commonly agreed, important feature of this system, was the wage restraint that was carried on for many years. This initiated an exceptional debate in the Autumn of 1994, when Kleinknecht firmly challenged the assumption of long-term benefits from wage moderation. According to him, Dutch wage moderation had only been advantageous to employment in so far as it had slowed down the demolition of existing employment (Kleinknecht 1994, 1996), because in the long run, it could lead to a serious slowing down of economically innovative activities. Entrepreneurs would not be encouraged to practice Schumpeter's 'creative destruction', that is, to seek improvements in products and production processes. By way of example, Kleinknechts pointed to the fact that high-quality investments had remained at levels lower than those of competing neighbouring countries, resulting in the Netherlands having lower economic growth and a less favourable employment development. To this he added the Keynesian view that wage moderation led to a downward pressure on expenditures, thereby jeopardising employment as well. In order to get more economic dynamism,

Kleinknecht therefore proposed an overall wage increase at a firm level. The majority of Dutch economists, employers, and politicians reacted in a rather irritated way, claiming that wage costs are extremely important in competition worldwide and that the lower they are, the more companies are able to compete. Therefore, wage increases should follow rather than precede innovation. This view, that wage moderation is a prerequisite for competition, is still the dominant view of Dutch economists.

4.3. The bargaining process

In the Netherlands, no extensive research has been carried out on the collective bargaining process. However, two comprehensive studies on the issue happened to appear in 1996. The first, by Van den Toren, deals with the question how unions can lay down and enforce qualitative terms of employment. Rojer, the author of the second study, models the bargaining process in order to come to predictions of the final results.

Van den Toren's qualitative terms are labour conditions reaching, as he puts it, beyond the contract wages, often expressing preferences in society at large, but frequently competing with wages. From these terms the author selected, for research purposes, working time, quality of work, labour participation of weak groups in the labour market and environmental protection. The question was: How and to what extent are these issues bargained in practice? Next to this, the author was much interested in a solid scientific establishment of the union's role in the process of collective bargaining. Both elements, the qualitative bargaining results and the role of the unions, have practical as well as scientific significance, not least as a contribution to the ongoing discussion about the economic effects of particular institutions.

A first conclusion, not very surprisingly, is that wage moderation has firmly been established for about fifteen years, shaped by still widely accepted forms of organisational coordination. Another finding was that, in practice, qualitative agreements differ according to the type of collective bargaining. Qualitative terms are most frequently found in the collective contracts of large branches and big companies. However, qualitative issues may approach but are not allowed to encroach on the employers' right to manage, while ideological differences may still function as important obstacles for bargaining about certain qualitative terms. Finally, on these and other findings, Van den Toren concluded that: 'Collective bargaining is not a predictable and logical rational process'.

The study is worthwhile for its outlook on contemporary bargaining issues, but unfortunately lacks sufficient explanatory strength. The relationship between the theoretical, neo-institutional approach and the empirical results is still unclear. Moreover, how the explanatory variables impact the bargaining outcomes remains obscure. It is indeed no wonder that the author came to the conclusion that the bargaining process remains a black box.

Whereas Van den Toren concluded that processes of wage negotiations are unpredictable, illogical and irrational, Rojer (1996) claimed, at the start of his thesis, that this statement is just a research subject worth investigating. His purpose was to inquire into the collective bargaining process itself, especially the transition or transformation of the actor's inputs into the real outcomes of the collective agreement, predicting these final outcomes and trying to explain them. For him, current theories of collective bargaining are either oriented too much towards the material ramifications of the bargaining processes or are too preoccupied with the actor's behaviour, both without close scrutiny of the bargaining results. In Dutch practice, moreover, bargaining processes are thought to be very closely related to the wider societal institutional context. In this respect, Rojer stipulated the broad bargaining agenda on which several issues, varying in weight, could be mutually exchanged. Moreover, in the Netherlands, workers' representation is plural: no union is allowed to act in the name of all workers, thereby by-passing other unions.

According to Rojer, for these reasons, the collective bargaining process in the Netherlands is a kind of political process. To explain multi-lateral negotiations, he therefore borrowed from political science two models of collective decision making which allow for empirical testing: a cooperative exchange model and a conflict model. Once some initial variables are known, the models can predict the outcomes of the collective bargaining processes concerned.

It is not really amazing that the cooperative exchange model has the best score for the Dutch collective bargaining cases. The model containing over 204 variables in 12 collective contracts, came to a score of 67 per cent good predictions, while the conflict-model got stuck at 40%.

Rojer came to the conclusion that these models are able to reconstruct the real bargaining results successfully, both retrospectively as well as prospectively. Moreover, because minor elements were eliminated, leaving just the paramount factors determining bargaining processes, the analysis seemed to shed light on the internal process of collective bargaining. This attempt at modelling the collective bargaining process is scientifically the most important contribution of this publication. However, it remains to be seen what the models will predict when actors are contesting each others' legitimate place in collective bargaining.

A notable difference between Van den Toren and Rojer is the degree of openness of the collective bargaining process. For Van den Toren, the skills and expertise of the bargainers are largely decisive for the outcome of the bargaining process. Since these prerequisites are difficult to assess, predictions are futile. Rojer, however, views predictions as feasible and important. When the context, that is, the distribution of power among the parties, the initial claims and the top priorities of both sides, is known, the prediction is a very simple task, it seems.

5. THE SYSTEM OF DUTCH CO-DETERMINATION WITHIN COMPANIES

Traditionally one of the most important issues in Dutch industrial relations research has been the system of co-determination of workers within the enterprise. Government, as the main commissioner, has always played a stimulating role in this research area. Until now, each amendment in law has been preceded by extensive surveys of co-determination practices, especially regarding the works council. Significant in this respect were the research projects of Hovels and Nas (1976) and Looise (1989). On the one hand, these projects aimed at assessing the practical effects of the amendments to the Works Council Act. On the other hand, they were directed at finding out what, in practice, were the obstacles and problems in co-determination, and how, subsequently, these could be accounted for in the new legislation.

Given this double perspective, it will be no surprise to learn that it was the actors on central (national) policy level who often formulated the central problem to be studied. The experiences and problems of the actors directly involved in putting co-determination into actual practice, were only of minor importance. This is why the research often overlooked the specific problems with co-determination, experienced by individual companies. As such, most research was heavily loaded politically, notably expressed in the urge to promote the process of democratisation within companies. Another political desire was the assessment of the relations between the different forms of workers' participation within the company. In particular, the link between the supervisory board and the works council attracted considerable political interest, specifically regarding the members of the supervisory board appointed through the works council, and the disputable demarcation of tasks between works councils and trade unions.

A lot of research on co-determination has remained inspired by these traditional questions in the present decade, such as, for instance, the empirical studies of Mulder (1992); Van der Knoop (1991), Van het Kaar (1993, 1995), and Smit et al. (1995, 1997). The most vital issue was whether or not co-determination actually contributed to the increase of workers' influence on the management of the company, and, secondly, whether a process of power levelling was taking place. However, another key problem was gradually gaining in significance. Co-determination was no longer exclusively looked upon from a structural point of view, but more frequently its functional significance was put on the research agenda. The functional perspective is focused on the question of whether co-determination contributes to efficient and effective company management, and, in particular, to organisational innovation. Many enterprises had been confronted with profound changes in their business environment to which they had to respond organisationally. A tendency then emerged for workers' participation research to become dominated by the aspect of economic performance, just as in other domains of industrial relations research in the Netherlands (see Sections 2 and 4). Among the authors who took up this subject, the following can be mentioned: Van Hees (1993); Goodijk (1993, 1995); Wissema et al. (1996) and Looise et al. (1996).

Mulder's study (1992) fits in the traditional research category. His dissertation has taken up the observation, as in many studies before, that, notwithstanding the activities of trade unions and works councils, Dutch workers can only exert a minimal influence on decisions determining the future development of their companies. The aim of Mulder's study was to find out what could be done to improve this form of workers co-determination. For that, seventy experts in labour relations and chairmen of works councils were interviewed on several issues.

One of the reasons for co-determination not performing well concerned, according to Mulder, the lack of adequate and effective co-operation between trade unions and works councils. With this conclusion, the author has touched upon a subject that would play a major role in the co-determination debate in the current decade. It concerned the division of tasks between works councils and trade unions, which grew in importance due to trends such as deregulation, decentralisation and flexibilisation. Smit et al. (1995) have gathered many opinions and options on this issue, putting them into three possible scenarios of workers' representation: (1) an Anglo–Saxon model with competition between unions and works council; (2) a Japanese model implying the replacement of trade unions by works councils, and (3) a kind of Dutch model in which the consultation economy is revitalised, trade unions provide collective agreements for different companies, and works councils act on behalf of the workers within the companies. For each of the models, the authors have found several plausible indications of actual industrial relations practices.

This theoretical sketch of scenarios has recently been put to a more thorough empirical test in a qualitative research project commissioned by the Ministry of Social Affairs (Smit and Miltenburg 1997). This exploratory research was based on five cases of co-operation between works councils and trade unions in the settlement of conditions of employment. For the case studies, sectors were taken showing great differences in the way trade unions and works councils were involved in the process of wage bargaining. Their most remarkable result was that they found that, in the branches studied, the decentralisation process had not fully been carried out. For instance, in the tourist industry, the first collective agreement had been introduced at industry instead of company level. The research indicated further, that within the branches under study no real debate was going on between trade unions and works councils with respect to each one's domain. Roughly speaking, the idea prevailed that works councils are willing to play a supportive role in the process of wage bargaining, but are not eager to take over the role of trade unions. Trade unions, however, were found to be willing to create more opportunities for greater differentiation in industry-level agreements, so as to give works councils more latitude to specify labour terms at company level. As such, the authors envisaged a less competitive relationship between trade unions and works councils, with the possible development of more cooperation and coordination.

The research discussed so far may indicate that there is no danger in the near future of the Dutch 'poldermodel' being startled by the introduction of Japanese or American customs and practices. We may expect that trade unions will maintain their precedence in settling employment conditions. The latest renewal of the Works Council Act (1997) formally validates this demarcation of competencies between trade unions and works councils. The provision has been made that works councils should have the right to negotiate with the employer on employment conditions. This can be laid down in a so called 'company agreement', which may, however, not include arrangements contrary to those already made in collective agreements between trade unions and the employer.

The relationship between trade union and works council was not the only subject for debate. Another problematic relationship stirred up the feelings of some researchers in the field of co-determination. It concerns the relationship between the supervisory board and the works council, and especially the role of those members on the board who are appointed on the works council's recommendation. The debate about the position and role of these members of the board cannot be detached from the criticism that broke out about the institution of the supervisory board in general. The tone regarding this institution has changed rather drastically during the last decade, with the debate linked increasingly with the controversy around constructions giving protection against take-overs. The current law results in the situation that acquiring the majority of shares does not automatically lead to gaining control over the company. The introduction of this principle would demand strengthening the shareholder's power at the expense of that of the supervisory board. This would imply a rather drastic change in the rationale behind the present regulation aiming at a more equal control of both capital and labour in the supervisory board. The approval of the works council with respect to the appointment of board members would then be finished. To make a stand against this, trade unions are pleading for a greater influence of the labour factor in the supervisory board and are proposing to replace the present system of co-optation by a system of direct appointment.

Van der Knoop's (1992) research on the supervisory board's role and influence on the management of an enterprise indicates that board members appointed on the recommendation of the works council experience difficulties in giving meaning to their special relationship with the works council. Almost all claimed to have the same task as 'normal' members. This situation has been confirmed in the more recent research of Van het Kaar (1995). Also this project, sponsored by the Dutch Trade Union Federation, revealed that only in a minority of cases could one speak of the existence of a special bond between the works council and the member of the board appointed on its recommendation.

According to Van het Kaar, most works councils fail to make optimal use of the possibilities offered by the present law. This can indicate that most works councils are not opting for another system of appointment. One can even conclude that if the actual regulation were to be changed so that shareholders would regain more influence, most works councils would not really be inclined to oppose this development.

The dissertation of Van Hees (1993) marks the beginning of a period in which research on co-determination has become more focused on the effects on enterprise performance. This change of direction cannot be disconnected from the drastic adjustments and innovations many companies have faced during the last decade. As a result, works councils are not only confronted with new questions such as flexibility, employability and internationalisation, but they also have to find new grounds and arguments for their very existence.

Van Hees developed a conceptual model to analyse the effects of workers' representation on firm performance. This model is an adaptation of the 'monopoly-and-collective-voice approach' of Freeman and Medoff to the Dutch situation. After critically analysing this approach and comparing the Dutch and US models of industrial relations, Van Hees presented his 'collective-consultation-and-collective-voice model'. He argues that this model is suitable for analysing the effects of worker representation on the functioning of firms in the specific Dutch context. The model discerns five types of activities of unions and works councils, which are related to four types of organisational effects: wages and employment, profit and investment, labour productivity, and resources in the environment of the firm. Although the model is applied to three cases, the study offers no empirical answer to the concrete organisational effects of worker representation since the empirical basis of the model is far too weak. The value of the study is mainly theoretical, that is, it offers entries along which research on the issue of organisational effects may take place. These issues still have to be tackled empirically and the Van Hees' model may render valuable services in this respect.

Seen from a business management-like perspective, a growing number of studies have appeared illuminating the role of the works council within modern work relations (Goodijk 1993 and 1995; Wissema et al. 1996; and Looise et al. 1996). These studies have tried to answer the question of whether or not the works council will retain a meaningful role, and if so, what its significance will be for the management of the firm. Quite distinct from Van Hees' study, these publications lack a thorough theoretical foundation. Their perspective is visionary and prescriptive, linked to conceptual schemes such as those of Kumpe and Bolwijn (see Section 3). This kind of framework is, however, of a rather normative and speculative nature, and has not been critically discussed.

Although the afore-mentioned studies have accentuated different aspects, they all agree that the works council of the future has a valuable role to play, although they see less emphasis being placed on the representation of worker's interests. Instead, it is anticipated that a works council will be more actively involved in the processes of strategic management and organisational renewal. The council's functioning will then be more tailored to the characteristics of the company it serves (Looise, Wissema), replacing the strategy of worker control for active involvement and co-management (Wissema), and will be equipped with professional management competencies (Goodijk). The authors forecast a future in which co-determination will be characterised by functional participation and, to a lesser degree, by the principles of opposition.

The value of these studies consists of their emphasis on a perspective long under-exposed in Dutch research on co-determination. Using this business management frame of reference, co-determination is analysed in terms of its contribution to the solution of business and work related problems.

6. NEW PRODUCTION CONCEPTS AND LABOUR RELATIONS

More or less the same phenomenon takes place in research on processes of integral organisation renewal and their effects on labour relations. Also in this domain, research is conducted from a business management frame of reference. Furthermore, one is confronted with a rather one-sided, and in a sense even technocratic, reasoning of unilateral adaptation of labour relations to the new and so called rational demands of modern systems of production. In particular, this tenor is present in the dissertation of Fruytier (1994). Among other things, this study explores the effects of the implementation of the so-called sociotechnical production concept on labour relations and wonders why a production concept like this, with so many economic and social advantages, has failed to break through. According to him, the application of this production concept will have huge repercussions for the character and structure of labour relations, not only in the enterprises themselves, but also for labour relations at the national level. One could even speak of a revolutionary transition. New production concepts give rise to labour relations founded on trust and loyalty and the rule-making process is concentrated on the enterprise level. This transition will have enormous outcomes, especially for the structure and policy of trade unions. Fruytier even postulates that without drastic changes in the trade unions and in the whole institutional complex of labour relations, new production concepts will never break through. From this line of reasoning, one could conclude that the actual system of labour relations (and the character and structure of trade unions) is the main barrier for the modernisation of business, and that, in the near future, the Dutch economy will be insufficiently equipped for international competition: a conclusion rather contrary to all the positive criticism currently conferred upon the Dutch system of labour relations.

From a labour relations frame-of-reference, several comments can be made on Fruytier's analysis—an analysis more or less symptomatic for studies originating from the scene of adherents to the modern sociotechnical system approach in the Netherlands.

One of the most important comments refers to the structural, deterministic angle hidden in the sociotechnical approach, which comes to the fore in the proposition that labour relations should be redesigned according to the imperative demands of the production system. What is overlooked is the insight that labour relations are not a construct of a strictly logical and technical rationality, but rather of political and even ethical rationality. For that reason, Vos and Buitelaar (1996) claim that the sociotechnical approach leaves no space for the political side of the employment relationship and does not offer any account of the societal aspect of the wage–work relationship. In their, empirically speaking, limited research on organisational renewal and labour relations in a few Dutch enterprises, they question the social and economic blessings of the sociotechnical production concept and do not envisage the kinds of drastic alterations in the structure of labour relations that Fruytier does. Instead of a development towards work-forms that promise more autonomy and job control for the workers, Vos and Buitelaar envisage a development towards a new kind of Taylorisation. The introduction of team-based work concepts is part of a more extensive restructuring process directed towards the creation of a flat and lean organisation. Teamwork offers workers more autonomy, but at the same time they are confronted with more intensive central regulation. New production concepts are part of what Vos and Buitelaar qualify as the extension of the assembly line. All parts and divisions of a company are linked to each other in a logistical chain leading to further standardisation and more work stress.

A completely different comment concerns the lack of assimilation between the theory of organisational redesign and the theory of labour relations. Fruytier's dissertation can be seen as an endeavour to combine two opposing theoretical approaches. The sociotechnical approach of redesign argues from the modern social system theory. Although, in industrial relations study, system theory is not unknown—albeit in its traditional and classical form—far more important are the so-called action (actor) approach and social constructivism. In research on the link between redesign work organisation and industrial relations, there is an urgent need for fine-tuning concepts and for integrating theoretical strands. In this field, some initiatives are noteworthy. In particular, Huiskamp (1992, 1995) is breaking fresh grounds with respect to a conceptual fine-tuning between the modern sociotechnical approach and industrial relations. In his endeavour to integrate both domains of study, he grants a key role to the employment relationship concept. The term employment relationship can be traced, in the UK tradition of the sociology of work, to authors such as Fox and Watson, who treat the employment relationship explicitly as distinct from the system of industrial relations. In their view, this term has to be reserved for the direct relationship between employer and employee and refers to the conditions under which the employer decides to hire labour and the employee decides to sell his manpower to the employer. These conditions are the result of continuous exchange and are related to different aspects of the deployment of labour, for example, wages and other employment terms, working hours and the working week, job security and career prospects, safety at the work place and job autonomy. Huiskamp expands the original focus on the individual and direct character of the relationship by establishing an analytical link between the employment relationship and industrial relations.

7. DUTCH LABOUR RELATIONS RESEARCH; AN ASSESSMENT

The selection of Dutch industrial and labour relations research presented here leads us to a number of evaluative remarks.

First, the studies reflect the changes in the system of industrial relations in the Netherlands. Factual developments, such as decentralisation, flexibilisation, membership changes, bargaining trends, as well as the change in dominant ideology towards neo-liberalisation, have been the main source of industrial relations research topics and directions. That may not be surprising, but the point here is that less research has been induced by industrial relations theory advancement. As such, industrial relations research is more driven by 'the empirical- and policy needs of the time' and far less by a theoretical coercion of research questions.

Secondly, undoubtedly more than in the past, recent research of industrial relations issues has been theoretically well-based, that is, the disciplinary theoretical departure to tackle a certain problem has generally been adequately stated. However, the problem here is that the theories used are so diverse that one could speak of a balkanisation of approaches. It seems common practice for each work to take the theoretical frame that seems to suit that research issue best. It is then hardly surprising that there is no integration of theoretical findings. At the same time, few attempts have been made to make progress on a multidisciplinary industrial relations framework.

Thirdly, economic research aspects of industrial relations have become significant in the nineties, just as economic reasoning has gained importance within the diversity of approaches just mentioned. Several important socio-economic institutions as well as the system of industrial relations as a whole have come to be evaluated, in particular, in terms of macro-economic performance. This has led to a vivid debate on the merits of the system of industrial relations and its various parts, in which the mere stereotype of mainstream economic reasoning has come to be transcended, leading to better economic consequences of institutional change. Yet, the discussion has suffered greatly from ideological overtones.

In analogy, fourthly, we observe a rise in importance of research into company issues, defined increasingly from a management perspective. This sharply contrasts with the character of the research questions before the nineties, which was clearly more worker-oriented.

Fifthly, the rise in importance of industrial relations issues in companies in the Netherlands has also been marked by a tendency to integrate domains of study that, previously, hardly interacted with each other. Notably, this occurs through socio-technical scientists attempting to integrate industrial relations issues with the process of workplace redesign. This interesting and promising endeavour still lacks an adequate conceptual match, that is, a closer theoretical correspondence between the prescriptive design approach and the analytical descriptive approach.

Moreover, it is remarkable that important segments of Dutch socio-economic systems, such as public and semi-public industrial relations, have received only scanty attention, as in the years preceding the nineties. The same holds for employers and the government as actors in the system of labour relations.

Finally, a development worth mentioning concerns the growing number of publications by Dutch authors in international books and journals. The growing curiosity from abroad about the Dutch model may certainly have contributed to this, but also domestic processes, such as university personnel policies and the activating role of the Open University, have been stimulating in this respect. Under the aegis of this institute, a number of books of Dutch and foreign authors have been issued by well-known publishing houses in Great Britain (Van Ruysseveldt et al. 1995; Harzing and Van Ruysseveldt 1995; and Van Ruysseveldt and Visser 1996).

All in all, we may conclude that, in the 1990s industrial relations research in the Netherlands has been creative and productive. New socially and politically relevant topics have been explored, the impact of Dutch researchers on the international scene of industrial relations has expanded and, last but not least, new paradigms fitting contemporary research subjects have been introduced. Yet, industrial relations research in the Netherlands will be confronted with new demands.

The first challenge is of a theoretical nature. Apart from the need to promote more theoretically induced research, it is becoming essential to update the theoretical framework of industrial relations in general. In particular, modern social system theory must be applied energetically to labour relations research, not only to renew classical system theory itself, which is still to be implicitly recognised in many contributions, but, above all, to develop a theoretical framework that allows researchers to interact fruitfully, including researchers engaged in workplace redesign. Such proactive theoretical work is the more important since, in contrast to the times of mass production, industrial relations transformations are likely to originate from changes at workplace level.

The second challenge follows more or less naturally from the line of argument just given. It is to be expected that the trend of decentralisation will continue. Within this context, differentiation and multiformity in industrial relations will increase. Finding out what is really going on in industrial relations practices will become rather complicated. To ensure that insight into developments in Dutch industrial relations will not depend on personal and speculative views, a comprehensive, representative survey over several years on developments in industrial relations at company level is badly needed.

NOTES

1 Also, when looking in textbooks, we find only a chapter in Albeda and Dercksen (1994), half a chapter in Nagelkerke and De Nijs (1996), and some subsections in Van Voorden et al. (1993). For a study on collective bargaining in the health and welfare sectors, see Plessen (1996).

2 This development could indeed be called robust since the consequences were such that around the middle of the 1990s the number of employed workers of 55 to 65 years of age was about 40%, and, most dramatically, between 60 to 65 years of age only 10%.

3 Later, in the second half of the nineties, other legal changes would follow, concerning, for instance, laws on working time, co-determination, and dismissals and probation periods. Most of these laws, if not all, were meant to enhance (economic) flexibility and the functioning of the labour market.

4 That means that for material on the role and significance of employers (organisations), we have to consult publications written mainly at the end of the eighties: Nobelen (1987), Van Voorden (1981, 1984, 1990), Van Waarden (1989), and De Vroom (1990).

5 Later, the Minister claimed that extension should only be granted when the collective parties wanted to negotiate about so-called 'good purposes', containing specific terms of employment such as training and measures to recruit long-term unemployed workers.

6 The debate touched upon other 'corporatist' elements as well, such as the minimum wage, the relatively large wage differences between minimum wages and the lowest contract wages (cf. Van Soest; Keuzekamp 1997; Vogels 1997). Even phenomena such as the collective agreement and the union were questioned (see also Section 2).

REFERENCES

Akkermans, A., R. Wielers and G. van Kooten, 1995. 'Vakbondscoalities en stakingen' (Trade union coalitions and strikes), *Tijdschrift voor Arbeidsvraagstukken* 11(2): 163-173.

Albeda, W., 1993. 'De toekomst van de overlegeconomie' (The Future of the Consultation Economy), in: Hofstra and Nobelen (eds.), pp. 23-31.

Albeda, W. and W.J. Dercksen, 1994. *Arbeidsverhoudingen in Nederland* (Labour Relations in The Netherlands), Alphen a/d Rijn / Zaventem, Samsom.

Becking, K.M., 1996. 'Arbeidsvoorwaarden en maatwerk bij de overheid' (The Terms of Employment in the Public Sector), *Sociaal Maandblad Arbeid* 51(3): 170-179.

Beke, J.O.M., 1996. *Flexible arbeidsrelaties en arbeidsbeloningen* (Rewarding Flexible Labour), Amsterdam, IBFD Publications.

Berg, A. van den, 1995. *Trade Union Growth and Decline in the Netherlands*, Amsterdam, Thesis Publishers Amsterdam.

Berg, A. van den, 1996. 'Vakbeweging, economische conjunctuur en institutionele veranderingen in Nederland' (Trade Unions, Business Cycle and Institutional Changes in the Netherlands), in: Visser, J. (ed,), pp. 54-72.

Bolwijn, P.T. and T. Kumpe, 1991. *Marktgericht ondernemen; Management van continuïteit en vernieuwing* (Modern Market Company Management: Continuity and Innovation), Assen/Maastricht, Van Gorcum.

Boos, C. and W. van Oorschot, 1998. 'Sociale zekerheid aan arbeidsvoorwaarden gebonden' (Social Security in Collective Agreements), *Publieke en private sociale zekerheid*, Den Haag (forthcoming).

Bottenburg, M. van, 1995. *Aan den Arbeid!* (To Work!), Amsterdam, Uitgeverij Bert Bakker.

Bruin, C. de and P.G. Klandermans, 1995. 'Uitkeringsgerechtigden en hun vakbond' (Social Security Beneficiaries and their Union), *Tijdschrift voor Arbeidsvraagstukken* 11(3): 280-291.

Buitendam, A., D.A.G. Dumas and A.C. Glebbeek (eds.), 1990. *Het Zweedse model, geschikt voor import?* (The Swedish Model, applicable in the Dutch case?), Assen/Maastricht, Van Gorcum.

Burgh, Y. van der, 1996. *De cao in de kappersbranche* (The Barber's Collective Agreement), Den Haag, EIM.

Central Planning Office, 1992. *Scanning the future. A long-term study of the world economy 1990-2015*. Den Haag, CPB.

Coenen, H. and P. Leisink, 1990. 'De structuratietheorie als theoretische oriëntatie bij de studie van de arbeidsverhoudingen' (Structuration theory as a theoretical vehicle for Industrial Relations study), *Sociale Wetenschappen* 33(1): 1-18.

Coenen, H. (ed.), 1995. *De Vakbeweging na 2000* (Trade unionism after 2000), Utrecht, Jan van Arkel.

Crouch, C., 1993. *European industrial relations and state traditions*. Oxford, Clarendon Press.

Daalder, A. and C. van Rij, 1996. 'Lidmaatschapsstromen; Een dynamische analyse van dertig jaar in- en uitstroom' (Membership developments; a dynamic analysis), in: Visser, J. (ed.), pp. 72-92.

Dankbaar, B., L. Delsen and W. de Nijs, 1998. *Collective bargaining and flexibility in the Netherlands*, Geneva, ILO (forthcoming).

Delsen, L., 1992. 'De vut: uitbreiden of afschaffen' (The Voluntary Retirement Regulation: extend or abolish), *Economisch Statistische Berichten* 77(3841): 46-48.

Delsen, L., 1997. 'Flexibilisering van de arbeid in Europa' (Flexibilisation of labour in Europe), *Tijdschrift voor Arbeidsvraagstukken* 13(1): 23-36.

Doremalen, H. van, 1996. *De handen ineen; geschiedenis van 100 jaar vakbeweging in Tilburg* (Hundred years of Trade Unionism in Tilburg), Tilburg, Stichting tot behoud van Tilburgs cultuurgoed.

Dijk, N. van and M. Punch, 1993. '"The Netherlands" in Management in Western Europe. Society, Culture and Organisation in Twelve Nations', in: David J. Hickson (ed.), pp. 167-190, New York and Berlin: Walter de Gruyter.

Eijl, C. van, 1997. *Maandag tolereren we niets; vrouwen, arbeid en vakbeweging 1945-1990* (Women, labour and trade unions 1945-1990), Amsterdam, IISG.

Elsendoorn, G.Th. and W.H.M. van der Hoeven, 1996. *De invloed van het algemeen verbindend verklaren van cao's voor jonge bedrijven* (The impact of the extension of collective agreements on young companies), Den Haag, OSA and EIM, SDU.

Esping-Andersen, G., 1990. *The three worlds of welfare capitalism*, Princeton, Princeton University Press.

Freeman, R.B., J. Hartog and C.N. Teulings, 1997. 'AVV, spil in het spel' (Extension of Sectoral Contracts; A central rule), *Economisch Statistische Berichten* 82(4115): 580-584.

Fruijtier, B., 1994. *Organisatieverandering en het probleem van de Baron van Münchhausen* (Organisational Transformation and the problem of the Baron of Münchhausen), Delft, Eburon.

Gier, H.G. de et al., 1991. *Gekantelde arbeidsverhoudingen* (Altered Industrial Relations), Alphen a/d Rijn, Samsom / H.D. Tjeenk Willink.

Glasbergen, M.P., 1994. *Flexibele en blijvende inzetbaarheid van machinebedieners in de grafische industrie* (Flexibility and employability of workers in the Printing Industry), Enschede, UT.

Goodijk, R., 1993. *Op weg naar een professionele ondernemingsraad?* (Towards a professional Works Council?), Assen, Van Gorcum.

Goodijk, R., 1995. *Ondernemingsraad en strategische besluitvorming* (Works Council and Strategic decision making), Assen, Van Gorcum.

Gradus, R.H.J.M., 1994. 'Nederlandse economie relatief rigide in Europa' (The Dutch economy in Europe: comparatively inflexible), *Economische Statistische Berichten* 79(3980): 921-924.

Haan, E. de, P. Vos and P. de Jong, 1994. *Flexibiliteit van de arbeid* (Flexibility of Labour), Amsterdam, Welboom.

Hartog, J., R. van Opstal and C.N. Teulings, 1994. 'Loonvorming in Nederland en de Verenigde Staten' (Wage formation in the Netherlands and the United States), *Economisch Statistische Berichten* 79(3964): 528-533.

Harzing, A.W. and J. van Ruysseveldt (eds.) 1995. *International Human Resource Management; An Integrated Approach*, London, Sage.

Heertum van-Lemmen, A.H. and A.C.J.M. Wilthagen, 1996. *De doorwerking van aanbevelingen van de Stichting van de Arbeid* (The Effects of Central Recommendations on Wage Negotiations), Hugo Sinzheimer Instituut Amsterdam, Den Haag, SDU.

Hees, G.B. van, 1993. *Bedrijfsmatige effecten van vakbonden en ondernemingsraden; de ontwikkeling van een conceptueel model en de toepassing daarvan op drie Nederlandse ondernemingssituaties* (The Economic Impact on Companies of Unions and Works Councils), Leuven/Apeldoorn, Garant.

Hemerijck, A., 1993. *The historical contingencies of Dutch corporatism*. Oxford.

Hemerijck, A., 1996. 'Let's make things better. Een apologie van het corporatisme' (An Apology of Corporatism), *Socialisme en Democratie* 53(4): 91-107.
Hofman, P.C., C. Compaijen and J.C. van Ours, 1992. *Sectorale loondifferentiatie en werkgelegenheid in internationaal perspectief* (Industrial Wage Differentiation and Employment: an International Comparison), Den Haag, OSA.
Hofstra, N.A. and P.W.M. Nobelen (eds.), 1993. *Toekomst van de overlegeconomie* (The Future of the Consultation Economy), Assen/Maastricht, Van Gorcum.
Hoof, J.J. van, 1995. *Arbeidsbestel op een keerpunt; Tien jaar veranderingen in arbeidsorganisatie, arbeidsmarkt en arbeidsverhoudingen vanuit een lange-termijnperspectief* (The System of Industrial Relations at a Cross-roads), in: L. Faase, M. Ott and C.J. Vos (eds.), *Nieuwe breukvlakken in het arbeidsbestel? Balans van 10 jaar veranderingen in Nederland en België*, Utrecht, De Tijdstroom, pp. 28-48.
Hooff, G. van (ed.), 1996. *Tot het hemelsch morgenrood; beelden en grepen uit honderd jaar vakbeweging Helmond 1896-1996* (Hundred years of Trade unionism in Helmond), Helmond, Stichting 100 jaar vakbeweging in Helmond.
Hovels, B. and P. Nas, 1976. *Ondernemingsraden en medezeggenschap* (Works Councils and Co-determination), Nijmegen, ITS.
Huiskamp, M.J., 1992. *De regulering van de arbeidsruil: analysekader* (The Regulation of the Employment Relation: an analytical framework), in: J. Ruysseveldt and J. van Hoof (eds.), *Part II*, pp. 9-31.
Huiskamp, R., 1995. 'Collective bargaining in transition', in: J. van Ruysseveldt, R. Huiskamp and J. van Hoof (eds.), *Comparative Industrial and employment relations*, London, Sage, pp. 135-155.
Huiskamp, R., 1996. 'De bedrijfstakcao heeft toekomst' (Collective Agreements by Industry do have a Future), *Gids voor personeelsmanagement* 75(5): 50-54.
Hurk, H. van den, 1995. 'Scholing in een moderne vakbond' (Schooling within a modern Trade Union), *Tijdschrift voor Arbeidsvraagstukken* 11(4): 374-382.
Jong, F. de and M. van Bolhuis, 1997. *Flexibilisering van de arbeid. Een onderzoek naar aspecten van (interne) flexibilisering in bedrijven* (Flexibilisation of Labour; the internal organisation dimension), Den Haag, Arbeidsinspectie.
Jong, H.W. de, 1996. 'Rijnlandse ondernemingen presteren beter' (Companies in Rhinelandic systems are performing better), *Economisch Statistische Berichten* 81(4049): 228-233.
Jong, J.A. and J. Paauwe, 1988. 'De toekomst van de Vakbeweging' (The Future of the Trade Union), *Economisch Statistische Berichten* 73(3657): 497-501.
Kaar, R.H. van het, 1993. *Medezeggenschap bij fusie en ontvlechting* (Co-determination in case of Merger or Separation), Amsterdam, Thesis.
Kaar, R.H. van het, 1995. *Ondernemingsraad en vertrouwenscommissarissen: structuurregeling en medezeggenschap* (Works Council and Workers Commissioner), Den Haag, SDU.
Kerkhof, P., 1997. *Van mediabericht naar politieke opvatting; Een onderzoek naar de opvattingen van CNV-leden over de verzorgingsstaat* (Views of Trade Union Members to the Welfare State), Amsterdam, VU.

Klamer, A., 1990. *Verzuilde dromen: 40 jaar SER* (Forty Years of Social Economic Council), Amsterdam, Balans.

Klandermans, B. and J. Visser (eds.), 1995. *De vakbeweging na de welvaartsstaat* (The Trade union after the Welfare State), Assen, Van Gorcum.

Kleinknecht, A., 1994. 'Heeft Nederland een loongolf nodig?' (Does the Dutch Economy require a Wage Wave?), *Tijdschrift voor Politieke Economie* 17(2): 5-25.

Kleinknecht, A., 1996. *Verborgen kosten van loonmatiging* (The hidden Costs of Wage Moderation), *Economisch Statistische Berichten* 81(4069): 694-696.

Knoop, J. van der, 1991. *Tussen toeschouwen en meesturen: de rol van commissarissen in en tussen grote vennootschappen* (The Role of supervisory Commissioners within and between big Corporations), Amsterdam.

Kooten, G. van and J.S.H. Stolk, 1992. *Arbeidsverhoudingen in balans* (Balanced Industrial Relations), Woerden, Bouw en Houtbond FNV.

Korevaar, K., 1990. *Funderingsherstel; Over vernieuwing, management en vakbondswerk in de bouw* (On the modern relations between Management and Unions in the Construction Industry), Amsterdam, Bouw en Houtbond FNV.

Kruif, C.G.M., 1996. *Flexibele arbeidsvoorwaarden* (Flexible Terms of Employment), Alphen aan de Rijn, Samsom.

Leemreize, H.J., 1992. 'Het belang van de algemeenverbindendverklaring' (The Significance of the Extension of Labour Contracts), *Economisch Statistische Berichten* 77(3855): 364-368.

Leisink, P. and L. Spaninks, 1994. 'Arbeidsverhoudingen zonder collectieve regulering' (Labour Relations without Collective Regulation), *Tijdschrift voor Arbeid en Bewustzijn* 18(1): 34-41.

Leisink, P., 1994. 'Belangenbehartiging door de grafische bonden; Tussen centrale dienstverlening en lokale cliëntenparticipatie' (Representation of Interests by the Unions of Printers), in: P. Leisink and H. Leisink (eds.), *'t Schild der solidariteit*. Amsterdam, Stichting FNV Pers.

Leisink, P., 1996. 'Dutch and Flemish Industrial Relations: Theory and Practice', *European Journal of Industrial Relations* 2(1): 69-93.

Leisink, P., J. van Leemput and J. Vilrokx (eds.), 1996. *The Challenges to Trade Unions in Europe; Innovation and Adaption*. Cheltenham, Edward Elgar.

Looise, J.C., 1989. *Werknemersvertegenwoordiging op de Tweesprong* (Representation of Workers Interests at a Cross-roads), Alphen aan den Rijn, Samsom.

Looise, J.C., 1992. 'Meer flexibel en terug naar de kern? Structuur en strategie van de vakbeweging in de jaren '90' (Unions: more flexibility and back to core business), *Sociaal Maandblad Arbeid* 47(7/8): 413-429.

Looise, J.C., J. de Leede and M. van Beusekom, 1996. *De Ondernemingsraad van de toekomst, de toekomst van de ondernemingsraad* (The Future of the Works Councils), Amsterdam, Welboom.

McKensie, 1997. *Een stimulans voor de Nederlandse economie* (An Incentive to the Dutch Economy), Amsterdam, McKensie and Company.

Meer, M. van der, 1996. 'Belangenbehartiging onder druk; De langste bouwstaking na de Tweede Wereldoorlog' (The longest post-war Strike in the Construction Industry: problems with the Representation of Interests), in: J. Visser (ed.), pp. 118-143.

Meeus, M., 1994. *Informatietechnologie: plaats en betekenis van arbeid* (The Impact of the Information Technology on Labour), Tilburg, Tilburg University Press.

Ministerie van Economische Zaken, 1997. *De toets op het concurrentievermogen 1997* (Testing Dutch Competitiveness), Den Haag, MEZ.

Nagelkerke, A.G., 1992. *Instituties en economisch handelen; een onderzoek naar de wetenschappelijke betekenis van de institutioneel-economische benadering* (Institutions and Economic Action), Tilburg, Tilburg University Press.

Nagelkerke, A.G., 1994. 'Institutioneel balanceren; decentralisatie in de Nederlandse arbeidsverhoudingen in de jaren tachtig' (Balancing Institutionally: Decentralisation of Dutch Industrial Relations), *Sociaal Maandblad Arbeid* 49(1): 20-31.

Nagelkerke, A.G. and W.F. de Nijs, 1996. *Regels rond arbeid; Arbeidsverhoudingen in Nederland en op het niveau van de Europese Unie* (Industrial Relations in the Netherlands and on European Union level), Houten, Educatieve Partners Nederland.

Nagelkerke, A. and P. Koijen, 1996. 'De postmoderne vakbeweging: tussen gefragmenteerde loonmachine en pluriforme arbeidsmarktorganisatie' (Postmodern Unionism: Fragmented Wage Machine or Pluriform Labour Market Organisation), in: A. Nagelkerke and J. van der Velden (eds.), *Erop of eronder; de strategie van de postmoderne vakbeweging*, Den Haag, Welboom, pp. 12-36.

Nagelkerke, A.G. and W.F. de Nijs, 1998. 'Institutional Dynamics in European Industrial Relations', *Labour*, (forthcoming).

Nobelen, P.W.M., 1987. *Ondernemers georganiseerd* (Organised Employers), proefschrift Erasmus Universiteit, Den Haag.

Paauwe, J., 1992. 'Participatie: Van werkvloer tot Brussel' (Participation; from shop floor level to Brussels), in: P. Hazenbosch (ed.), *Het vlees op de botten; over structuur en participatie in vakbondsland*, Kampen, Kok.

Paping, R.H.M. and H. Stegeman. 'Niet het corporatisme zorgt voor problemen' (It is not corporatism that causes problems), *Economisch Statistische Berichten* 82(4121): 721-723.

Peijpe, T. van, 1990. *De conjunctuur van het arbeidsrecht* (The Business Cycle of Labour Law), Groningen, Wolters Noordhoff.

Plessen, W.G.M., 1996. *Collectieve onderhandelingen in de zorgsector* (Collective Bargaining in the Health and Care Industry), Deventer, Kluwer.

Praag, B.M.S. van and J.P. Hop, 1995. *De matigende invloed van de Nederlandse vakbeweging* (The Impact of Dutch Unionism on Wage Moderation), in: *Economisch Statistische Berichten* 80(4032): 996-1000.

Reynaerts, W.H.J., 1985. *Kantelende posities, arbeidsverhoudingen in een keertijd* (Industrial Relations at a Turning Point), Den Haag, OSA.

Reynaerts, W.H.J. and A.G. Nagelkerke, 1986. *Arbeidsverhoudingen, theorie en praktijk Deel I* (Industrial Relations, Theory and Practice Part I), Leiden, Stenfert Kroese (1982).

Riel, B. van, 1995. *Unemployment divergence and coordinated systems of industrial relations; a comparative analysis of six countries*, Frankfurt am Main, Lang.

Rij, C. van, 1994. *To join or not to join; an event-history analysis of trade union membership in the Netherlands*, Amsterdam, NIMMO.

Rij, C. van and B. van den Putte, 1992. 'Wanneer en waarom worden werknemers lid van een vakbond? Een empirische confrontatie van sociologische en economische theorieën' (To become an Union member: When and Why; An empirical confrontation of sociological and economic theories), *Tijdschrift voor Arbeidsvraagstukken* 8(3): 265-275.

Rojer, M., 1993. *Hoe meer zielen hoe meer vreugd; De invloed van plurale representatie in collectieve onderhandelingsprocessen* (Plural representation of Interests in Collective Bargaining), Amsterdam Working Papers in Sociology, 93(1), University of Amsterdam.

Rojer, M. and J. Visser, 1993. 'De ene sector is de andere niet. Keuzegedrag, netwerkvorming en werknemersorganisatie' (Sectoral differences in Workers Attitudes towards Trade Unions), *Tijdschrift voor Arbeidsvraagstukken* 9(2): 182-199.

Rojer, M., 1996. *Cao-onderhandelingen: een voorspelbaar, logisch en rationeel proces* (Collective Bargaining: a predictable, logical and rational process), Amsterdam, Thesis Publishers.

Rojer, M., 1996b. 'De reparatie van het WAO-gat; Een dynamische analyse van CAO-onderhandelingen' (The case of the Law on Disablement: A dynamic analysis of Collective Bargaining), in: J. Visser (ed.), pp. 92-118.

Roorda, W.B. and E.H.W.M. Vogels, 1997. 'Arbeidsmarkt, bescherming en prestaties' (Labour Market, Protection and Performance), *Economisch Statistische Berichten* 82(4099): 245-249.

Ruysseveldt, J. and J. van Hoof (eds.), 1992. *Arbeidsverhoudingen in Europa. Deel I en II* (Industrial Relations in Europe Part I and II), Heerlen, Open Universiteit.

Ruysseveldt, J. van, R. Huiskamp and J. van Hoof (eds.), 1995. *Comparative Industrial and employment relations*, Sage, London.

Ruysseveldt, J. van and J. Visser (eds.), 1996. *Industrial Relations in Europe; Traditions and Transitions*, London, Sage.

Schilstra, K. and E. Smit, 1996. 'Drie scenario's voor de belangenbehartiging van werknemers' (Three Scenario's of Representation of Workers Interests), in: *Sociaal Maandblad Arbeid* 51(2): 116-127.

Schrover, M.L.J.C., 1991. *Het vette, het zoete en het wederzijds profijt; Arbeidsverhoudingen in de margarine-industrie en in de cacao- en chocolade-industrie in Nederland 1870-1960* (Industrial Relations in the Margarine, Cocoa and Chocolate Industry 1860-1960), Hilversum, Verloren.

Smit, E. and J. Miltenburg, 1997. *Competitie of coalitie; samenwerkingsrelaties tussen ondernemingsraad en vakbeweging in de arbeidsvoorwaardenvorming* (Competition or Coalition; Works Councils and Trade Unions in Wage Negotiations), Den Haag, Vuga.

Sociaal-Economische Raad, 1992. *Convergentie en overlegeconomie* (Convergence and the Consultation Economy), Den Haag, SER.

Soest, A. van and A. Kalwij, 1996. *Loonvorming en werkgelegenheid in Nederland; een dynamische analyse* (Wage Formation and Employment in the Netherlands; a dynamic analysis), Den Haag, Vuga.

Steeg, G. ter, 1994. 'Flexibele binding: moderne arbeidsverhoudingen in de audiovisuele branche' (Flexible Commitment; Modern Labour Relations in the Audio Sector), *Tijdschrift voor Arbeid en Bewustzijn* 18(1): 27-34.

Stenvert, T., 1992. *'Zwarte kunst'; 100 jaar grafische vakbeweging in Groningen 1892-1992* (Hundred years of Printers Union in Groningen), Groningen, Druk en Papier Groningen.

Stoop, S., 1992. *De sociale fabriek; Sociale politiek bij Philips Eindhoven, Bayer Leverkusen en Hoogovens IJmuiden* (The Social Plant; Company Social Policy at Philips, Bayer and Hoogovens), Leiden/Antwerpen, Stenfert Kroese.

Stichting van de Arbeid, 1993. *Een nieuwe koers* (Changing Course), Den Haag, SvdA.

Streeck, W., 1992. *Social institutions and Economic Performance*. London, Sage.

Streeck, W. and P.C. Schmitter, 1992. 'From National Corporatism to Transnational Pluralism: Organised Interests in the Single European Market', in: Streeck, 1992.

Teulings, C.N., 1995. 'Efficiënte loonvorming door sociale partners' (Efficient Wage Formation of Trade Unions and Employers Organisations), *Economisch Statistische Berichten* 80(4010): 460-465.

Teulings, C.N., 1996a. 'Corporatisme in de loonvorming' (Corporatism and Wage Formation), *Socialisme en Democratie* 53(4): 79-87.

Teulings, C.N., 1996b. *De plaats van de vakbeweging in de toekomst* (Unions in the Future), Amsterdam, Welboom.

Tijdens, K. and N. Goedhart, 1996. 'Kwaliteit van de arbeid en rol van de vakbond in de schoonmaaksector' (Unions and Quality of Work in the Cleaning Industry), *Tijdschrift voor Arbeidsvraagstukken* 12(1): 31-43.

Toren, J.P. van den, 1996. *Achter gesloten deuren? CAO-overleg in de jaren negentig* (Behind close doors; Collective Bargaining in the 90s), Amsterdam, Welboom.

Trommel, W.A., 1995. *Korter arbeidsleven; De wording van een rationele mythe* (A shorter Working Life: the Genesis of a Rational Myth), Den Haag, SDU.

Valkenburg, B., 1995. 'Trade unionism in the Netherlands: back to the future'. *Transfer* 1(1), Brussels.

Veersma, U., 1992. *Technologie en arbeid in verandering; Case-studies in de grafische sector* (Technology and the Transformation of Labour; case-studies in the Printing Industry), Brussels, VUBPRESS.

Visser, J., 1987/1990. *In search of inclusive unionism, a comparative analysis*, Amsterdam, Universiteit van Amsterdam.

Visser, J., 1991. 'Trends in Union Membership'. in: OECD, *Employment Outlook 1991*, Paris, pp. 97-134.

Visser, J., 1992a. 'The Netherlands: The End of an Era and the End of a System', in: A. Ferner and R. Hyman (eds.), *Industrial Relations in the New Europe*, Oxford (UK) / Cambridge (USA), pp. 323-357.

Visser, J., 1992b. 'The Strength of Union Movements in advanced capitalist Democracies'. in: M. Regini (ed.), *The future of Labour Movements*. London, Sage.

Visser J., 1994. 'European Trade Unions; The Transition Years', in: R. Hyman and A. Ferner (eds.), *New Frontiers in European Industrial Relations*. Oxford, Basil Blackwell.

Visser, J. (ed.), 1996. 'De vakbeweging op de eeuwgrens' (Trade Unions at the Turn of the Century), Special number *Mens & Maatschappij* 71, Amsterdam, Amsterdam University Press.

Visser, J. and B. Ebbinghaus, 1996. 'Een halve eeuw verandering; Verklaringen voor convergentie en diversiteit van werknemersorganisaties in West-Europa' (Half a century of Change; Convergence and Diversity of Trade Unionism in Western Europe), in: J. Visser (ed.), pp. 20-54.

Visser, J. and A. Hemerijck, 1997. *A Dutch Miracle; Job Growth, Welfare Reform and Corporatism in the Netherlands*, Amsterdam, Amsterdam University Press.

Vogels, E.H.W.M., 1997. 'Minimumbeloningen en werkloosheid' (Minimum Wages and Unemployment), *Economisch Statistische Berichten* 82(4121): 716-721.

Voorden, W. van, 1981. 'Werkgeversorganisaties, een poging tot plaatsbepaling' (Employers Organisations; an Assessment), in: W. van Voorden (ed.), *Arbeidsverhoudingen uit model*. Alphen aan den Rijn, Samsom.

Voorden, W. van, 1984. 'De werkgeversorganisatie in het krachtenveld van de arbeidsverhoudingen' (Power and Significance of Employers Organisations in the System of Industrial Relations), *Sociaal Maandblad Arbeid* 39.

Voorden, W. van, 1987. 'De cao als spiegel der arbeidsverhoudingen' (The Collective Agreement: A Mirror of Industrial Relations), *Sociaal Maandblad Arbeid* 39(10): november.

Voorden, W. van, 1989. 'Arbeidsverhoudingen bij de overheid, de toekomst in beeld' (Changing Industrial Relations in the Public Sector), *Economisch Statistische Berichten* 25-10-1989.

Voorden, W. van, 1990. 'De ondernemersorganisatie, conjuncturele invloeden en strukturele kenmerken' (The Organisation of Employers; the Impact of the Business Cycle and Structural Characteristics), in: A. van Doorn (ed.), *Ondernemer, onderneming en omgeving*. Eindhoven, Stichting Toekomst Middelgrote Ondernemingen.

Voorden, W. van, 1991. 'Algemeen-verbindendverklaring onterecht mikpunt' (The Inappropriate Attack on the Extension of Collective Agreements), *Economisch Statistische Berichten* 76(3790): 53-54.

Voorden W. van, A.G. Nagelkerke and W.F. de Nijs, 1993. *Macht in banen; Arbeidsverhoudingen in theorie en beleid* (Balanced Power; Industrial Relations, Theory and Policy), Leiden/Antwerpen, Stenfert Kroese.

Vos, P. and W. Buitelaar, 1996. *Arbeidsorganisaties en arbeidsverhoudingen in beweging* (Changing Organisation of Work and Changing Labour Relations), Amsterdam, Welboom.

Vroom, B. de, 1990. *Verenigde fabrikanten* (United Manufacturers), Groningen, Wolters-Noordhoff.

Waarden, B.F. van, 1989. *Organisatiemacht van belangenverenigingen* (The Organisational Power of Interests Groups), Den Haag.

Waarden, F. van, 1995. 'Breekt Nederland zijn dijken door?' (Is Holland breaking down the Dikes?), *Economisch Statistische Berichten* 80(3993): 52-58.

Waarden, F. van, 1997. *Institutions of socio-economic coordination: a European style?* Document, prepared for the Ministry of Social Affairs and Employment, The Hague.

Warning, J., 1992. 'Modernisering van vakbondsdemocratie. Dienstenbond FNV op zoek naar nieuwe wegen om leden bij beleid te betrekken' (Modernising Union Democracy), *Tijdschrift voor Arbeidsvraagstukken* 8(3): 252-265.

Wijngaert, R., 1994. *Trade Unions and Collective Bargaining in The Netherlands*, Amsterdam, Tinbergen Institute Research Series.

Williams, A.R.T., J. Paauwe and J.C. van Ham, 1989. 'De toekomst van de vakbeweging' (The Future of the Trade Union), in: Bolweg J.F. and F. Kluytmans (eds.), *De noodzaak van nieuwe verhoudingen; beschouwingen over arbeidsverhoudingen en personeelsmanagement*. Deventer, Kluwer.

Wissema, J.G. et al., 1996. *Medezeggenschap op maat: van toetsende naar interactieve medezeggenschap* (Taylored Participation; substituting checking for interactive participation), Assen, Van Gorcum.

Zalm, G., 1992. 'Betekenis en toekomst van de algemeen verbindend verklaring' (The Significance and Future of the Extension of Collective Agreements), *Economisch Statistische Berichten* 77(3842).

AUTHORS

Dr. A.G. Nagelkerke
Tilburg University, Faculty of Economics
P.O. Box 90153, 5000 LE Tilburg
tel. 013-4662549 (or 2013), fax: 013-4663042
e-mail: a.g.nagelkerke@kub.nl

Dr. W.F.M. de Nijs
University of Nijmegen, Nijmegen Business School
P.O. Box 9108, 6500 HK Nijmegen
tel: 024-3612880, fax: 024-3611933
e-mail: W.deNijs@bw.kun.nl

RESEARCH INTO THE QUALITY OF WORK

Peter Oeij, Ben Fruytier and Inge van den Broek

1. INTRODUCTION

Given the immense quantity of research literature on the quality of work in the Netherlands, it is not possible to present a complete overview. Nonetheless, a good picture of the 'state of the art' can be arrived at by focusing on the most important contributions in a particular area. We have therefore defined a clear-cut field of interest—the content of work—since this is the most fundamental element of the quality of work. This restriction implies that little attention is paid to industrial relations, the remuneration system (employment relationship), and the working environment (physical working conditions). We have further restricted ourselves to research that has been published in the years 1991-1996. For overviews of the preceding period, we refer to the work of other authors.[1] Thirdly, we have focused on scientific articles in the two leading Dutch specialist journals, *Tijdschrift voor Arbeidsvraagstukken* (*TVA*, Journal for Labour Issues) and *Gedrag en Organisatie* (*G&O*, Behaviour and Organisation).

The main question addressed in this paper is: What developments have occurred or are occurring in the research into the quality of work and how should they be evaluated?

After the seventies, research into just the quality of work virtually ceased, with two books closing off this period, *Kwaliteit van de arbeid* (Quality of Work) (Van Dijck et al. 1980) and *Humanisering van de arbeid* (Humanising Labour) (De Galan et al. 1980). Articles on the duty and the right to engage in meaningful labour (e.g. Kuiper 1976) also became scarce, and only from an ideological perspective can these views still be heard (Muskens 1997).

In the eighties, the quality of work research was dominated, in general, by socio-economic developments. The change was marked by the WRR reports *Vernieuwingen in het arbeidsbestel* (Innovations in the labour relations system) (1981) and *Kwaliteit van de arbeid* (Quality of work) (1982).[2] In these reports, the quality of work is connected with absenteeism and disablement (incapacity to work) and with processes of technological innovation.

Our description begins at the point where Van Klaveren's study *Trends en keuzes in het onderzoek naar de kwaliteit van de arbeid* (Trends and choices in the research on the quality of work) (1994) ends. Van Klaveren's mood is gloomy when commenting on the social status of the research into the quality of work: 'To all appearances, the field has hardly succeeded in acquiring a position of its own in government and business policy and, as a rule, it remains a derivative of other policy goals' (1994: 67). In fact, in describing the main trends, Van Klaveren presents a 'state of the art' review of the research on the quality of work in the Netherlands in the year 1993. In the present article, we want to determine whether there has been a shift in emphasis in recent years, and, if so, to what extent.[3]

We begin by outlining the concept 'quality of work' (Section 2). To fully understand the discussion in the Netherlands, it is important to know the context of quality of work research. This context is the socio-economic development and, in particular, the development of the labour factor (Section 3). We will specify four themes within this framework which we believe play a role in the quality of work research.

Next, we shall describe the framework, constructed on the basis of the four themes and on a characterisation of the kind of research done, that was used to analyse the articles (Section 4). Separate sections deal with psychological research into the quality of work (Section 5) and with accents stressed by the government (Section 6). The findings of our research are illustrated with examples. In our conclusions (Section 7), we answer the following questions: (1) Where have the accents been in quality of work research and how are these related with socio-economic development? (2) What is lacking in the quality of work research?

From an empirical perspective, the article presents only limited support for the answers to our questions. Nevertheless, we hope that by putting forward some propositions, we will stimulate discussion on quality of work research.

2. THE QUALITY OF WORK

There are many definitions of the quality of work.[4] Van Klaveren (1994: 31-46), for instance, makes a distinction between quality of work as a factor of the work situation and of the worker (the person involved). While it certainly makes sense to distinguish between these two factors, we prefer another distinction, that between a definition of the quality of work on the basis of the objective characteristics of the working situation and a view that takes the quality of work to be an effect of the relationship between work and worker (or task and performer).

In the development of quality of work as a characteristic of the work situation, there is a similarity between sociotechnics (De Sitter 1981) and the WEBA method.[5] Both methods are characterised by an objective approach to the quality of work. Quality of work depends on the structural characteristics of the work[6] and is independent of the attitudes and behaviour of those performing the job. WEBA has been criticised for failing to consider mental pressure, work stress, and the coping mechanisms of individuals by those interpreting the quality of work as an effect of the relationship work-worker (Grunveld 1992; Furda and Meijman 1992).

Judging by their insistence on the systematic listing of risk factors,[7] those focusing on the 'fit' between work and worker in quality of work research have also been looking for ways to objectify the quality of work. Psychic and physiological risks can be determined by representative population surveys, so these too can be considered as objective factors, in other words, as aggregated knowledge not based on individual judgements (of how respondents feel).

The quality of work approach focusing on the relationship work–worker is dominated by subjective operationalisations such as subjectively founded norms on the quality of work and intersubjective task characteristics (Van Klaveren 1994: 39). The point of departure is frequently judgements and perceptions of workers, as in job satisfaction research. In the action–theoretical approach, subjective and objective factors coincide. Thus, besides job satisfaction, work stress and well-being are also measured and objective task characteristics determined.

In recent years, a convergence[8] has been taking place between, on the one hand, the ideas of quality of work as a property of the work situation (the conditional approach) and, on the other hand, as a property of psychological and physiological human behavioural reactions to work situations (the action–theoretical approach). The conditional approach focuses increasingly on the reactions of workers, whereas the action–theoretical approach is becoming more aware of, let us say, the individual–independent (objective) characteristics of labour. In addition to these, there is still labour satisfaction research, but there is no convergence of ideas in this area.

3. SOCIAL CONTEXT

After the seventies, the emphasis in research and policy in the quality of work field shifted (Fruytier 1986). At the time, the dominant approach was based on the view that labour offered a way to develop one's abilities and that work could give social meaning to a person's life. Quality of work corresponded with quality of life. In the eighties, new concepts for economic management, combining the ability to meet flexible market demands and the recognition of the need for skilled workers, began to dominate research. Taylorism was questioned. In practice, however, this has not resulted in an evident improvement in the quality of work (Fruytier 1986; 1994).

The question is: What has happened in recent years? We shall try to describe the main contextual developments in broad outline and to point out the relationship, if any, with the research into quality of work.

3.1. A bird's-eye view of the general socio-economic development in the Netherlands

In several respects, the oil crises of the seventies were a point of no return. For the Western world, these events marked the beginning of economic decline and rapidly increasing unemployment. Not until the second half of the eighties did the first change for the better set in. Between 1984 and 1992, employment increased by about 70,000 man-years each year. On the one hand, this growth was largely produced by the increase in part-time work and the reduction of working hours. On the other hand, it was the result of mainly government efforts to control wage growth and decrease the financial burden of companies caused by taxes and premiums. The government cut down its expenditures. Unemployment, however, still remained critically high. Between 1990 and 1993, the economic motor stalled for the second time. The number of unemployed rose again and remained high even when, somewhat later, the economy improved and employment increased (Faase et al. 1995b: 138). All in all, the employment issue has been an important item on the agenda for the last two decades. Between 1970 and 1993, the number of man-years did not or hardly increase in the Netherlands (Schmid 1997).

An important political development that took place in the eighties was that government interference decreased substantially. This has resulted in a liberalising of industrial relations and less government interference in consultations about the terms of employment.

Cut-backs in expenditure and the government acting in conformity with market demands contributed to the restructuring of the social security system. The growing working population, high unemployment, the high rate of inactivity, and the high volumes of benefits resulting from increasing absenteeism and the reduction of working hours led to a 'labour market-stimulating social security policy'. This is a break with the past (Faase et al. 1995a: 16-17).

Now, in the nineties, the government's policy on the labour market and social security is being dictated by the desire to achieve greater labour participation and more flexibility. An effort is being made to create an additional demand for low-skilled and low-paid work. This policy entails new risks of segmentation. Examples are the creation of starter functions by splitting up tasks, including new lower wage scales in the collective labour agreements, and the government's threat not to give recognition to the results of collective bargaining unless a fair degree of labour market flexibility is included. This flexibility is further enhanced by making employment relations more flexible. Relaxing the Act on working hours, adaptations in employment protection, and deregulating the terms for temporary employment are examples of this. The government must find the balance between a social security system cut down to the bone and social pressure on labour participation. 'Thus, the government is heading for minimum protection norms (...)' (Faase et al. 1995a: 17-18).

3.2. Industrial relations, the labour market, and labour organisations

In his article on changes in the system of industrial relations over the last ten years, Van Hoof (1995: 28-36) observed that such issues as the reduction of working hours and the redistribution of work were already topical a decade ago, but that nowadays the socio-political scene has changed structurally, judging by the confidence placed in the salutary effect of the market. This is accompanied by a business-like hard line against those who are trying to escape their duty. He examined the developments within the labour organisations, within the industrial relations, and on the labour market.

Radical changes on markets, particularly labour markets, have marked the 'crisis' of the Tayloristic labour organisation. A search for new organisational concepts has begun, Van Hoof notes, in which not only flexibility and quality but also efficiency serve as the guidelines. Examples of new organisational concepts, usually old wine in new bottles, are numerous: socio-technical integral organisational change, 'lean production', 'total quality management', human-resources management, Toyotism, the learning organisation, and 'business process re-engineering', to mention just a few (Vaas 1995: 130).

Characteristic of the new concepts is the view of human capital as the source (critical resource) of flexibility, quality, and innovation. Employees are required to approach their jobs in a more flexible way. Besides their traditional professional skills, a lot is demanded of their social skills. They must be more capable of cooperating with those operating at other functional levels and with persons from other disciplines, and they must be capable of working in a group (Bosch et al. 1994: 68; Dagevos et al. 1996: 160-165). However, this is only one part of the picture. To promote flexibility, the bond between organisations and employees is also made much looser. This is manifested in industrial relations and on the labour market.

Within the system of industrial relations, the trend towards decentralisation cannot be ignored. The central government is interfering less and less directly with collective bargaining processes; there is no longer a need for nation-wide agreements to be settled; during the collective bargaining on the branch level, there is increasingly room for a more detailed interpretation by the individual companies, with the result that the works councils come to play a bigger part. In this view, the trade unions' position is substantially weakened. According to Van Hoof, there has been no real de-institutionalising as yet, but the appreciation of the collective bargaining economy by the parties involved is certainly shifting. The discussions about a more flexible regulation of social security and about a more individual approach to collective bargaining clearly indicate this.

Throughout the eighties and nineties, flexibility and deregulation have characterised the labour market. Deregulation, or discouraging regulation, for instance, can be observed in matters such as working and rest hours, employment protection and reviews of dismissal, and the *de facto* abolition of the concept of 'proper labour' (adapted or fitting work) for the unemployed.

Both employer and employee are developing different views about the permanent, full-time nine-to-five job. We speak of increasing flexibility when (temporary) staff can be more easily employed and dismissed. The turnover of employment agencies has set new records. This often involves externalisation of permanent staff. A mobility policy mainly addressing external outflow and flanked by provisions regarding 'out-placement' and the increase of 'employability' is becoming common property.

These developments lead to a number of conclusions with respect to labour. In the new production concepts, the care of the skeleton staff or core workers is a fundamental concern for organisations. These core workers work with a fair degree of autonomy and are highly paid. On the other hand, these organisations demand a lot of such staff. Increasing labour productivity goes together with a high work-load. The risk of the work-load exceeding the limits seems to have increased (Van Hoof 1995: 39-40; also see Nijhuis 1995; Kompier 1996). The shell of employees with temporary contracts around this core of permanent staff is growing. The work performed by this temporary staff may vary considerably in character. While it may be high quality work, it can also be low quality work at the same time. Government policy to raise labour participation has contributed to the creation of this low-skilled work. Starter jobs for the underprivileged have been created on a large scale.

3.3. Socio-economic development and the quality of work

Four themes for research into the quality of work can be gathered from the developments in labour organisations, industrial relations, and the labour market.

The first theme is *employment and the division of functions*. The government's goal is to increase participation. Since the WRR in its report on labour participation (1990: 170) mentioned the division of functions, there has been a lot of fuss about its consequences for the quality of work—witness the editorials of no less than three issues of *TVA*,[9] each of which underlined the risks for the quality of work.

The second theme is *organisational change*. Under this heading new production concepts, technology, and flexibility are taken together. The concepts of organisational innovation, described before, also result in changes in the nature of work. In particular, we have in mind the emergence of working in whole task-groups and further flexibility in the deployment of labour. Related to innovation within organisations is the increasing technological push to which work processes are subject. Computerisation, in particular, is increasingly leaving its mark on the nature of the tasks.

The third theme is the *development of functions*. Personnel policy (human-resources management), training, and qualifications fall under this heading. When organisations concentrate on their core businesses and respond to the demands of the market and the restrictions of the labour market, a new situation emerges which affects the way the inflow and outflow of labour is regulated. With respect to the quality of work, new research into the nature of personnel management, training, and the development of the demand for qualifications is to be expected. Roughly speaking, we are dealing here with developments and changes in functions.

The fourth, and last, theme is: *health and well-being*. Partly in view of the immense political attention that was paid to the problems of absenteeism and the inability to work at the beginning of the nineties, the changes in the content of work have stimulated research into the quality of work in terms of physical and psychological well-being. The policy focus of these themes can be seen in, among other things, the 'Arbo-wet' (Working Environment Act) and the social security regulations.

4. INVENTORY AND ANALYSIS

4.1. Framework of analysis

The four themes discussed above constitute the first pillar of the framework of analysis. The second pillar is the type of research done. In spotting the developments in the research into quality of work, we have distinguished, partly following Berting's approach in his analysis of sociological research in the Netherlands (1979: 67-80), the following types of research: (1) theoretical-explanatory research; (2) descriptive research; (3) action research; (4) evaluation research.

Using these types as variables for the framework of analysis is interesting for the application of a type and leads to a better understanding of the nature of the knowledge that one is trying to find in the research into the quality of work. Thus, the types that are used give us information about the aim of the research. These types are explained below.

In *theoretical–explanatory research*, we are dealing with two variants of research. The first, the 'deductive' variant, is oriented towards the development of theory by the testing of (valid) hypotheses. The second, the 'inductive' variant, refers to research aiming at acquiring more understanding of empirical phenomena, for instance, in order to be able to determine similarities and differences between specific research units.

Descriptive research is meant to provide precise and reliable information on social reality. Its aim is to determine to what extent a phenomenon occurs. This type of research is also very suitable for exploring (statistical) relations between social phenomena. It may yield empirical generalisations that can be important for the development of theory. The case study also belongs to this category.

The main aim of *action research*, or transformative research, is to explore how social reality can be changed. Tracing manipulable factors is what it is usually about. This type of research is policy oriented and is not concerned with increasing scientific knowledge. The manipulation of phenomena should contribute to the solution of problems observed. Consequently, research has been designed on the basis of the problem situation. Under the heading 'action research' we are taking together design-oriented research, intervention research, 'research-based consultancy', and forms of policy research.

Evaluation research is mainly oriented towards the evaluation of decision processes in order to determine the extent to which policies focused on transformation or maintenance contribute to the achieving or changing of goals. In our analysis, we understand evaluation research especially as research commissioned by policy makers like the government.

4.2. Inventory

In the issues of the scientific journals *TVA* and *G&O* in the years 1991-1996, we found 39 articles[10] related to the content of work. In our study, we have adopted a fairly broad definition of research into the work content, namely, all the research that is related to work or the evaluation of work. Research into labour mobility, work motivation, and the development of employment have not been taken into consideration, but articles on labour satisfaction, organisation development, and qualification processes have been included.

In the inventory, we focused on five issues: (1) the statement of the problem or the research question; (2) the principal aim of the research; (3) the nature of the research; (4) the research method, the data collection method, and the data analysis method; (5) the results of the research.

We have tried to classify the articles with the help of the four themes and the four types of research: thus, we have 8 cells. It appeared that some articles could not be readily classified in a specific theme or type. These were included more than once. Consequently, in these cases, there was overlap. Of the 39 articles, seven dealt with two themes and 17 could not be exclusively classified in one single type.

We present our findings divided as to theme and type in Table 1.

Table 1. Themes and types of research

Classification	*No. of articles (in %)*
Theme	
Employment and division of functions	0
Organisational change	20
Development of functions	25
Health and well-being	55
Total (n=44)	100
Type of research	
Theoretical–explanatory research	25
Descriptive research	48
Action research	7
Evaluation research	20
Total (n=56)	100

Health and well-being is the theme of more than half of the articles (55 per cent). Almost a quarter deal with a subject related to development of functions and a fifth with organisational change. Not a single article has employment and division of functions as its subject from the perspective of quality of work.[11] It is worth mentioning that the Ministry for Social Affairs and Employment—in other words: the Ministry of Labour—published a *Manual of Task Division for Creating Functions on a Low-skilled Level* (*TVA* 11(2): 99).

If we sub-divide the types of research, almost half of the articles appear to have a descriptive character (48 per cent). A quarter may be characterised as theoretical–explanatory, a fifth represent the evaluative type and action research is less than a tenth (7 per cent) of the total.[12] The distinction between descriptive and theoretical–explanatory articles is most difficult to make. Ten articles fit into both categories.

Approximately three quarters of the articles refer to a problem in which the quality of work is a dependent variable. In the remaining articles, the quality of work is a predictor variable.[13]

4.3. The articles

We then examined the extent to which the four themes varied within the four types of research. An unambiguous categorisation was not feasible. We therefore gave up our ambition to achieve a consistent systematic approach. In this section, we present an impression of the content of the articles within the types and themes. We selected articles that we believe to be illustrative for the present research.

We shall present our impressions by describing specific articles, using as our point of departure the type of research that is most common, i.e., *descriptive* research.

4.3.1. Descriptive research

In some cases, it was hard to decide whether the article reported descriptive research or theoretical–explanatory research. Two articles by Steijn and De Witte (1993, 1996) on the theme of *organisational change* can be used as illustration. In these articles an attempt was made to quantitatively test the 'internal differentiation hypothesis' that had already been presented as a thesis. The hypothesis was that the content of functions directly affected by computerisation become more complex, whereas, at the same time, the degree of freedom within the function decreases. Increasing complexity (more procedures, broader tasks, a higher level of knowledge, and experience) corresponds to decreasing autonomy.[14]

This hypothesis can be placed within the broad debate on economic, political, and technological developments and the effects on degradation, regradation, and polarisation of labour. However, the authors did not directly derive their hypothesis from the theories commonly used in this debate. Their notion of internal differentiation of labour fits into the 'older' technological debate in which the quality of work is the result of computerisation.

In their second article, Steijn and De Witte (1996) anticipate the reproach that this is technological determinism by arguing that, according to the 'organisational choice approach', management has the choice to influence the consequences of computerisation. The fact that, in practice, management seldom seizes this opportunity leads to the question of what effect this 'organisational conservatism' has on the quality of work, a question that remains unanswered. The internal differentiation hypothesis is the more interesting because it can give us more information on the *development of functions*, the third theme.

In neither case is the hypothesis confirmed. It is true that in comparing computerised functions (functions in which many tasks have been taken over by computers) and non-computerised functions of technicians in the metallurgical industry, the computerised functions appear to be more complex, but the autonomy, which is supposed to decrease, remains approximately the same. But Steijn and De Witte concluded, nevertheless, that the hypothesis had to be rejected.

A general internal differentiation process also failed to occur in their subsequent research among wage-workers from a panel of households. The expected internal differentiation pattern of the degree of computerisation (complexity) and the content of the function (autonomy) was always different from what the hypothesis predicted. This was investigated for manual workers, white-collar workers, and professionals. The authors speak of 'chaotic patterns in the regradation of labour'.

Another article characterised by us as descriptive, also comes close to the theoretical-explanatory type of research. This research also regards the quality of work as an effect of new technology. Zijlstra et al. (1996) assume that a new form of labour has developed, named 'Mental Information Work' (MIW). MIW is work involving information and such information objects as computers and software, in which mental operations dominate. It deals with work in which the production and distribution of information is central. The work mainly refers to the collecting, operating, filing, and distribution of data. Computerisation changes the nature and manifestation of the work. It strongly appeals to the imaginative powers of the workers, increasing the importance of their perceptive and cognitive skills. Zijlstra et al. observed that in a sample of the Dutch professional population, MIW is relevant for 15 per cent of the respondents, particularly people on the 'MBO' (intermediate vocational education) level or higher. They work in the services industry, both in white-collar and blue-collar professions, especially in functions having to do with administration.

It was predicted that MIW would be less bound to time and place than other work. One could work anywhere as long as there is a PC. Indeed, it appears that MIW people have more freedom to manage their working hours and do outwork more often.

The research is based on data from 1991. The authors expected the phenomenon to have increased since then because of the development of mobile communication, laptop computers, and the rapid expansion of the internet. There is assumed to be a relationship between the intensification of the working day due to the increased accessibility and availability of staff through information technology, and the increasing number of workers complaining of work stress. Ever increasing mental stress may be at the root of this.

Some contributions within the descriptive type of research focus on the theme of function development. Warmerdam's research (1992, 1994) takes technological development as a point of departure. He asks how companies, branch organisations, and trainers anticipate technological changes and deal with new developments they have not brought about themselves. Here the question is what possible choices are there with respect to the designing of technology, organisation, and labour. Warmerdam is especially interested in the consequences of technology for the development of qualifications and functions and how those involved deal with it. In one of his contributions (1992), three companies were 'tested' on two occasions—in 1985 and in 1991. Here it was not so much a direct measurement of the quality of work that was intended. Rather it was the question of whether management considered these changes to be an opportunity for job enrichment or whether management strove to increase their control of labour by task differentiation. Warmerdam concluded that there was first a tendency towards social integration by way of task integration. In the following years, a process of task differentiation occurred, that is, workers began once more to specialise and employers began to carry out a training policy focused on division of labour. In part, this had to do with changes on the market, in part also with the limited opportunities for employees to be trained or to cope with mental pressure. According to Warmerdam, the tendency towards task differentiation is a compromise between company and employees and one cannot speak simply of a control strategy.

This contrasts with Steijn and De Witte's remark about 'organisational choice'. They argue that there is room for managerial choices, but that they seldom avail themselves of the opportunities. Steijn and De Witte characterise this as 'organisational conservatism'. Warmerdam's article, however, gives the impression that the options are limited and that management's actions are more or less dictated by the market. Van Hoof, averse to economic determinism, cannot believe this, because there are always strategic choices to be made (1995: 37).

In Warmerdam's second article (1994), the economic position of the enterprise appears to determine the room for narrow or broad qualification. What is examined are the consequences of the 'electronification' of the car for enterprises that have to anticipate new technologies, such as the car-repair branch, which is dependent on innovations in the automobile industry. Therefore, the qualification profile of the function mechanic in the 'dependent' branches depends on various (external) factors. Warmerdam examined three of them. The first was the new workshop machinery needed for the electronified car. This is expensive. Secondly, he looked at the choices garages make in their own organisation of labour, which is partly determined by car producers and importers. Their freedom to choose is limited. Finally, the mechanic's qualification profile is dependent on choices in the training policy within the branch. Several parties are involved in these decisions.

All these factors affect the actual freedom of choice of entrepreneurs. For example, this can mean that the option for a team of all-round mechanics with a high quality of work, such as Warmerdam sketches, is not always a real option for management owing to the (business–economic) context of the organisation.

This brings us to another descriptive article situated at the intersection of the themes *organisational change* and *function development*. Here the question is why the opportunities for improvement of the quality of work offered by team production (self-regulating teams) are often not realised. To answer this question, Van Klaveren and Tom (1995) investigated their own research and consultancy practice. In 'all-round' team work, the members of the team perform a coherent whole of operations, where tasks are integrated both horizontally and vertically and the division of labour is substantially reduced.

The problems these so-called 'self-regulating teams' have with the quality of work are determined, according to the authors, by power-processes.[15] Thus, it appears that executives are quite averse to delegating power to the teams. The power that is delegated is characterised by segregation. Only a few members of the team are given control and managing tasks, or the number of people qualified to become all-rounders is restricted. Increasing labour costs owing to the 'upgrading' of employees is not infrequently used as an argument to slow down decentralisation. Moreover, power processes are also found to occur within the teams. Those with a strong position best succeed in having their own interests and wishes recognised in the group.

This results in a new form of segregation on these new internal labour markets.

Less important, but still relevant, according to Van Klaveren and Tom, is that design mistakes have been made from a sociotechnical perspective. Often too few control tasks have been designed to really enrich the work, partly because the order flows are not adequately streamlined ('parallelised').

A final, but not unimportant, problem with the quality of work is the increase of work stress, either as a result of the introduction of team work or as an additional symptom, for example, because there is insufficient time to learn the new tasks. Van Klaveren and Tom found that the combination of executive tasks with regulating or managing tasks for a number of employees of groups functioning for a somewhat longer period is accompanied by increasing work stress. It seems that it is not so much the accumulation of tasks which causes this, but chiefly the high and ever increasing performance norms. For instance, they show that the work force is often too tight. In their conclusions, they refer to the findings from psychological research, pointing out that the simplistic prescription whereby control possibilities are increased does not automatically reduce work stress. On the contrary, regulating activities as a result of task enrichment can be a source of stress, if they exceed the skills of the person concerned. Tasks with too many possibilities to choose are, by definition, complex and therefore require a great deal of mental effort (Furman and Meijman 1992: 139). In team work, individual differences must be taken into account. 'Pretending that everyone is equal' does not result in really all-round employable people (Van Klaveren and Tom 1995: 32).

The majority of descriptive research is related to the theme *health and well-being*. A relatively large amount of research on this topic has been published by psychologists, particularly clinical psychologists, industrial and organisation psychologists, and medical psychologists. In the last few years, this field has expanded enormously. This has resulted in a new discipline, namely, Work and Health Psychology (Winnubst and Schabracq 1992).

In the *descriptive* 'psychological' research on health and well-being, the objective is usually to determine the relations between phenomena occurring with persons of a specific population, such as stress, pressure, burnout, and satisfaction. It may concern relations with jobs, but also relations with specific forms of behaviour. For example, the goal of some research projects is to establish the job satisfaction of professional groups.

An example of a predictive research project is De Winter's (1992) research. He asked himself how an increased risk of incapacity for work could be established. The author used a longitudinal approach. By combining data collected with the help of 'Vragenlijst Arbeid en Gezondheid' (VAG, 'Questionnaire on Labour and Health') and actual data on absenteeism and outflow, De Winter succeeded in establishing the risk of incapacity for work for some people. It appeared that there was a relation between the work situation, health, and outflow to the 'WAO-Act', the Disablement Insurance Act.

4.3.2. Theoretical explanatory research

Theoretical explanatory research focuses almost exclusively on the theme of *health and well-being*. The theoretical models frequently tested are the job-demand-control model (Karasek) and the job-characteristics model (Hackman and Oldham). In testing the models, it appears quite regularly that the factor social support has an additional value. Social support affects the extent to which health risks manifest themselves, as in the case of stress and burnout. This is an important addition for the development of theory. It is difficult to determine whether it is always a case of theoretical–explanatory research. In quite a number of articles, the emphasis is on establishing relations between factors. Christis noted that relations between factors as such do not explain anything, but need themselves to be explained by the context in which these relations occur (1988: 60).

The 'psychological' articles deal with various subjects within the broad field of health and well-being for which the term the quality of work is, in fact, not an appropriate label. The articles are also diverse with respect to types of research. Among others, explanatory models and diagnostic questionnaires are put to the test. Quantitative research designs are also frequently found in which hypotheses, whether or not derived from theories, are examined and correlations determined. It would not be very helpful for our overview if we were to describe all these publications. We have opted for sketching some general trends within psychological research in a separate section (see Section 4).

4.3.3. Action and evaluation research

There were but few examples of action and evaluation research in the field of the quality of work, in the journals we studied. It is remarkable that little action research has been published in these journals. This may have to do with the fact that (these) scientific journals do not cover these topics and with the slow speed at which this type of research is being systematically documented (Vaas 1995). Thus, there has been a need for examples of sociotechnical action practices for years. Only with the recent publication of a collection of case studies in which sociotechnics has been practised has this need at last been met (Van Hooft 1996).

Organisational change and *the development of function* are dealt with within the action type of research. An example of function development is Vogelaar and Van der Vlist's literature study that investigated the extent to which the job-characteristics model can actually be used in task design. It is a description and analysis of research done, with conclusions for transformational practice. The authors write that, in research using the job-characteristics model, it is mainly the perceptions of the task characteristics that are noticed (the dimension task complexity) and the reactions to the work resulting from it, such as job satisfaction and performance. In addition to the dimension task complexity, so they argue, the quality of functions can be evaluated by other dimensions as well, such as efficiency, contacts, and safety. The dimension task complexity pays relatively little attention to these kind of changes in the functions that are also affecting the perceptions of employees. Illustrations of these are the image of the function and all kinds of uncertainties, such as being exposed to unexpected and unwanted situations. Moreover, redesigning a task, based on changing the task complexity, also has consequences, in particular, in matters such as wages, leadership, qualification, and the like. These consequences in turn affect the perception of the employee. Therefore the consequences must be taken into account in designing the task. Task design, to paraphrase the authors, should be an integral part of the broader organisation design. In fact, the employee has a greater range of problems than is supposed in the job-characteristics model. Arguing from the task design, the employee should have more room to determine how problems must be coped with. This is consistent with the idea that a strict assessment of the tasks in functions does not tell us everything about the behaviour someone will exhibit. This is a very relevant notion for transformational practice in designing functions.

The *evaluation* research within our inventory of articles also focuses on the themes *organisational change* and *development of function*. Within the theme organisational change, Benders and Aertsen (1993) have made an analysis on the basis of the bibliography in the bestseller *The Machine that Changed the World: The Story of Lean Production* (Womack et al. 1990).

The article is not concerned with the quality of work as such but with, among other themes, the consequences of 'lean production' for employees in terms of qualifications, work pressure, and the meaningfulness of the work. Compared to De Sitter, who puts the message of 'lean production' on a par with the well-known 'newspeak' of George Orwell's *1984* (1994: 60), the authors are lenient in remarking that both pros and cons are involved. According to the authors, it is difficult to determine whether work is meaningful. There are, for instance, ample opportunities for learning, but work stress is a risk. The various authors they deal with in their literature study contradict each other, except on one issue: It is most likely to be superior economic performance that determines the choice of lean production methods.

Within the *development of function* theme, Smit-Voskuil (1993) discusses the measurement of the quality of work within the framework of the so-called 'well-being' clause in the Working Environment Act (WEA). Various instruments have been evaluated. In doing so, a distinction has been made between measurement instruments characterised by the task characteristics approach and measurement instruments characteristic of the socio-technical approach. The author believes that none of these are suitable instruments for measuring the well-being aspects of the WEA. However, the two approaches might well complement each other.

A method especially developed in the context of the WEA is the WEBA method (Well-being at Work). This method has been evaluated with respect to its applicability in health care (Grunveld 1993). As an instrument for analysis and discussion, the WEBA is useful and appropriate to operationalise the quality of work. As a measuring instrument, the user can influence the outcomes too much, according to Grunveld. The WEBA is developed to diagnose organisational aspects in relation to work and is not designed as a (survey) instrument to collect data on the opinions of individual workers.

In the meantime, the WEBA method has been revised and expanded. Apart from the quality of work, the method deals with, among other things, the designing of functions as well as organisations, the working environment policy, the prevention of illnesses, work disability, and turnover (Vaas et al. 1995). In addition, there are sector-specific variants, and a questionnaire for quantitative research (NOVA–WEBA)[16] has been developed. Moreover, the WEBA has been evaluated in 20 organisations and has, according to the researchers, proved to be quite usable (Rozemond et al. 1996).

5. PSYCHOLOGICAL RESEARCH INTO THE QUALITY OF WORK

Research into the quality of work in the psychological discipline is very extensive. In general terms, research is focused on the relation between labour (work content, jobs, the working environment) and the functioning of individuals (constitution, behaviour, and attitudes). As such, psychological and sociological research are complementary. Sociological research mainly deals with labour tasks and work situations.

It is not simple to define the research into the quality of work within the psychological discipline. The research is mainly concentrated on the perception of the work and, in many cases, it is not published under the label of the quality of work. On the other hand, a lot of medical, physiological, and ergonomic research is ranked under this denominator. In our analysis, we only took into account task perception research and task-analytical research.

A central issue in psychological research is the task analysis dealing with determining psychologically relevant characteristics of tasks, such as mental and emotional demands (Van Ouwerkerk et al. 1994: 76; see also, Algera 1991: 10-12). Roughly speaking, there are three approaches: the task-characteristic approach, the action-theoretical approach, and the cognitive task analysis (Van Ouwerkerk et al. 1994: 89 ff.).

In the first case, the task characteristics are assessed from an organisational psychological approach in relation to, for example, job satisfaction, well-being, and health. Examples are the job diagnostic survey and the Organisational Stress Questionnaire.

In action-theoretical task analysis, it is not merely the task characteristics which are taken into consideration, but also the task performance of the person being studied.

In the third case, arguing from a cognitive-psychological approach, the task performance is taken as the point of departure. The aim is to understand, for instance, the mental processes or the skills required: the behaviour on the job, the behaviour required for a specific performance, and the skills required to realise a specific performance. Several divergent approaches can be mentioned, all of them having their origin in experimental psychology.

The divergent research within the psychological discipline has passed through a stage of integration. The outlines, themes, and issues of recent research in this field can be retrieved within the NWO priority programme *Psychological fatigue in the working situation* (Meijman et al. 1995; Meijman and Schaufeli 1996), which was started in 1995.[17] This six-year programme brings together medical, health, and psychological perspectives on the subject of acute and chronic fatigue. Psychological fatigue is defined as the phenomenon that occurs in the case of progressive physical and/or mental activity that has resulted in such psychological stress that one is no longer able to react adequately to the demands of the task situation or the environment; one can only do so at the expense of increasing mental stress and by overcoming psychological resistance (Meijman et al. 1995: 11). The acute psychological fatigue can usually be made to disappear by taking a break or by a change of tasks. Chronic fatigue is much less task-specific.

It must be observed that a coherent theory on psychological fatigue is not yet available. 'Some notions are being sketched that might serve as a framework for a theory on psychological fatigue', so it is said. 'This framework is descriptive and still has a lot of gaps' (Meijman et al. 1995: 11). Christis warns us about empirical research that is insufficiently based on theory, because 'each discovery of new factors and relations reduces our understanding of the process of psychological work stress and increases our helplessness with respect to the phenomenon' (1988: 59).[18]

The concepts mental pressure, effort, fatigue, and stress come together in the NWO programme (Meijman and Schaufeli 1996: 237-240). These concepts come close to the quality of work. Mental pressure concerns the appeal that is made from the job situation to mental processes needed to perform well. Effort has to do with psychological and physiological mechanisms needed to cope with the mental pressure required by the job situation. Fatigue refers to the psychological and physiological consequences of the effort a person must make to function well. Fatigue can affect the capacity for adequate job behaviour. In that case, we are speaking of psychological fatigue. This may change into stress, but need not do so. Stress is described as a misguided adaptation reaction characterised by psychological, physiological, and behavioural disfunctioning if the coping mechanism for handling problems fails. That is, one cannot, or one thinks that one cannot, come up with the required job behaviour. Psychological fatigue is dependent on the balance between compensation mechanisms and capacity. Thus, a fatigued employee may slow down his working speed or pay less attention to details. The aim is to control the mental effort within acceptable boundaries. As a result of psychological fatigue, people may be confronted with overstrain and 'burnout'. Burnout is a combination of extreme fatigue or emotional exhaustion and aloofness, cynicism, and little commitment to one's work, or demotivation.

The research programme focuses on three fields (Meijman et al. 1995: 21-33). The first is the research into acute psychological fatigue in the job situation. This includes experimental and field research into determinants and mechanisms of psychological fatigue on the job and its consequences for functioning, well-being, and health. It is about spotting the factors affecting acute fatigue and the effects of acute fatigue on behaviour and judgements. This type of research design is applied in many of the research projects examined within the theme of well-being and health.

Secondly, there is the research into long-lasting psychological fatigue in relation to work. This concerns epidemiological and health psychological research into the origins and development and significance of long-lasting psychological fatigue for, among other things, overstrain and burnout. High demands on cognitive and emotional functioning, time pressure, lack of control possibilities and job autonomy, role conflicts and role overload, are regarded as important risk factors for long-lasting psychological fatigue. Indicators of this phenomenon include the lack of job satisfaction and commitment. Moderating factors between these relations include knowledge and skills, social support, and coping style. These separate relations, already established empirically, must also be established in time. Concretely, it concerns work- and person-affiliated determinants of chronic fatigue, risk factors turning acute fatigue into burnout, and intervention possibilities and moments preventing chronic fatigue.

Thirdly, the programme deals with the research into diagnostics, treatment, supervising and reintegration. This joint programme of the Universities of Groningen, Utrecht, Amsterdam, Limburg, and Nijmegen (and third parties who are going to participate) is ambitious and broadly designed, the more so, because one of the goals is to form a bridge between the industrial psychological research on job performance, mental (work) pressure, and effort, on the one hand, and the organisational psychological research into work stress, on the other. Thus, the programme covers a great part of the psychological research into the quality of work (see also: Kompier 1996; Nijhuis 1995; Schaufeli 1995).

So far, the research has been descriptive. There is little theory-directed research. The final aim is to achieve both theoretical-explanatory and policy-directed research.

6. THE GOVERNMENT: ACCENTS IN THE RESEARCH INTO THE QUALITY OF WORK

Research into health and well-being has been a booming affair for years now, or so it would seem from the weight of the NWO programme discussed above. The social interest in absenteeism and incapacity for work at the end of the eighties was a major stimulus for this research. The emphasis on this 'branch' of the research into the quality of work can be illustrated by the activities of the Ministry for Social Affairs and Employment. At the beginning of the nineties, Social Affairs had two research programmes *Quality of work 1991-1995* (halfway through the programme was renamed *Work content and ergonomics 1991-1995*), and *Stress in the working situation.*[19] The programme *Work content and ergonomics* strongly focused on the development of instruments, the revision of the WEBA method among them, which was the method developed by three Dutch research institutes (NIA, TNO/NIPG and IVA) for the assessment of the quality of work. The programme fitted quite well into the government policy aimed at prevention, namely, the prevention of health damage through work and the prevention of disability to work. It focused on the development of instruments with which the self-motivation of enterprises could be stimulated. The further implementation of the Working Environment Act (WEA) in this period played a major role in this programme. The WEA compels employers to develop an active policy to reduce risks to physical and mental health.

The *Stress in the working situation* programme focused on stimulating and supporting the self-motivation of organisations in stress prevention. The emphasis has been put on the development of instruments, exemplary projects, and monitoring. The *Work Stress Handbook (Handboek werkstress)* (Kompier and Marcelissen 1990) is a well-known example of such an instrument.

Once these research programmes had been concluded, research into the quality of work financed by Social Affairs was given a low profile.[20] Insofar as it is still undertaken, it is subordinate to the labour market and social security. For instance, within the TNO/PG-programme *Working environment 1996-2000*, which is partly financed by Social Affairs, the theme working environment is no longer characterised as an autonomous field of interest.[22] Partly because departmental policy is now concentrating on labour market and social security, more emphasis has been put on the relation between these two fields and the policy on the working environment in the TNO/PG programme. The issue of the quality of work is only mentioned as a result of this relation: for instance, as a consequence of flexible working hours, new information technology, and the development of employment at the bottom half of the labour market.[22]

To complete the picture of government policy, it should be noted that, apart from Social Affairs, the Ministry of Education, Culture and Science and the Ministry of Health, Well-being and Sport have also initiated research into the field of the quality of work. The last mentioned, for instance, is participating in the NWO programme *Psychological fatigue in the work situation.*

7. CONCLUSION AND DISCUSSION

On the basis of the articles in *TVA* and *G&O*, an answer can be given to the two questions formulated at the beginning of this paper, viz: (1) Where have the accents been in the quality of work research and how closely are these linked with socio-economic development? (2) What is lacking in the quality of work research?

After a general socio-economic analysis of the Netherlands focusing on the three aspects, labour organisation, industrial relations, and labour market, we expected that the research into the quality of work would focus on four themes: employment and division of functions, organisational change, development of functions, and health and well-being.

One of these themes stands out in a positive sense: more than half of the articles deal with health and well-being. One theme does not receive any attention at all: employment and division of functions.

Conclusion 1: What is lacking is research into the relation between employment (policy) and the quality of work. Fully concentrating the policy on creating more employment without giving any attention to the effects on the quality of work is too one-sided a goal.

Of the four types of research we distinguished, namely, theoretical–explanatory, descriptive, action, and evaluation research, the descriptive type of research is the most frequent: almost half of the articles examined were of this type. The theoretical–explanatory research, a quarter of the contributions, is restricted to the theme of health and well-being. We have found very little action research. It is assumed that this has to do with the selection of the sources. There are probably more articles on action research in the scientific journals on management and in the professional journals on personnel policy. Evaluation research, a fifth of the total, can also be considered scarce.

Conclusion 2: Evaluation research is almost totally lacking. As a result, an adequate picture of policies related to the quality of work as well as a clear picture of the factual quality of work are likewise lacking.

Conclusion 3: The fact that there is almost no explanatory research on the themes organisational change and the development of functions means that theory development in this field is not being stimulated.

In our view, in the nineties, two main lines in the field of the quality of work can be distinguished: (1) quality of work and organisational change (including function development); (2) quality of work and health and well-being.

Within the first main line, there is a great deal of design-oriented research. The reason is that labour is regarded as a *critical resource* for the success of the organisation. Therefore, a lot of attention is paid to the structure of the organisation and to human resources management.

Within the second main line, two kinds of research can be distinguished. First, there is research in line with the WEBA method. This research concentrates on the improvement of the quality of work by measuring and adapting jobs. Secondly, there is the research into psychological fatigue in the labour organisation (including mental pressure, stress, and effort). This is an attempt to collect quantitative data on the man–work relationship.

These two kinds of research within the second main line are usually undertaken for the following reasons. Due to the strive for more financial control, both politically and socially there is a broad basis for problems surrounding absenteeism, incapacity for work and related social security issues.

Improvements in the quality of work and the working environment correspond to managers' and policy makers' latest views on human resources in labour organisations. These views see labour as a critical resource for achieving flexibility, quality and innovation. This is especially the case with regard to the WEBA research.

The search for variables that can be measured objectively as indicators of the relation between man and work is in line with the dominant trend in (experimental) psychology to make the discipline more scientific in terms of the natural sciences. This is valid for the research into psychological fatigue.

Conclusion 4: The research into the quality of work is dominated by a management perspective and a psychologistic perspective. The socio-logical perspective is lacking.

The sociological perspective implies attention to the quality of work and such social issues as social inequality, individualisation, distribution issues, and problems of solidarity. This perspective is necessary because the quality of work not only has a financial–economic impact on society but also a social–cultural impact. For the cultural emancipation of society, a high quality of work is essential (De Sitter 1981).

NOTES

1 In particular, Van Ruysseveldt and Van Grumbkow (1990), Heming (1992: Chapter 3) and Van Klaveren (1994). In these publications, an overview can be found of the main developments, i.e., Humanisation of Labour, the Leiden approach of Humanisation and Employee Participation, the Delft Quality of Work Measure Box, the Flexible Labour Systems Approach, the Labour Process Approach, and Modern Sociotechnics. These approaches cover the research into the quality of work in the psychological, sociological, and organisation disciplines to a very large extent.

2 WRR is the Scientific Council for Government Policy.

3 We fully realise that in studying a few volumes of only two leading journals we are not nearly covering all the research done. We do not, for instance, pay much attention to the many dissertations, inaugural addresses, studies, and policy reports that appeared in this period. We do assume, however, that the articles analysed represent recent trends.

4 For quality of work approaches in relation with the concepts objective–subjective, level of measurement and property or characteristic, see, e.g., Fruytier and Ter Huurne (1983), Van Ruysseveldt (1990), Van Klaveren (1994) and Jetten and Van Kooten (1994, 1995).

5 WEBA stands for well-being at work, a method used to assess the quality of work. It is an instrument designed for evaluating the quality of work and for creating jobs that offer both learning opportunities and minimal stress.

6 Structural characteristics securing a good quality of work are defined by experts on the basis of a theory of psychic stress and development of human skills. These can be determined in the desired relation between control capacity and control requirements resulting from the design of the function (the division of labour). Thus, instead of an 'objective' approach we can also speak of 'objectified' (expert-)approach.

7 Especially within industrial and health psychology.

8 The many references by both sociotechnicians and psychologists in the Netherlands to R. Karasek's 'job-demand-control approach', is illustrative of this.

9 J. van Hoof in 1991: 7(1); F.D. Pot in 1992: 8(3); and M.C. de Witte in 1995: 11(2).

10 There were 15 in *TVA* and 24 in *G&O*.

11 What has been published was a quantitative article on labour participation in response to the 1990 WRR report, with reply and rejoinder (*TVA* 12(2)). However, it does not refer to the work content.

12 The small number of articles on action research might well be related to the selection of the journals. Possibly this type of research occurs more frequently in journals such as *Bedrijfskunde* (Journal of Management Studies) and *M&O* (Journal for Management and Organisation). We did not check this.

13 Sometimes a definition problem occurred. For instance, when a work situation results in an evaluation in terms of satisfaction: Is the quality of labour to be regarded as a characteristic of the situation (independent variable) or as a person's subjective view on work (dependent variable)?

14 The reason they speak of 'internal differentiation' is that there are differential consequences for the different functions (relevant for one function, but not for another) and that contradictory effects occur within the functions (e.g., that the qualifications required are very high, but that the skills that are in fact required correspond with limited autonomy). A good example of a function combining high complexity and little autonomy is the process operator in the chemical industry.

15 It is relevant to mention the article by Boonstra (1994) in this context, who from an action perspective deals with the failure of change processes and concludes that power processes may affect these. However, Boonstra relates his findings to other terms such as the way decisions are made and communication processes.

16 For an application, see Jetten and Van Kooten (1994, 1995).

17 NWO is the Dutch Organisation for Scientific Research. NWO controls most of the grants for academic research projects.

18 In his enumeration of the objections to the psychological stress theory as an interaction model, with so many interaction possibilities that factor models of gigantic proportions are threatening, he expresses his anxiety that 'this runs the risk of becoming a research programme with a "tendency towards a decreasing surplus"' (Christis 1988: 59).

19 Apart from this, there is the 'Regulation subsidising scientific research trade union federations' (FNV and CNV). It is not easy to understand the kind of research done within this regulation. Projects are partly carried out on the quality of work, particularly sectoral research, but this kind of research seems to be in the minority. The unions also carry out

research, beyond these subsidy regulations, but we have no systematic picture of these efforts (see also, Van Klaveren 1994: 17-21).

20 A project financed by Social Affairs that does refer to the quality of work is the report *Innovation and Labour* (Dhondt et al. 1996). In this report, it has been established on the basis of literature study and ten case studies that good quality work, c.q. decentralisation of control tasks (a form of production with little division of labour, demanding relatively much knowledge and skills) is a condition for improving the capacity for innovation of companies. Investing in knowledge and skills has a stimulating effect, progressive numerical flexibility has a contrary effect. Improvement of innovation capacity, for that matter, is an 'unintended' positive consequence of improvement of the quality of work. In other words, in the companies examined, the quality of work was not improved in order to enhance the innovation capacity. The companies adapted their way of producing because of problems with functional design or owing to the modern trend for flow-like production forms (Dhondt et al. 1996: 95).

21 Since 1996, TNO/PG (Institute for the Prevention of Health and Safety) has merged with NIA (Dutch Institute for Working Conditions) into NIA/TNO. TNO also has Social Affairs target-funding.

22 See for instance: 'The bottom half of the labour market: new jobs for low-skilled workers' (March 1996), in which the permanence of new, low-level jobs has been investigated, especially the quality of labour and future career perspectives.

REFERENCES

G&O = *Gedrag en Organisatie* (Behaviour and Organisation)
TVA = *Tijdschrift voor Arbeidsvraagstukken* (Journal for Labour Issues)

Algera, J.A., 1991. 'Het gebruik van arbeidsanalysemethoden voor verschillende systemen van personeelsmanagement' (The use of methods to analyse work for different systems of personnel management), in: J.A. Algera (ed.), *Analyse van arbeid vanuit verschillende perspectieven* (Analysing work from different perspectives), Amsterdam/Lisse: Swets & Zeitlinger, pp. 9-15.

Benders, J. and F. Aertsen, 1993. 'Aan de lijn of aan het lijntje: wordt slank produceren de mode?' (Is lean production becoming popular?), *TVA* 9(3): 263-272.

Berting, J., 1979. 'Sociologisch onderzoek in Nederland' (Sociological research in the Netherlands), in: L. Rademaker (ed.), *Sociologie in Nederland* (Sociology in the Netherlands), Deventer: Van Loghum Slaterus, pp. 61-97.

Bloemhoff, A. and P.G.W. Smulders, 1991. 'Kwaliteit van de arbeid van vrouwen en mannen: verschillen en trends in de periode 1977-1986'(Quality of work among men and women: differences and trends in the period 1977-1986), *TVA* 7(1): 4-17.

Boonstra, J., 1994. 'Herontwerp, reengineering en ontwikkeling' (Redesign, reengineering and development), *G&O* 7(6): 331-351.

Boonstra, K.A., I.T. Bousema, A.J. Schoneveld and S. Siero, 1993. 'Determinanten van arbeidsmotivatie, taakkenmerken, taakdoelen en gerichte beloning' (Determinants of the motivation to work, taskcharacteristics, taskgoals and rewarding), *G&O* 6(3): 169-179.

Bosch, G.J.T., P.M.M. Hulsinck, P.R.A. Oeij and M.A.C.M. van der Westerlaken, 1994. *Toekomstige opleidingsbehoefte van het bedrijfsleven* (The need for education of companies in the future), Tilburg: EIT/ETIN/IVA.

Buunk, A.P., M. Peeters and K. Verhoeven, 1991. 'Sociale interacties en stress bij politieagenten, een microanalytische benadering' (Social interaction and stress by policemen, a microanalytic approach), *G&O* 4(3): 170-184.

Christis, J., 1988. 'Psychische arbeidsbelasting' (Mental workload), *G&O* 1(4): 55-71.

Dagevos, J., M. Vermeulen and P. Oeij, 1996. *Tussen raakvlak en breukvlak. De aansluiting onderwijs-arbeidsmarkt in Rotterdam* (The relationship between the education system and the labour market in Rotterdam), Tilburg: IVA.

Demarest, S., E. Henderickx and J. Bundervoet, 1994. 'Personeelbeleid en werkbelasting in Belgische ziekenhuizen' (Personnel policy and workload in Belgium hospitals), *TVA* 10(2): 156-164.

Dhondt, S. et al., 1996. *Innovatie en arbeid. Een onderzoek naar de synergie tussen kwaliteit van de arbeid en het innovatievermogen van bedrijven* (Innovation and work. A research on the synergy between the quality of work and the capacity of enterprises to innovate), 's-Gravenhage: VUGA.

Dijck, J.J.J. van, J.A.P. van Hoof, A.L. Mok and W.F. de Nijs (eds.), 1980. *Kwaliteit van de arbeid. Een sociologische verkenning* (Quality of work. A sociological exploration), Leiden/Antwerpen: Stenfert Kroese.

Emmerik, IJ.H. van, 1993. 'Overeenkomsten en verschillen tussen de voorkeuren, werktevredenheid en commitment van mannen en vrouwen op verschillende functieniveaus in een dienstverlenende organisatie' (Resemblances and differences in the aspirations, job satisfaction and commitment of men and women on varying levels of functions in a service organisation), *G&O* 6(5) 254-267.

Faase, L., M. Ott and C.J. Vos (eds.), 1995. *Nieuwe breukvlakken in het arbeidsbestel? Balans van tien jaar veranderingen in Nederland en België* (New changes in the societal system of work? The balance of a decade of change in the Netherlands and Belgium), Utrecht: De Tijdstroom.

Faase, L., M. Ott and C.J. Vos (eds.), 1995a. 'Breukvlakken in het arbeidsbestel. Terugblik en voorbeschouwing' (New changes in the societal system of work. Looking back and ahead), in: Faase et al., pp. 11-27.

Faase, L., M. Ott and C.J. Vos (eds.), 1995b. 'De breukvlakken beoordeeld' (The new changes evaluated), in: Faase et al., pp. 135-145.

Fruytier, B., 1986. 'Het einde van de humanisering? Kwaliteit van de arbeid in de jaren tachtig' (The end of humanisation? Quality of work in the eighties), *TVA* 2(4): 50-58.

Fruytier, B., 1994. *Organisatieverandering en het probleem van de Baron van Münchhausen* (Organisational change and the problem of the Baron of Münchhausen), diss. KUN, Delft: Eburon.

Fruytier, B. and A. ter Huurne, 1983. *Kwaliteit van de arbeid als meetprobleem. Een vergelijkende literatuurstudie*, (The problem to measure quality of work. A comparative literature study), Tilburg: IVA.

Furda, J., J. de Jonge, P. Le Blanc, T. Meijman, P. Scheurs and J. Scheenen, 1994. 'Het demand-control-support model in relatie tot gezondheidsklachten en herstelklachten' (The demand-control-support model related to complaints on health and recovery), *G&O* 7(2): 225-238.

Furda, J. and T. Meijman, 1992. 'Druk en dreiging, sturing of stress' (Pressure and threat, control or stress), in: J.A.M. Winnubst and M.J. Schabracq (eds.), *Handboek arbeid en gezondheid psychologie. Hoofdthema's* (Handbook work and health psychology. Central themes), Utrecht: Lemma, pp. 127-144.

Galan, C. de, M.R. van Gils and P.J. van Strien (eds.), 1983 [2]. *Humanisering van de arbeid* (Humanising labour), Assen: Van Gorcum.

Gier, H.G. de, 1993. 'Kwaliteit van de arbeid tussen eenheidsmarkt en nationale economie: 1970-2000' (Quality of work: 1970-2000), *TVA* 9(1): 28-39.

Grunveld, J.E., 1993. 'Ervaringen met de WEBA bij functieontwerp in de gezondheidszorg' (Experiences with the WEBA method to design functions in health care), *G&O* 6(1): 1-9.

Haasnoot, M., D. de Gilder and M. Schabracq, 1996. 'Arbeidstevredenheid onder oudere werknemers' (Job satisfaction amongst older workers), *G&O* 9(4): 225-239.

Heming, B.H.J., 1992. *Kwaliteit van arbeid, geautomatiseerd..... Een studie naar kwaliteit van arbeid en de relatie tussen automatisering, arbeid en organisatie* (Quality of work, automated..... A study in the quality of work and the relation to automation, work, and organisation), diss. TUD.

Hoof, J.J. van, 1995. 'Arbeidsbestel op een keerpunt. Tien jaar veranderingen in arbeidsorganisatie, arbeidsmarkt en arbeidsverhoudingen vanuit een lange-termijnperspectief' (The societal system of work at a turning point. A decade of changes in work organisations, labour market and working relations from a long term perspective), in: Faase et al., pp. 28-47.

Hooft, M.C.G. van (ed.), 1996. *Synergetisch produceren in praktijk. Toepassingen van structuurbouw in industrie en dienstverlening* (Synergetic production in practice. Applying structural systems in industry and services), Assen: Van Gorcum.

Jans, E.J.G.M., A.P. Buunk, E.J. Doosje and H. van der Flier, 1991. 'Beheersingsoriëntatie en sociale ondersteuning bij werkstress' (Control attitude and social support by stress), *G&O* 5(1): 1-9.

Janssen, P.M., B.P. Buunk and F.J.N. Nijhuis, 1994. 'De invloed van sociale steun ten aanzien van relatieve deprivatie en stressreacties bij hoger opgeleide mannen. Een vergelijking tussen drie leeftijdsgroepen' (The effect of social support on relatieve deprivation and stress reactions by high educated men. A comparison of three age cohorts), *G&O* 7(2): 71-87.

Janssen, P.M., F.J.N. Nijhuis, M.C.W. Peeters and J. de Jonge, 1996. 'Intrinsieke werkmotivatie, een heroriëntatie op het begrip en een verklaring vanuit de motivatie- en taakkenmerken benadering' (Intrinsic motivation to work, a reorientation on the terminology and an explanation with the motivation- and task characteristics approach), *G&O* 9(5): 290-303.

Jetten, B. and G. van Kooten, November 1994. 'Kwaliteit van de arbeid. Van theorie naar toetsing' (Quality of work. From theory to testing), paper presented at the WESWA-conference, Enschede: SISWO/TU Twente.

Jetten, B. and G. van Kooten, 1995. 'Quality of work: from theory to test' (Quality of work: from theory to test), in: G.B. van Hees, F. Huijgen, Th. van der Krogt and J.J. Schippers (eds.), *Work from the lowlands: labour and organisation research*, Amsterdam: SISWO, pp. 67-92.

Jonge, J. de and J.A. Landeweerd, 1993. 'Toetsing van de job demand-control benadering bij werknemers in de gezondheidszorg' (Testing the job demand-control approach among workers in the health care sector), *G&O* 6(2): 78-91.

Jonge, J. de, J.A. Landeweerd and G.J.P. van Breukelen, 1994. 'De Maastrichtse Autonomielijst: achtergrond, constructie en validering' (The Autonomy checklist from the University of Maastricht: background, construction, and validation), *G&O* 7(1): 27-41.

Jonge, J. de, W.B. Schaufeli and J. Furda, 1995. 'Werkkenmerken : psychologische arbeidsvitamines?' (Working characteristics: psychological vitamines for work?), *G&O* 8(4): 231-248.

Klaveren, M. van, 1994. *Trends en keuzes in het onderzoek naar de kwaliteit van de arbeid* (Trends and choices in the research on the quality of work), Amsterdam: SISWO.

Klaveren, M. van and T. Tom, 1995. 'All-round groepswerk: doen of doen alsof?' (All-round team work: do or act?), *TVA* 11(1): 21-33.

Kompier, M.A.J., 1996. *'The best of both worlds'. Arbeids- en organisatiepsychologie tussen theorie en praktijk* (The best of both worlds'. Work and organisation psychology and organisation psychology between theory and practice), address KUN, Nijmegen: KUN.

Kompier, M.A.J. and F.H.G. Marcelissen, 1990. *Handboek werkstress* (Handbook work stress), Amsterdam: NIA.

Kuiper, J.P., 1976. 'Arbeid en inkomen, twee plichten en twee rechten' (Work and income, two obligations and two rights), *Sociaal Maandblad Arbeid* (Social Monthly Review on Work) 3(9).

Kuipers, H. and R. van Eybergen, 1994. 'Expertise en anti-expertise in de sociotechniek' (Expertise and anti-expertise in socio-technics), *G&O* 7(6): 316-330.

Linden, G. van der, 1992. 'Toetsing van het Job Characteristics Model en de Job Diagonistic Survey als meetinstrument van de taakstructuur' (Testing the Job Characteristics Model and the Job Diagonistic Survey as instruments to measure the structure of tasks), *G&O* 5(3): 184-202.

Meijman, T. and W. Schaufeli, 1996. 'Psychische vermoeidheid en arbeid. Ontwikkelingen in de A&O-psychologie' (Mental fatigue and work. Developments in work and organisation psychology), *De Psycholoog* (The Psychologist) 31(6): 236-241.

Meijman, T.F., W.B. Schaufeli, F.J.H. van Dijk and H.J. van den Elzen, February 1995. *NWO-prioriteit-programma Psychische vermoeidheid in de arbeidssituatie* (NWO-priority programme Mental fatigue in working situations), Den Haag: NWO.

Morée, M. and M. Vulto, 1995. 'Zorgarbeid als zorgenkind? De kwaliteit van de arbeid in de gezinsverzorging' (Caring about care work? The quality of work in family care work), *TVA* 11(1): 48-59.

Muskens, M., 1997. 'Heeft honger voorrang op de wet? (May hunger violate the law?), in: K.-W. Merks (ed.), *Stropen, stelen, beunen... Over de grenzen van de wet* (Illegal hunting, stealing, illegal production... Tresspassing the law's borders), Aalsmeer: Dabar-Luyten, pp. 13-18.

Nandran, S.S. and P.G. Klandermans, 1995. 'Burnout onder vakbondskaderleden' (Burnout amongst leading union members), *G&O* 8(2): 128-145.

Nijhuis, F.J.N., 1995. *De paradoxale gezondheidseffecten van arbeid. Van gezondheidsbedreiging naar gezondheidsbevordering* (The paradoxal effects of work on health. From threatening health tot stimulating health), address RULi, Maastricht: RULi.

Oeij, P., B. Fruytier and I. van den Broek 1998. 'Quality of work: research in the Netherlands in the nineties', paper for the 14th World Congress of Sociology, Montréal (Canada), July 26-August 1, International Sociological Association (ISA).

Ouwerkerk, R.J. van, T.F. Meijman and G. Mulder, 1994. *Arbeidspsychologische taakanalyse* (Work psychological analysis of tasks), Utrecht: Lemma.

Peeters, M., 1992. 'Nieuwe produktieconcepten in de confectie-industrie. De wankele schreden van een traditionele bedrijfstak op weg naar integrale vernieuwing' (New concepts for production in the textile industry. From traditionalism towards integral renewal), *TVA* 8(2): 130-143.

Roe, R.A., R. Schalk and F. Zijlstra, 1995. 'Veranderingen in arbeid. Consequenties voor de Arbeids- en organisatie-psychologie' (Changes in work. Effects on work and organisation psychology), *G&O* 8(4): 209-220.

Rozemond, P., M. Peeters and V. Vrooland, 1996. *Gezonde arbeid, gezonde organisatie. WEBA in de praktijk, effecten op kwaliteit van arbeid en organisatie in twintig ondernemingen* (Healthy work, healthy organisation. WEBA method in practice, and effects on the quality of work and organisation in twenty enterprises), Amsterdam: NIA.

Ruysseveldt, J., 1990. 'Kwaliteit van de arbeid' (Quality of work), in: J. van Ruysseveldt and J. von Grumbkow, pp. 1-19.

Ruysseveldt, J. van and J. von Grumbkow, (eds.), 1990. *Kwaliteit van de arbeid. Hedendaagse stromingen* (Quality of work. Current mainstreams), Assen: Van Gorcum.

Schabracq, M.J. and J.A.M. Winnubst (ed.), 1993. *Handboek arbeid en gezondheid psychologie. Toepassingen* (Handbook work and organisation psychology. Applications), Utrecht: Lemma.

Schaufeli, W. 1995. *Burnout: dwaallicht of lichtpunt?* (Burnout), address UU. Utrecht: UU.

Schaufeli, W.B., R.J.J.M. van den Eijnden and H.M.G. Brouwers, 1994. 'Stress en burnout bij penitentiaire inrichtingwerkers. De rol van sociaal-cognitieve factoren' (Stress and burnout by penitentiary institution workers. The effects of social cognitive factors), *G&O* 7(2): 216-224.

Schmid, G., June 1997. '"Jobwunder" Niederlande. Eine moderne Arbeitsmarkt- und Beschäftigungspolitik' ("Jobwunder" Niederlande. Eine moderne Arbeitsmarkt- und Beschäftigungspolitik, *WZB-Mitteilungen* 76: 3-6.

Scholten, A., C.J. van Oel, D. Oort-Marburger, S.H. Schmidt and T.F. Meijman, 1994. 'Welbevinden in de arbeid en verandering van baan na revalidatie' (Well-being at work and job change after revalidation), *G&O* 7(2): 90-100.

Sitter, L.U. de, 1981. *Op weg naar nieuwe fabrieken en kantoren* (Towards new factories and offices), Deventer: Kluwer.

Sitter, L.U. de, w.t.c.o. J.L.G. Naber and F.O. Verschuur, 1994. *Synergetisch produceren. Human resources mobilisation in de produktie: een inleiding in structuurbouw* (Synergetic production. Human resources mobilisation in production: an introduction in designing structure), Assen: Van Gorcum.

Smit-Voskuil, O.F., 1993. 'Het meten van welzijn in het kader van de Arbo-wet' (Measuring well-being in the framework of the act on working conditions), *G&O* 6(3): 121-133.

Steijn, B. and M. de Witte, 1992. *De januskop van de industriële samenleving. Technologie, arbeid, en klassen aan het begin van de jaren negentig* (The two faces of industrial society. Technology, work, and class at the beginning of the nineties), diss. EUR, Alphen a/d Rijn: Samson.

Steijn, B. and M. de Witte, 1993. 'De interne-differentiatie-hypothese. De invloed van automatisering op complexiteit, autonomie en arbeidsbeleving' (The internal-differentiation-hypothesis. The effect of automation on complexity, autonomy and job satisfaction), *TVA* 9(3): 253-272.

Steijn, B. and M. de Witte, 1996. 'Chaotische patronen in de regradatie van arbeid. Een toetsing van de interne-differentiatie-hypothese' (Chaotic patterns in the regradation of work. Testing the internal-differentiation-hypothesis), *TVA* 12(2): 108-123.

Tijdens, K. and N. Goedhard, 1996. 'Kwaliteit van de arbeid en rol van de vakbond in de schoonmaaksector' (Quality of work and the role of unions in the clean-up sector), *TVA* 12(1): 31-42.

Vaas, S., 1995. 'Nieuwe produktieconcepten. Nieuwe vormen en gedachten over arbeid?' (New concepts for production. New forms and thoughts about work?), in: Faase et al., pp. 128-134.

Vaas, S. et al., 1995. *WEBA-methode. Deel 1 WEBA-analyse handleiding, Deel 2 Herontwerp, Deel 3 De aanpak van verbetering van organisatie en arbeid, Deel 4 Werksoorten* (WEBA-method. Part 1 WEBA-analysis handbook, Part 2 Redesign, Part 3 Approach to improve organisation and work, Deel 4 Types of work), Alphen a/d Rijn / Zaventem: Samson.

Vlerick, P. and D. Goeminne, 1994. 'Onderzoek naar de gevolgen van verpleegkundige functie-ontwerpen op de arbeidsbeleving' (Research into the effects of the design of nursing functions on job satisfaction), *G&O* 7(2): 101-113.

Vogelaar, A.L.W, E.H.M. Eurelings-Bontekoe and I.F. van de Velde, 1991. 'Persoonlijkheidsstructuur en gevoeligheid voor werkstress, suggesties ter aanvulling van het Michiganmodel' (Personality structure and sensitivity for work stress, proposals in addition to the Michigan model), *G&O* 4(2): 100-112.

Vogelaar, A.L.W. and R. van der Vlist, 1995. 'Het Job Characteristics Model en taakontwerp' (Job Characteristics Model and task design), *G&O* 8(2): 65-87.

Vuuren, V. van, 1991. 'Bouwen aan kwaliteit van de arbeid in de bouw. Een onderzoek naar de gevolgen voor het welzijn en de gezondheid van de werknemers in de bouwnijverheid' (Building on the quality of work in the construction sector. An investigation into the effects on the well-being and health on workers in the construction sector), *TVA* 7(2): 44-51.

Warmerdam, J., 1992. 'Flexibilisering binnen grenzen. Een onderzoek naar organisatie- en kwalificatieprocessen in een drietal grote ondernemingen in de voedingsmiddelen-industrie, het verzekeringswezen en het omroepbedrijf' (Limited flexibilisation. A research into the organisational and qualification process in three large enterprises in the food industry, insurances and the broadcasting sector), *TVA* 8(3): 213-225.

Warmerdam, J., 1994. 'Technologische vernieuwing en scholing in de autobranche' (Technological renewal and education in the automobile industry), *TVA* 10(4): 292-305.

Wetenschappelijke Raad voor het Regeringsbeleid (Scientific Council for Government Policy), 1981. *Vernieuwingen in het arbeidsbestel* (Innovations in the labour relations system), 's-Gravenhage: Staatsuitgeverij.

Wetenschappelijke Raad voor het Regeringsbeleid (Scientific Council for Government Policy), 1982. *Kwaliteit van de arbeid. Preadviezen bij het rapport Vernieuwingen in het arbeidsbestel* (Quality of work. Pre-advices to the report Innovations in the labour relations system), 's-Gravenhage: Staatsuitgeverij.

Wetenschappelijke Raad voor het Regeringsbeleid (Scientific Council for Government Policy), 1990. *Een werkend perspectief. Arbeidsparticipatie in de jaren '90* (A working perspective. Participation in the work process in the 90's), 's-Gravenhage: SDU.

Winter, C.R. de, 1992. 'Arbeidsongeschiktheid: voorspellen en voorkómen' (Disability to work: predicting and preventing), *TVA* 8(3): 196-201.

Yperen, N.W. van, 1996. 'Burnout en werkrelaties in de verpleegkunde, de rol van een hulpverleningsoriëntatie' (Burnout and working relations in nursing, the function of a help oriented attitude), *G&O* 9(2): 100-114.

Zijlstra, F.R.H., M.J.D. Schalk and R.A. Roe, 1996. 'Veranderingen in de arbeid. Consequenties voor werkenden' (Changes in work. Effects on working people), *TVA* 12(3): 251-263.

AUTHORS

Drs. P. Oeij
Dr. B. Fruytier
Drs. I. van den Broek
Tilburg University, IVA, Institute for Social Research,
P.O. Box 90153, 5000 LE Tilburg
tel. +3113 4668070, fax: 4662959
e-mail: P.R.A.Oeij@kub.nl

HUMAN RESOURCES MANAGEMENT
Evolving paradigms and research issues from an integrated stakeholder perspective

Jan Kees Looise and Jaap Paauwe

1. INTRODUCTION

According to the *Wetenschapsverkenning Personeelswetenschappen* (Scientific Review of Personnel Science in the Netherlands) (1993), HRM research in the Netherlands has largely disintegrated, has an overwhelmingly monodisciplinary character and is dominated by short-term and instrumental perspectives. When we started to compose this state-of-the-art paper (in 1996), we did not expect radical changes in the short term, and our findings confirm this. Our inventarisation also shows many of the aspects indicated by the *Wetenschapsverkenning*. On the other hand, we also discovered some new and more positive signals. One of these is a growing focus in Dutch HRM research on core issues within the HR field. The research thus becomes of more interest to practitioners, who, up to now, have experienced a large gap between their own needs and existing HR research. Last, but not least, interesting developments seem to be taking place in the form of more multi-disciplinary approaches and integrated theory development. In our opinion, these multi-disciplinary approaches and integrated theories can make an important contribution to a more balanced position of HRM in the Netherlands (and elsewhere). Compared to the position of HRM in the Anglo–Saxon countries, HRM in the Netherlands still has a strong institutional focus, although, in some respects, radical changes are taking place in the direction of HRM, Anglo–Saxon style.

In making an overview of the position of HRM[1] in a country, of necessity, a number of choices have to be made. Not all aspects of HRM can be dealt with in this paper, so we decided to focus our attention on the following aspects:

- a brief overview of the historical development and context of HRM in the Netherlands;
- a rather extensive overview of Dutch HRM research;
- an overview of the existing theories and paradigms;
- a research agenda for further HRM research.

HRM in the Netherlands is both an old and a new phenomenon. It is old in the sense that examples of the earliest forms of systematic HRM in our country can already be found in the 1880's; new in that full HRM—in terms of a function that encompasses all aspects of dealing with personnel (including wage conditions)—is rather new for most Dutch companies. As a point of reference, we discuss the development of HRM in the Netherlands compared to that in an Anglo–Saxon context (especially the UK and the US). The starting point is the idea that HRM in a (continental) European or Rhineland (Albert 1991) institutional context—as in the Netherlands—has a different meaning from HRM in a market context, as in the Anglo–Saxon countries. The question is whether this situation still can be found in the Netherlands or whether current changes are causing the Anglo–Saxon model to become dominant in the Netherlands too (and in continental Europe generally). Based upon an inventory of research projects carried out in the Netherlands (SISWO 1993; complemented with our own inventory of two related academic journals) we analyse the kinds of issues that have received attention from the academic community. Our findings will be confronted on the one hand with issues emphasised by practitioners and, on the other, with an overview of issues that have received attention in two UK/USA HRM journals.

The next step is to contrast our findings with theory and paradigm development in the area of HRM and the organisational sciences. Whereas, in the past, many personnel management and HRM topics were being studied from a monodisciplinary point of view, our analysis indicates the increased tendency in the last decade to use more multidisciplinary approaches across related disciplines (such as psychology, sociology, economics, etc.). On the other hand we also discern a shift towards management initiated topics or models that emphasise (explicitly or implicitly) managerial interests. The perspective of industrial relations, trade unions and workers' interests and the importance of related institutional settings seems to fade away. A noticeable Anglo–Saxon influence might account for that. However, we strongly believe that, in this way, no full justice is done to the (continental) European institutional setting which has both converging and diverging claims from the various stakeholders involved, including workers and their representative bodies such as works councils and trade unions. Consecutively, we need to develop more integrative conceptual frameworks, which combine, amongst others interactive, resource based, institutional and behavioural paradigms. Examples of those kinds of interactive models will be presented and—more importantly—linked to a research agenda for the next decade, which justifies diverging claims from the various stakeholders involved in HRM processes and outcomes.

2. THE HISTORICAL DEVELOPMENT AND CONTEXT OF HRM IN THE NETHERLANDS

In order to set the scene (especially for an international audience) some brief information is given here on historical developments in industrial relations, managerial trends and personnel management in the Netherlands. For those familiar with the setting in the Netherlands, we refer directly to our evaluative remarks at the end of this section.

2.1. Historical situation (until the 1980's)

Dutch industrial relations are traditionally characterised by neo-corporatist arrangements (Visser 1992: 323 ff; Smit et al. 1995). Organised interest groups were deeply involved in governmental decision making, and the federations of trade unions used to be centralised and hierarchically structured. The trade union movement opted for legal enactment and participation in neo-corporatist policy, which had several consequences for labour unionism. A first consequence was that trade unions used to be weakly represented at the company and plant level. The company level is the domain of works councils, whereas collective bargaining was located outside the company. Secondly, the organisation of production used to be kept separate from wage bargaining. The unions concentrated on the determination of the terms and conditions of employment and never questioned the Tayloristic mode of organisation. Thirdly, the government had an enormous influence on wage policies.

For personnel management, in the past, this implied only a limited role; the personnel manager was the most active in the application and translation of national CBA (collective bargaining agreements)-and legal regulations at the company level. There was hardly any room left for an autonomous personnel policy from the company itself (Buitendam 1979). Personnel management in the Netherlands is of long standing. It is probable that the first personnel manager was appointed by the Yeast and Methylated Spirits Works in Delft (1880). This company took the lead in experimenting with industrial democracy in the form of so-called 'kernels'. These may be seen as precursors of the works councils which were eventually introduced across the Netherlands, by statute. Personnel management itself developed from personnel administration in the post second WW II years to a period (in the sixties and seventies) when social issues, such as industrial democracy, job consultation and job structuring moved centre stage. This period ended rather abruptly with the advent of what is known as the no-nonsense phase, prompted by the economic recession towards the end of the seventies and the early eighties. This trend was modified by the rise of the idea of human resources management, which stressed integration with corporate strategy and with line management, and sought to contribute to flexibility, quality and customer orientation.[2]

2.2. Drastic changes from the 1980's

Since the 1980's, the Netherlands has experienced a number of drastic changes in industrial relations, the most important of which are flexibilisation and decentralisation. Some well-known developments formed the backdrop for these flexibilisation and decentralisation tendencies. Firstly, the neo-liberal policies of deregulation became dominant in the 1980's. Secondly, European unity and economic internationalisation renders the national level increasingly more obsolete, which promotes willingness to accept US- or Japanese-based elements into industrial relations practices. Thirdly, employers increasingly seek flexibility and tailor-made terms of employment —standard clauses in collective agreements discourage this. For this reason, Bolweg (1989) concludes that industrial relations, which had previously been kept outside the firm, now are becoming increasingly internalised. At the same time, personnel management is becoming more subject to processes of 'political debate' among the various parties involved, such as top and line management, the personnel department itself, and the employees, primarily represented by the works council. The national bilateral agreement of 1982 meant a watershed in Dutch industrial relations and the beginning of the decline of national concertation. Confronted with high unemployment, trade unions and employers' organisations agreed on wage moderation, job-sharing and reduction of working hours. As Visser (1992) notes, for the first time since 1945, collective bargaining at the meso-level (industries and large corporations) had become legally and factually liberalised from nation-wide controls. Employers and trade unions both recognised the worth of collective agreements, but pursued larger potentialities for choices. This implied a development in the direction of more general sectoral agreements, which allow firm-specific arrangements to be negotiated by either unions or works councils.

There are at least two reasons why the works council assumed greater importance at company level. Firstly, legislation extended its responsibilities in 1979. Secondly, the tendency towards decentralisation of collective bargaining implies that unions are reassessing the standard character of labour contracts. They have taken initiatives to propose two-tier models of industry-wide collective labour agreements which leave room for company- and works-specific arrangements and/or individual differentiation. Naturally, works councils are involved in this process, especially since trade unions were unable to develop strong roots within the companies. At present, the tide is turning, but from the end of the 1970s the rate of unionisation was dropping sharply from 35 per cent in 1980 to 25 per cent in 1990. On account of this, trade unions lack manpower to staff their labour-intensive decentralisation policies and to strengthen their visibility at shop floor level. Increasingly, therefore, trade unions cooperate closely with their trade union representatives in the works council. Most works councils (70 per cent) are dominated by union members (Looise and De Lange 1987), who constitute a majority. In fact, works councils appear to have developed into the primary form of union activity at company level.

2.3. Recent developments

Recent developments in the area of management and organisation in the Netherlands are not very different from those taking place elsewhere in Western Europe, the United States and Southeast Asia. At the most, one may note a certain time lag. CEO's, managers and consultants are eager to gain inspiration through new developments in management, as presented in Anglo–Saxon business and professional journals. In the Netherlands, too, there is tension between, on the one hand, the demand to counter increasing complexity by way of greater autonomy at every level in the organisation and, on the other hand, the need to retain overall control.

A first line of current development, therefore, consists in seeking alternatives for the bureaucratic, large-scale organisation, based on Taylorism. Examples of widely applied alternatives include de-layering, decentralisation, the creation of entrepreneurial internal market systems such as unit-management and the socio-technical redesign of the organisation (Paauwe 1994: 17; Van Hoof 1995: 6; De Sitter 1981). However, structural adjustments in themselves are useful, but insufficient. Management and employees need to be equipped with greater autonomy, which is reflected in a second current line of development aimed at expanding tasks and increasing competencies and responsibilities at every level of the organisation. More specifically, we refer to (more or less fashionable) approaches such as empowerment, policy deployment, self-managing teams, introduction of forms of direct participation and improvements in order to enhance the combined quality of organisation and working life. The two organisational trends mentioned above have one thing in common, namely that—within the framework of strategic policy—they aim at bringing about an increase in the self-regulating capacity of managers and employees. At the same time, they intensify mutual dependence. Exchange of information and ready access to it is necessary in order to establish coordination, both in a formal and an informal way. It goes without saying that the manner in which human resources are treated is crucial in bringing about this self-autonomy of managers and employees (Looise 1996).

2.4. Evaluation

The above described developments demonstrate quite clearly that the present setting of HRM in the Netherlands is a mixture of both the traditional Western European institutional context and Anglo–Saxon influences. The position of the workers is historically safeguarded through institutional arrangements such as widespread CBA coverage and all kinds of legal regulations. For personnel management in the past, this implied only a limited role; the personnel manager was the most active in the application and translation of national CBA- and legal regulations at the company level. There was hardly any room for an autonomous personnel policy by the company itself. Since the 1980s, however, we see drastic changes in the traditional institutional setting, and therefore also in the role of personnel management and the position of workers, which brings them more in line with the situation in the Anglo–Saxon countries. Especially during the last 5 years, developments are evident that promote flexibility, including a revision of legislation and institutional arrangements in the area of social security, labour laws, etc. Such developments may form a threat to the position of the workers and their interests (Looise et al. 1997). Moreover, trade unions are quite willing to cooperate in order to stimulate CBA agreements that fit the business situation of a specific company. Both from a practitioners' point of view (employers in charge), and from an academic point of view (the present hype on HRM and performance), workers/employees and trade unions increasingly run the risk of their interests being neglected.

The main question is: In what direction will the development of industrial relations and personnel management in the Netherlands (and other Western European countries) go? On the one hand, it is clear that the traditional institutional context is not longer suitable for ongoing developments. On the other hand—seen the historical and cultural background of these institutional arrangements—one cannot expect that they will be fully replaced by another (Anglo–Saxon) system. This leads to the need for a (continental) European or Rhineland model of industrial relations and personnel management (see also, Brewster 1993, 1994). Within such a model there must be room for a proper alignment between personnel management and business, without the historically grown patterns and practices of CBA arrangements and legislation forming a hinderance. Also, the developments with respect to new forms of work organisation, which imply an increased level of autonomy for workers in their job and direct work environment, fit very well into this model. However, with respect to the introduction of HRM initiatives aimed at strengthening the link between market development, strategic issues and the shape of HRM policies and practices, research evidence demonstrates that the establishment of those kinds of linkages is still not very widespread (albeit based upon '89 data, see Ten Have 1993; Paauwe 1995; and Kluytmans and Van Sluijs 1993).

3. AN OVERVIEW OF DUTCH RESEARCH

As already indicated in our introductory section, we can make use of an inventory by SISWO, compiled during the period 1991-1992 (Maenhout and Van Hoof 1993). Their overview and classification is based on 291 research projects with the following 7 categories/themes:

- organisational embedment/shaping of the personnel function;

- industrial relations;
- quality of work (with sub-categories such as: general, job content, working conditions and labour conditions);
- external labour market;
- internal labour market (sub-categories: inflow, throughflow, outflow);
- motivation and commitment;
- effects and performance.

Table 1. Research projects personnel management to themes

	SISWO (1991-1992)		*TVA/M&O (1993-1996)*	
	abs.	*(%)*	*abs.*	*(%)*
Organisational embedment (personnel function)	43	15	15	16
Industrial relations	14	5	7	7
Quality of work	69	24	28	30
- general	(4)	(1)	(8)	(8)
- job content	(19)	(7)	(8)	(9)
- working conditions	(31)	(11)	(4)	(4)
- labour conditions	(15)	(5)	(8)	(9)
External labour market	23	8	8	8
Internal labour market	103	35	30	32
- general	(26)	(9)	(6)	(6)
- in flow	(16)	(5)	(2)	(2)
- through flow	(51)	(18)	(22)	(24)
- out flow	(10)	(3)	(-)	(-)
Motivation and commitment	24	8	5	5
Effects and performance	15	5	2	2
Total	291	100	95	100

Table 1 shows the distribution of the various research projects across the different categories. The internal labour market category features most prominently, with a special focus on the sub-category 'throughflow'. More specifically, we can discern an emphasis upon topics such as training and development, career- and management development and general aspects of internal labour markets. The category 'quality of work' has the second best score, with a special emphasis on sub-categories such as working conditions and job content. Ranking thirdly is the organisational embedment of the personnel function, focused on question such as: Where should it be located?;

How should it be organised?, etc. Topics such as motivation/commitment, external labour market, industrial relations and effects/performance of personnel management have a strikingly low score. Based on this overview, we can conclude that in the period 1991-1992 the majority of HRM research was still a of rather institutional and instrumentalist (i.e. focused on HRM activities/practices/policies) nature in that it emphasised topics such as the quality of work and the various personnel management practices and policies related to the throughflow of staff. Key HRM issues (see Paauwe 1995) as put forward by practitioners (mainly from a management perspective), such as the importance of HRM in generating added value, the shift from staff to line, and measuring and monitoring the performance of HRM were hardly represented in the research projects carried out at the beginning of the nineties.

Based on an inventory of two related academic journals in the Netherlands, *Tijdschrift voor Arbeidsvraagstukken* (*TVA*/Journal for Labour Issues), and *M&O* (Journal for Organisational Sciences and HRM), we have updated the overview in order to include the period 1993-1996. This update is also included in Table 1, column 2, however with the obvious disadvantage that our update is based upon publications in only two journals and not upon an overview of all research in progress. This means that this update cannot be seen to be fully representative of the HRM research in our country. However, it gives a reasonable base from which to subtract the main tendencies. With this limitation in mind, we can see that, in the first instance, there are no radical changes in HRM research compared to the previous period. There is an increase in topics related to quality of work (especially in the sub-category 'general', and a striking fall in the topic 'working conditions'), but the other categories have more or less maintained their share. Inspite of the increasing importance of performance management and performance measurement—at least if the commercial conferences and popular articles featured in professional journals are used as a base—the interest of the academic community in the Netherlands with respect to measuring and monitoring the effects/performance of personnel management is still lagging behind. Research in the area of the linkage between HRM and value generating corporate strategies and the shift in the position of the personnel function has hardly found a footing. In summary, we can conclude that there is a more or less fifty/fifty distribution, with, on the one hand, institutional HRM research (quality of work, industrial relations and external labour market issues), and, on the other hand, more focused and/or instrumentally oriented HRM research (organisational embedment, throughflow HRM practices).

3.1. HRM research projects and their customers

Additional insights into the state-of-the-art of HRM research can be gained if we try to analyse the 'customers' or target groups of HRM research in the Netherlands. Will it be the employers/managers who benefit most from the outcomes, or will it be society at large, or the personnel managers themselves or is it just meant to please the academic community by finishing another Ph.D. project. Last but not least, do the workers/employees themselves benefit from it as subjects or are they only being considered as 'research elements' or 'objects', which generate a promising or disappointing response rate.

Trying to answer these questions is not easy. At first, one might tend to favour topics—especially those related to internal labour market (throughflow) and quality of work—that reflect the interests of practitioners (i.e. mainly personnel managers). That was also the conclusion reached by the SISWO analysis: *the field of personnel management research in the Netherlands is heavily dominated by practitioner-oriented issues which are instrumentally and short term oriented.* However, a further analysis of the available data reveals a different image or picture. Only a limited part (19 per cent) is initiated from a personnel management, and thus practitioner-oriented, perspective. Almost half of all research projects is initiated for 'societal' reasons, for example as preparation or evaluation of government policy, legislation, and/or inventories at regional or sectoral level. More than one quarter (28 per cent) of all research projects is targeted at the academic community itself in the form of Ph.D. projects, the development and testing of (parts of) theoretical models and the further refinement of testing and measurement tools, for instance in the field of personnel planning, recruitment, selection, job classification, career development, and remuneration, etc. Finally, the workers' perspective is only represented to a minor degree (2 per cent). Our own update, based on the aforementioned content analysis of two journals in the area of labour studies, organisational analysis and HRM (see Table 2, the right hand column) does not reflect any clear changes. We see an increase in articles from an academic perspective, but that can be attributed to the fact that both journals can be considered as academic journals. Internationally comparative research features in our update as a new, although modest category.

Table 2. Research projects personnel management to customers or target groups

	SISWO (1991-1992)						TVA/M&O (1993-1996					
	P	*G*	*A*	*W*	*O*	*T*	*P*	*G*	*A*	*W*	*O*	*T*
Organisational embedment (personnel function)	19	-6	14	0	4	43	3	3	7	1	1	15
Industrial relations	-	-4	-5	4	1	14	-	4	1	1	1	7
Quality of work	7	41	18	1	2	69	3	7	13	2	4	29
- general	(1)	(1)	(1)	(-)	(1)	(4)	-	(2)	(4)	-	(2)	(8)
- job content	(2)	(9)	(7)	(-)	(1)	(19)	(1)	(1)	(6)	-	-	(8)
- working conditions	(2)	(25)	(4)	(-)	(-)	(31)	(2)	-	(1)	-	(1)	(4)
- labour conditions	(2)	(6)	(6)	(1)	(-)	(15)	-	(4)	(3)	-	(1)	(8)
External labour market	1	20	-2	-	-	23	-	4	2	-	2	8
nternal labour market/	19	59	25	-	-	103	1	10	16	-	2	30
- general	(2)	(11)	(13)	-	-	(26)	-	-	6	-	-	(6)
- in flow	(4)	(9)	(3)	-	-	(16)	-	(2)	-	-	-	(2)
- through flow	(10)	(33)	(8)	-	-	(51)	(1)	(8)	(10)	-	(2)	(22)
- out flow	(3)	(6)	(1)	-	-	(10)	-	-	-	-	-	-
Motivation and commitment	4	-8	11	1	-	-24	-	-	5	-	-	5
Effects and performance	5	3	-5	-	2	-15	1	-	1	-	-	2
Total	55	141	80	6	9	291	8	28	45	4	10	95
Percentage	19	48	28	2	3	100	8	30	47	11	4	100

3.2. An international comparison

Our overview of Dutch HRM research based on the SISWO inventory, and including our journal-based update has been used as a starting point for a comparison with articles/topics that have featured in the past 5 volumes of the UK *Human Resource Management Journal* and the US journal *Human Resource Management.* Both journals each encompass over a 5-year period more than 100 articles. With respect to the UK, we have deliberately excluded the *International Human Resource Management Journal,* because it explicitly addresses an international forum and receives contributions—very often with a comparative perspective—from authors of different nationalities.

Taking a closer look at Table 3, a *first* striking difference between UK/US research and Dutch research is the theme of organisational embedment. This topic features prominently and twice as much as in the Netherlands. More specifically, we see that in the United States and in the United Kingdom there is a lot of interest in topics such as the linkage between the personnel function and strategy, the organisational setting of the personnel function, the different HRM roles and required competencies. The theme of effects of HRM is also more prominently present in both the UK and US setting of HRM research. A *second* striking difference is the degree of attention for the so-called institutional HRM research (encompassing quality of work, external labour market and industrial relations), which is lower in the United Kingdom and the United States. With respect to the theme of industrial relations, we need to be careful, because both the United Kingdom and the United States have a number of specialised academic journals in this respect, which we did not include in our analysis. For the time being, however, we safely assume that the Dutch emphasis upon the topic of quality of work—also due to the prominence in Dutch research of the so-called socio-technical systems approach and the labour process theory—is a distinctive characteristic of Dutch research. A *third* difference is related to the theme of the internal labour market, and especially to the topics under the heading 'throughflow'. In the Netherlands, these topics are mainly related to training, career and management development. However a further analysis indicates that in the United States and the United Kingdom—next to these topics—issues such as performance appraisal, self assessment, feedback- and reward systems have quite a good coverage. Moreover, research in these areas aims to develop or analyse links between these HRM activities and their subsequent effects on individual and firm performance. Interpreted in this way, these topics/articles could alternatively be included in the category of effects. A *last* difference is the lack of interest of Dutch research in internal HRM. Seen the position of the Netherlands as a small country, with a number of large international companies and an impressive tradition of foreign trade, and also seen the developments within the European Union, it is difficult to understand why more attention is not given to international or European aspects of HRM. The institutional character of Dutch HRM research may again provide the underlying explanation.

Table 3. A comparison of personnel research / publications between NL, UK and US for the period 1990-1995

	SISWO (1991-92)		*TVA/M&O (1993-96)*		*UK/HRMJ (1991-96)*		*USA/HRM (1991-96)*	
	abs.	*%*	*abs.*	*%*	*abs.*	*%*	*abs.*	*%*
Org. embedment / strategy	43	15	15	16	35	30	34	30
Industrial relations	14	5	7	7	14	12	2	2
Quality of working life	69	24	28	30	3	3	13	11
External labour market	23	8	8	8	4	3	1	1
Internal labour market								
- general	26	9	6	6	1	1	1	6
- in flow	16	5	2	2	5	4	6	5
- through flow	51	18	22	24	35	30	27	24
- out flow	10	3	-	-	-	-	1	1
Motivation and commitment	24	8	5	5	12	11	6	5
Effects and performance	15	5	2	2	7	6	13	12
Comparative/international	-	-	-	-	-	-	5	4
Total	291	100	95	100	116	100	114	100

In summary, we can—albeit provisionally—conclude that, in the Anglo–Saxon countries, HRM research seems to have a less institutional character and is more focused on HRM activities such as the redesign of HRM tools in the area of throughflow and performance management (appraisal, reward systems, feedback mechanisms), the monitoring of the effects of HRM and the organisational setting and design of the HRM function in relationship to strategic issues and the performance of the firm. In this way, it does more justice to key HRM issues as being put forward by practitioners from a managerial point of view. Following this line of reasoning, we can expect that Dutch

HRM research in the years to come will be intensified in the direction of strategic issues from a managerial point of view. However, looking at the Dutch tradition with respect to industrial relations and personnel management, a full convergence of Dutch research on these topics with an Anglo–Saxon approach is unlikely to take place. The challenge for Dutch research on personnel management is to find the right combination or balance between market forces and institutional arrangements, including the position of the workers. Promising examples of this kind of research are new projects on the interrelatedness of changes in the legal, social and individual aspects of the employment relationship and to the interrelatedness of the effects of these changes. At the end of this paper, when we present our conclusions and proposals for a research agenda, we will return to this point. An important aspect of new research is also the development of new integral theories and models of HRM which offer an escape out of the present (US/UK dominated) unidimensionality/single mindedness of HRM research.

4. BUILDING THEORETICAL FRAMEWORKS: UNITY IN DIVERSITY

Theory building in the area of personnel management initially developed out of the traditional disciplines that focused on separate and distinct parts of personnel management, such as psychology, sociology, law and economics. Within these disciplines, special branches or sub-disciplines took root like, for example, the sociology of work, industrial psychology, labour economics and labour law. Well-known examples in this respect are:

- theories about motivation and satisfaction, as developed by industrial or organisational psychologists and subsequently applied to personnel management in the areas of work design, participation, leadership, career development, training and reward systems;
- theories about labour markets and power within organisations, as developed within the sociology of work and organisation and applied in areas such as recruitment, staffing, industrial relations, participation, distribution of rewards, etc.;
- models about personnel costs, human capital, labour productivity as developed in the area of labour economics and econometrics and applied to topics such as planning, staffing, training and development, and performance.

In Table 4, we give an overview of the development and contributions of the various disciplines and their contribution to the applied discipline of personnel management. In short, we can conclude that there has been a lot of theory development with respect to the various parts of personnel management, however, until the eighties, this was rather fragmented, lacking alliances and cross fertilisation.

Table 4. Contribution disciplines to theory building personnel management

	Fields of Personnel Management (Beer et al. 1985)					
Disciplines and Theory Building	*Personnel Flow*	*Work System*	*Reward*	*Partici- pation*	*Embedment - Personnel - Function*	*Effects/ Perform- ance*
Industrial psychology						
- motivation,	x	x	x	x		
satisfaction	x	x				
- pers.characteristics				x		
- leadership						
Sociology of work						
- labour markets	x					
- industrial relations				x	x	
- quality of labour		x	x			
Labour economics						
- personnel/			x			x
transaction costs	x				x	
- labour market	x		x		x	
- labour relations						
Labour law						
- labour contract	x		x		x	
- labour conditions		x				
- co-determination				x	x	

We have deliberately restricted our conclusion to the eighties, because, since then, it has been possible to discern an increased tendency to look for interfaces and cross-border activities across related disciplines. This development has mainly been caused by the resurgence of personnel management in the disguise of HRM, in particular, *strategic* HRM. Yet many researchers complain about the lack of integration and the still highly fragmented nature of the PM/HRM discipline despite its proclaimed strategic importance. Wright and

McMahan (1992), for example, refer to the 'relative infancy of the field' and the lack of coherent theoretical frameworks. Steyart (1994) is also critical about the present state-of-the-art and makes a plea for a thorough discussion, which should be linked to the present discussion about paradigms in the organisational sciences. However, many authors are also worried about the diverging paradigms in the organisational sciences. Before being able to test and further develop existing paradigms, the next one is already being presented and attracts—as in fashion—many 'believers'. Needless to say, this causes a lot of fragmentation, which hinders scientific progress and sincere recognition. By way of illustration we cite Pfeffer (1993):

> 'Proponents of functionalism, postmodernism, critical theory, realism and many other theoretical approaches contend vigorously in the study of organisations. Whatever else one might think of this state of the affairs, it is by definition a state that signifies a field that is fragmented and that does not share the consensus characterising more paradigmatically developed disciplines.' (Pfeffer 1993: 608)

4.1. Competing paradigms in the organisational sciences

Reed (1996: 34) distinguishes a range of paradigms, that have dominated the organisational sciences in the past 100 years. Subsequently, he describes the following frames of reference and interpretation (between brackets we indicate the central problem in italics and then give typical examples of theoretical thought):
- rationality (*'order'*, e.g. scientific management, decision theory);
- integration (*'consensus'*, e.g. human relations, contingency, functionalism);
- market (*'liberty'*, e.g. economic organisation theory, population ecology);
- power (*'domination'*, e.g. marxism, labour process approach);
- knowledge (*'control'*, e.g. ethnomethodology, postmodernism);
- justice (*'participation'*, e.g. ethics, critical theory, industrial democracy).

The overview of central problems clearly has relevance for an applied discipline such as personnel management, and taking them into account in proper theoretical frameworks would do justice to the various stakeholders and their interests *vis à vis* personnel management. However, we should not be too negative about the present fragmentation and diversity. Albeit partially a 'fashionable' and normative stream in PM thinking, the very essence and importance of human resources management has acted, at the same time, as an attractive and inspiring umbrella concept, bringing together many researchers from a variety of backgrounds in their search for cooperation across related disciplines. Using Table 4 once more we can discern—albeit slowly and hesitantly—patterns of integration along both the horizontal and vertical axis of our schematic overview.

By horizontal integration, we refer to the tendency to integrate and coordinate the various HRM activities or tools. Thanks to the impetus of the phrase 'strategic', there is a lot of theorising and model building (without, sometimes, very much testing) in order to align market developments, corporate and business strategies with HRM policies and practices in a consistent manner (see, amongst others, Beer et al. 1985; Fombrun et al. 1984; Dyer 1983; Ackerman 1986, Paauwe 1997). In general, the problems facing these kinds of strategic theories (see also Guest 1996 for a clear categorisation) is that they:

- are rather normative and prescriptive in nature (Legge 1989);
- have a strong ideological character (Horwitz 1990);
- incorporate a number of inconsistencies (Horwitz 1990);
- have a weak theoretical base and are often formulated in a way which inhibits empirical testing (Hendry and Pettigrew 1990);
- are strongly management oriented (Looise 1996); and
- hardly take into account industrial relations (Kluytmans and Paauwe 1991).

Adding up all these critical remarks might generate enough ground to skip HRM theorising all together. A more positive stance, however, is to use these critics to strengthen and improve the theoretical body of knowledge. For this reason, we will elaborate on the aspect of integration across related disciplines and sub-disciplines (see Table 4, vertical axis). Wright and McMahan (1992) have given an important stimulus/impetus in this area. They distinguish the following six paradigms (theoretical frameworks), which they consider to be important for theory development in the area of HRM:

- behavioural perspective;
- cybernetic models;
- agency/transaction cost theory;
- resource-based view of the firm;
- power/resource dependence models;
- institutional theory.

Following Kamoche (1991) and inspired by Burrell and Morgan (1979), Steyart (1994) makes a strong plea for a multi-paradigmatic approach of personnel management (preferably labelled by him as Post-HRM). The different paradigms such as radical humanism, radical structuralism, interpretative sociology and functionalism (the latter being currently the most dominant one in the field of HRM) should be used next to each other and intermingled. In this way, Steyart emphasises pluriformity to create a multiplicity of perspectives on HRM. Only then can full justice be done to management reality (including personnel management), which is far too complex to be included/grasped by one single perspective or paradigm (see also Morgan 1986). However, these kind of approaches, which we would like to support, do not preclude the necessity to develop models or frameworks, which highlight and interconnect the various approaches, especially if our aim is to emphasise issues and research topics from a worker's point of view. Nowadays, the functional or economic perspective seems to dominate the scene. Combined with an increasing emphasis on managerial- and performance-related issues (Anglo–Saxon influence), we can expect that the dominance from a manager's point of view will last, unless we succeed in developing theoretical frameworks, which will do full justice to the various stakeholders involved, including employees themselves and their representative bodies (such as trade unions and works councils).

4.2. Towards integrative theory development

The prevailing dominance of the functional or economic paradigm and its accompanying organisational imperative (with its emphasis upon performance, profitability, and cost efficiency, Kamoche 1994) seems to be paralleled by overlooking a number of elements that are also extremely relevant. The following listing[3] is indicative of these missing elements and the incomplete images of HRM theory development resulting from it:

- *Human resources are not just resources.* They are acting individuals with a history, internalised values and norms (not necessarily those of the employing organisation), who belong to different groups inside and outside the organisation and whose behaviour is partially governed by institutions.
- *Human resource management is more than being strategic and performance oriented.* The HRM or personnel function, as one of the organisational functions, is also involved in the process of rendering professional

services and establishing a sense of corporate citizenship. Many of these activities are by no means strategic and do not relate at all to the performance of the firm. They must be fulfilled, however, in a proper way, due to all kinds of legislation, national and industry agreements and administrative/accounting practices. More importantly—especially from a Dutch or continental European perspective—personnel management activities arise in order to meet demands from corporate social responsibility and related legislation and institutions (so we not only need a flexible or innovative firm, but also a responsible one).

- *The yardstick of human resource outcomes is not just economic rationality.* At the beginning of this section, we already referred to the dominance of the organisational imperative, with its emphasis on efficiency, effectiveness, etc. (Kamoche 1994: 32). Based on a stakeholder's perspective and recognising the importance of values and institutions in the employment relationship, economic rationality should not be the exclusive base. A broader perspective of business performance is needed, which is also based on *relational rationality* (Eelens 1995; Schipper 1993)—a concept that refers to the development and maintenance of sustainable relations with relevant stakeholders, which includes more than just customers and shareholders.
- *HRM is not just about optimising/maximising performance.* Rather, it is about satisficing the different aspiration levels of the various stakeholders involved, such as the different categories of employees, shareholders, works council members, trade union activists, etc. One sometimes gets the impression that research in the area of HRM and performance is all about generating added value, and profits. However, an important aspect of HRM—especially if one focuses on the employment relationship—is not so much involved with 'generating' as with bringing about a system of 'distributive justice' with respect to work, time, rewards, information, training opportunities and (career)development and finally participation.

Theoretical models are needed therefore, that take into account the institutional setting and allow reality to emerge and enable us to analyse the underlying processes between the various stakeholders involved. One way of achieving this might be to opt for models which combine different theoretical perspectives such as systems theory, interactive models, institutional theory, organisational behavioural theory and the resource based theory of the firm (see also Wright and McMahan 1992; Guest 1996; and Paauwe 1996). The latter one, especially, seems to offer a good way of integrating a multidimensional view on HRM, because it takes into account the competencies and capabilities of the (human) resources instead of exclusively focusing on dominant business-like criteria as being dictated by the industry-based demands of the specific product/market combination. Kamoche strongly advocates this view because, it gives more potential to take into account the specific nature and complexities of human resources:

> '... this paradigm emphasises that the skills of employees are conceived of as a vital resource, which the firm is able to build upon rather than simply to exploit rationally and ideologically. Therefore the full potential of HRM can be realised and can be a key determinant in a firm's performance, without the *a priori* imposition of the organisational imperative.' (Kamoche 1994: 41)

Within a Western European socio-economic setting, it is important to do full justice to the various stakeholders that represent their claims *vis-à-vis* the management of human resources. Contrary to US and UK approaches, in which personnel management is increasingly seen as merely representing the line management perspective in meeting strategic demands, the Dutch and continental Western European institutional context offers a unique proposition for reconciling both strategic demands of the market place and justified claims from the 'human resources' themselves in terms of fairness and legitimation. The last can be expressed by the members of the works council—in combination with local trade union activists—who play an increasingly important role in shaping industrial relations and human resource management policies and practices at local plant and office level. Moreover, the 'creative merging' of these apparent paradoxes could create insights into a unique (firm-specific) approach to the management of human resources.

The following conceptual framework (see Figure 1) brings these two forces—next to the administrative heritage of the organisation—into contact with the dominant coalition, in order to bring about a unique synthesis of strategic demands and the characteristics and aspirations of the workforce itself, including relevant stakeholders, their interaction and related institutions inside and outside the domain of the organisation.

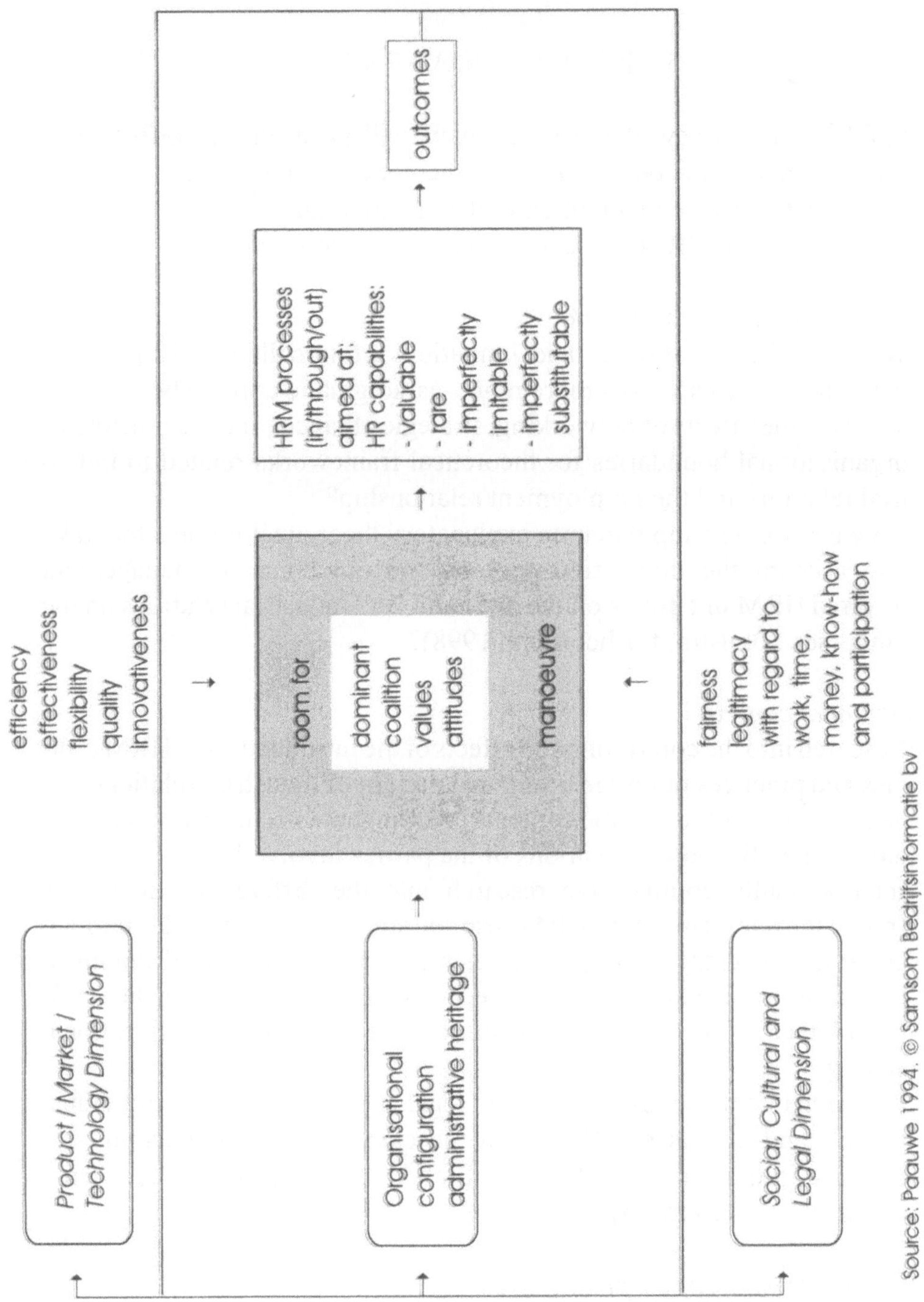

Figure 1. The human resource based theory of the firm

5. RESEARCH AGENDA

In the following overview of research issues we will make a distinction between:
- issues related to the development of theoretical frameworks;
- issues that pay special attention to the institutional context;
- issues related to HRM, as seen from a worker perspective.

Building theoretical frameworks
- What are the possibilities and limitations of so-called multi-paradigmatic frameworks versus more mono-paradigmatic approaches?
- What are the effects of networking, strategic alliances and the blurring of organisational boundaries for theoretical frameworks related to industrial relations and the employment relationship?
- How can we develop dynamic explanatory theoretical models that take into account the interaction patterns and outcomes of management inspired HRM initiatives on the one hand, and industrial relations on the other (see Schilstra, forthcoming, 1998)?

Institutional context
- Research into the conditions and effects of the introduction of HRM policies and practices upon the traditional pattern of industrial relations, for example with respect to the contents of arrangements, the process of bargaining and the power positions of the parties involved.
- Internationally comparative research into the differences in leeway (room for manoeuvre) of HRM inspired initiatives, if we take into account the different systems of industrial relations, degree of unionisation, degree of legislation with respect to industrial democracy, degree of compliance to EC directives and subsequent differences in institutional setting.
- Research into the interrelatedness of legal, organisational and individual aspects and effects of changes in the employment relationship—for instance in the form of all kinds of labour flexibilisation—between a company and its employees.

HRM seen from a worker perspective
- Research which focuses on the attitude and well-being of workers/employees in situations where they are confronted with the introduction and practice of HRM-inspired so-called high performance, high involvement

work systems. Can any consequences be discerned in terms of increased stress, role overload and a subsequent rise in absenteeism due to illness.

- Research on the influence of employees and employee representatives (such as works councils, trade unions) on HRM strategies and HRM instruments and the effects of this influence on company performance, employee satisfaction, commitment, etc.
- Research on personnel management in a 'responsive firm' (seen as a next phase in the phase model of companies (Bolwijn and Kumpe 1996).

NOTES

1 We use the term HRM here in a 'neutral' way. We see HRM as the management function directed at the relationship between an organisation and its employees (the employee relationship); as a function comparable with other management functions such as production management, financial management, etc.

2 Nearly 50 per cent of the personnel officers are members of the NVP, the Dutch Association for Personnel Management. The association has been flourishing since the end of the 1980s; its membership (1996: 4800 members) is expanding and much attention is given to the issue of professionalising. This leads to a greater concern for the quality of the personnel function, making a real contribution to the bottom line (competence and performance oriented) and more interaction between theory and practice.

3 The following listing is based on a discussion paper by Paauwe (1996) for the ESRC-funded series of seminars on HRM and Performance. Needless to say, we have been inspired in this respect by a number of critical authors and their writings, such as Keenoy (1992), Legge (1995), Storey (1989, 1995), Kamoche (1994), and Kluijtmans and Paauwe (1991).

REFERENCES

Akkermann, K.F., 1986. 'A contingency model of HRM strategy', Paper presented at EIASM, Brussels.

Beer, M., B. Spector, P. Lawrence, D. Mills and R. Walton, 1984. *Human Resources Management: A General Manager's perspective*, New York, Free Press.

Bolweg, J.F., 1989. 'Internalisering van de arbeidsverhoudingen en politisering van het personeelsmanagement' (Internalisation of labour relations and the politising of personnel management), in: J.F. Bolweg and F. Kluytmans, *De noodzaak van nieuwe verhoudingen* (The necessity of new relations), Deventer, Kluwer.

Bolwijn P.T. and T. Kumpe, 1990. 'Manufacturing in the 1990's—productivity, flexibility and innovation', *Long Range Planning* 23(4).

Bolwijn, P.T and T. Kumpe, 1996. 'About facts, fiction and forces in Human Resource management', *Human Systems Management* 15(3).

Brewster, C., 1993. 'Developing a "European" model of human resource management'. *International Journal of Human Resource Management* 4(4).

Brewster, C., 1994. 'European HRM. Reflection of, or challenge to, the American concept?', in: P.S. Kirkbride (ed.), *Human Resource Management in Europe. Perspectives for the 1990s*, London, Routledge.

Buitendam, A., 1979. *Personeelsafdelingen in de industrie. Een empirisch onderzoek naar de structuur en het functioneren van personeelsafdelingen in industriële ondernemingen in Nederland* (Personnel departments in industry, an empirical research to the structure and functioning of personnel departments in industrial enterprises in The Netherlands), Groningen, Konstapel.

Bartlett C. and S. Goshal, 1989. *Managing across borders: Transnational solutions*, Boston, MA, Harvard Business School Press.

Burrell, G. and G. Morgan, 1979. *Sociological paradigms and organisational analysis*, London, Heinemann.

Dyer, L., 1983. *Human resource management: evolving roles & responsibilities*, ASPA/ BNA series.

Eelens, L., 1995. 'The fallacy of fit'. *Paper for the seminar group on HRM master course 1994/5.* Erasmus University Rotterdam.

Flood P., M. Cannon and J. Paauwe, 1996. 'Managing without Traditional Methods: International Innovations in Strategic Human Resource Management', London, Addison Wesley.

Fombrun, C., N.M. Tichy and M.A. Devanna, 1984. *Strategic Human Resource Management.* Chichester, Sussex, John Wiley.

Guest, D.E., 1996. 'Human resource management and performance: a review and research agenda', *The international Journal of Human Resource Management* 8 (June).

Have, K. ten, 1993. *Markt, organisatie en personeel in de industrie. Een empirisch onderzoek naar produktieregimes als configuraties van arbeidsdeling en arbeidsrelaties* (Market, organisation and personnel in industry. An empirical research to production regimes as configurations of division of labour and labour relations), Tilburg, Tilburg University Press.

Hendry, C., and A. Pettigrew, 1990. 'Human Resource Management: an agenda for the 1990s'. *International Journal of Human Resource Management* 1(1).

Hoof, J.J. van, 1995. 'Arbeidsbestel op een keerpunt' (Labour relations at a turning point), in: L. Faasse, M. Ott and C.J. Vos (eds.), *Nieuwe breukvlakken in het arbeidsbestel?* (New cracks in the labour relations?), Utrecht, De Tijdstroom.

Horwitz, F.M., 1990. 'HRM, an ideological perspective', *Personnel Review*, 19(2).

Kamoche, K., 1991. 'Human Resource Management: A Multiparadigmatic Analysis', *Personnel Review*, 20(4).

Kamoche, K., 1994. 'A critique and an proposed reformulation of strategic human resource management'. in: *Human Resource Management Journal* 4(4).

Kluytmans, F. and J. Paauwe, 1991. 'HRM denkbeelden: De balans opgemaakt' (HRM ideas: making-up of accounts), *M&O, Tijdschrift voor Organisatiekunde en Sociaal Beleid* (Journal for Organisation Management and Social Policy) 45(4).

Kluytmans, F., and E. van Sluijs, 1995. 'De relatie tussen bedrijfsbeleid en personeelsmanagement' (The connection between company policy and personnel management), *Tijdschrift voor Arbeidsvraagstukken* (Journal for Labour Issues) 11(1).

Legge, K., 1995. *Human Resource Management. Rhetorics and Realities*. Houndmills, MacMillan Business.

Looise, J.C. and F.G.M. de Lange, 1987. *Ondernemingsraden, bestuurders en besluitvorming. Eindrapport onderzoek ondernemingsraden* (Works councils, (top)managers and decision making. Final report research on works councils), Nijmegen, ITS.

Looise, J.C., 1996. *Sociale innovatie moet, maar hoe?* (Social innovation is needed, but how?), Oratie (Inaugural oration), University of Twente.

Looise, J.C., F.G.M. de Lange, J. de Leede and M. van Riemsdijk, 1997. 'Balancing between Cost Effectiveness and Commitment: Labour Flexibility Strategies in an Institutional Context'. Paper presented at the 13th EGOS Colloquium, Budapest, July 1997.

Macduffie, P.C., 1995. 'Human resource bundles and manufacturing performance', *Industrial and Labor Relations review* 48(2).

Maenhout, J.M.M. and J.J. van Hoof, 1993. *Personeelsresearch in kaart gebracht. Een overzicht van personeelsonderzoek en uitvoerende organisaties in Nederland* (Mapping personnel research. An overview of personnel research and research organisations in The Netherlands), SISWO-Informatief, nr. 1, Amsterdam.

Morgan, G., 1986. *Images of Organisation*. London, Jossey-Bass.

Paauwe, J., 1991. 'Limitations to freedom: is there a choice for human resource management?' *British Journal of Management* 2.

Paauwe, J., 1994. *Organiseren, een grensoverschrijdende passie* (Organising, a border crossing passion), Oratie (Inaugural oration), Alphen aan den Rijn.

Paauwe, J., 1995. 'Kernvraagstukken op het gebied van strategisch HRM in Nederland' (Key issues in HRM in the Netherlands). *M&O, Tijdschrift voor Organisatiekunde en Sociaal Beleid* (Journal for Organisation Management and Social Policy) 49(5).

Paauwe, J., 1997. 'Afzetmarkt, organisatie en personeelsmanagement' (Market, organisation and personnel management), in: F. Kluytmans (ed.), *Personeelsmanagement, omgeving en personeel* (Personnel management, environment and personnel), Heerlen, Open University.

Pfeffer, J. and G.R. Salancik, 1978. *The external control of organisations: A resource dependency perspective*. New York, Harper and Row.

Pfeffer, J., 1993. 'Barriers to the advance of organisational science: paradigm development as a dependent variable', *Academy of Management Review* 18(4).

Reed, M., 1996. 'Organisational theorising: a historically contested terrain', in: S.R. Clegg, C. Hardy and W.R. Nord, *Handbook of Organisation Studies*, London, Sage.

Schilstra, K.M. and E.J. Smit, 1994. 'Changing forms of interest representation in the Netherlands.' Paper presented at the IIRA Regional European conference, Helsinki.

Schilstra, K.M., 1998. *The relationship between industrial relations and HRM: a dynamic conceptual framework.* Rotterdam, Ph.D. dissertation, (forthcoming).
Schipper, F., 1993. *Zin in organisaties* (Sense in organisations), Amsterdam, Boom.
Sitter, L.U., 1981. *Op weg naar nieuwe kantoren en fabrieken* (The road to new offices and factories). Deventer, Kluwer.
Smit, E., K. Schilstra and J. Paauwe (1995), *Belangenbehartiging van werknemers: een toekomstverkenning* (Interestrepresentation of workers: an exploration of the future), Den Haag, VUGA Uitgeverij BV.
Steyaert, C., 1994. 'Post-Human Resource Management: Personeelsmanagement in meervoud?' (Post-Human Resource Management: Personnel Management in plural), *M&O, Tijdschrift voor Organisatiekunde en Sociaal beleid* (Journal for Organisation Management and Social Policy) 48(6).
Storey, J., 1989. *New perspectives in Human Resource Management.* London, Routledge.
Storey, J., 1995. 'Human Resource Management: still marching on, or marching out?' in: J. Storey (ed.), *European Industrial Relations. The challenge of Flexibility*, London, Sage.
Visser, J., 1992. 'The Netherlands: The end of an Era and the end of a System'. in: G. Baglioni and C. Crouch (eds.), *European Industrial Relations. The challenge of Flexibility*, London, Sage.
Watson, T.J., 1977. *The personnel managers, a study in the sociology of work and employment.* London, Routledge & Kegan Paul.
Wright, P.M. and G.C. McMahan, 1992. 'Theoretical Perspectives for Strategic Human Resource Management', *Journal of Management* 18(2).
Zuthem, H.J. van, 1979. *Inleiding in de economische sociologie* (Introduction in economical sociology). Amsterdam, De Bussy.

AUTHORS

Prof.dr. J.C. Looise
University of Twente, Dept. of HRM
P.O. Box 217, 7500 AE Enschede
tel: 053-4893508, fax: 053-4892159
e-mail: j.c.looise@sms.utwente.nl

Prof.dr. J. Paauwe
Erasmus University of Rotterdam, Human Resource System-Research Unit
P.O. Box 1738, 3000 DR Rotterdam
tel: 010-4081352, fax: 010-4526094
e-mail: paauwe@few.eur.nl

APPENDIX

Further explication of the model (Figure 1)

On the one hand, HRM is largely determined by demands arising from relevant product/market combinations and the appropriate technology (P-M-T dimension). These demands are usually expressed in terms of criteria such as efficiency, effectiveness, flexibility, quality and innovativeness. This dimension represents the tough economic rationality of national and international competition.

On the other hand, it is important to remember that the so-called 'free market' is embedded in a social, cultural and legal context (S-C-L dimension). Prevailing values and norms and their institutionalisation channel the outcomes of the market process in ways that simultaneously do justice to the dictates of fairness and legitimacy. By *fairness* (see also Watson 1977) we refer to a 'fair' arrangement in the agreed exchange between the individual as an employee and the organisation as employer. Elements in this exchange are not only time, money and labour, but also information, know-how, and voice.

Legitimacy refers to the same elements, but collectively, whereby the parties involved are interest groups (employees, unions, government through legislation) rather than individuals.In addition to the above-described two dimensions, historically grown configurations of firms also have their bearing on the structuring of HRM. The concept of administrative heritage (Bartlett and Ghoshal 1989) refers to the influence of structures, methods, competencies, values and so on, which originated in the past and can still be considered as an important influential factor (for better or worse) in continued organisation structuring, including the structuring of HRM (Flood et al. 1996: 317).

Dominant coalition and room for manoeuvre

Together with the two dimensions, these three forces have an impact upon the so-called dominant coalition and it's room for manoeuvre. From a pluralistic perspective, the dominant coalition is made up of a number of key actors. Examples of these are the various executive and governing boards, works council and the human resources department. These actors all have their own norms and values, shared with others to a greater or lesser degree.

The shaded area in Figure 1 represents the available room for the dominant coalition to manoeuvre in shaping HRM. Depending on the situation this leeway may be expansive or restricted.

Examples of relevant circumstances are the market position, the degree of unionisation, labour–capital ratio, and the financial health of the company (for a more extended treatment of contingencies governing the degree of leeway, see Paauwe 1991). Based on the available room for manoeuvre, actors involved in the dominant coalition develop initiatives to shape human resources policies. Whether they succeed in that depends, amongst others, upon the kind of resources they control and the power relations involved (Pfeffer and Salancik 1978). In this respect, however, it is important to note that also the interaction between the parties involved and their shared ideology *vis à vis* each other's position and role are important elements in creating understanding and credibility. Social credibility, in itself generates possibilities for innovative approaches in the area of human resources management. Approaches are aimed at furthering or strengthening a sustainable competitive advantage.

The resource-based approach focuses on the key success factors of individual firm behaviour by applying a portfolio of differential core skills and routines, coherence across skills and unique proprietary know-how and values.

Important in this respect is the role that can be fulfilled by human resources professionals. Amidst the pressures for profit maximising, they are able to emphasise the long-term perspective in building commitment, by taking into account not only justified claims in the areas of fairness and legitimacy as put forward by interest groups, but also the capabilities and specific characteristics of the human resources and their possibilities for training and development. Emphasising these elements offers insights in competitive strategies that are unique, firm-specific and difficult to imitate by competitors. The works council can also play an important role in this whole process of developing unique approaches. Based on its legally prescribed two-fold task of both representing the interests of the enterprise in all its objectives and the interests of workers it can help to reconcile different claims put forward by, for example, management and unions.

In this way, it can help to bring about a unique synthesis of strategic demands and the characteristics and aspirations of the workforce itself. In this respect, its not surprisingly that in our case studies among leading Dutch companies, we very often encounter a cooperative and creative —albeit sometimes due to conflicts and diverging opinions—working relationship between HRM specialists and representatives of the works council.

Outcomes
HRM activities structured according to the above described analyses and processes are, of course, oriented to the realisation of certain objectives or outcomes, for which we developed the distinctions between strategic, societal and professional dimensions. More specifically, we can refer to Beer et al. (1984), who mention the following four dimensions:

- *Commitment*: To what extent are HR policies aimed at strengthening the bond employees have with their work and with the organisation of which they are a part?
- *Competence*: To what extent are HR policies able to recruit, retain and develop personnel with the capabilities, skills and knowledge needed by the organisation and society now and in the future?
- *Cost-effectiveness*: How effective and efficient are the results of the HRM policies as implemented in relation to labour costs, secondary labour conditions, personnel turnover, strikes, and so on.
- *Congruence*: To what degree does the HRM policy and its activities achieve congruence or harmonisation among the distinct personnel categories, in the relation between organisation and society, between employee and family and the relation with the personal aspirations of individuals.

These outcomes, in turn, should contribute to the realisation of long-term objectives such as individual well-being, effectiveness of the organisation, and social well-being. Both HRM objectives and long-term goals fit nicely into the context of the aforementioned P-M-T and S-C-L dimensions.

THEORY AND RESEARCH ON WORK AND ORGANISATION

Ad H. van der Zwaan[1]

1. INTRODUCTION

It is very intriguing, though rather complicated, to describe the recent developments in the study of work and organisation in the Netherlands. It is not the recent history of just organisation theory or organisation sociology, which forms the core of this article. In that case, we could easily have followed Lammers et al. (1997), who especially focus on the developments in organisational sociology and even on its impact on the theory of organisation design and intervention. Our mission is a little more difficult, because our task stems from a labour perspective, so the sociology (or socio-psychology) and economics of work closely linked with organisation theory is the very object of our analysis. Our aim is to deal with organisation theory, but theory that is as close as possible to work and the work organisation itself. The objective is not so much to describe actual 'concrete' developments about items in the field, such as gender, employment relationship, internal labour market, co-determination, etc. The aim is rather to survey the work and organisation area from a more abstract theoretical and methodological perspective. At this level of abstraction, we shall try to formulate a number of guiding questions and the related suppositions will be submitted to some sort of test. These will be articulated in Section 3 of this article.

We shall first give a brief and global sketch of what has happened in the study of work and organisation over the last approximately thirty years (Section 2). It forms the background for interpreting our relevant data.[2] In addition to the journals, we have surveyed many dissertations, conference proceedings and textbooks, the outcomes of which can be found in Section 6. The final section, 7, is an outline of our conclusions.

2. SKETCH OF DUTCH HISTORY

When overviewing approximately thirty years of developments in work and organisation theory, and when attempting to categorise themes and periods, we can roughly formulate the following propositions, while referring to the graphical representation in Figure 1.

In the Netherlands, the *seventies* were dominated by three major fields of interest. They are, firstly, the mostly socio-psychological endeavours of leadership, motivation, influence, attitudes, and group dynamics; secondly, a broad interest in the concept of technology; and thirdly, a great many attempts to construct organisational structure typologies.

We have already illustrated the first category by mentioning a number of socio-psychological variables that enjoyed great popularity in the seventies.[3]

The second category (technology) looks a little more complex, as its composition is very heterogeneous. It featured at least three independent frames of reference: the Tavistock or sociotechnical approach, the Woodward type of research, and the Bravermanian or labour process way of theorising. Each frame of reference was entirely independent of the others regarding its conceptual frame, method of analysis, and socio-economic ideals, notwithstanding the fact that all the frames of reference fully embraced and shared the common notion of technology. With respect to the third category (structural contingency), we only need to refer to the Aston school, their predecessors Burns and Stalker (1961) and Lawrence and Lorsch (1969), and their contingency paradigm, which is still vivid and strong (Lammers et al. 1997).

The category of technology has been positioned in the middle of the seventies' column of Figure 1, since it produced multiple continuities during the eighties, especially in the Netherlands.

With respect to the *eighties*, the following is of interest. Technology follow-ups (from the seventies) are the broad industrial-democracy field experiments in ten Dutch firms. These experiments, based partly on sociotechnics, and subsidised by the government (De Man 1988), were also a continuation of the socio-psychological small-group research tradition. The other line in the eighties is the quality-of-working-life research stream, which, among other things, also fed the well-known and particularly Dutch debate between the labour process proponents and those dedicated to sociotechnics (Buitelaar

1988; Van Klaveren 1994; Mok 1990; De Sitter 1987, 1994).[4] A closely related item is the segmented internal labour market (Van Hoof 1987; Glebbeek 1993). The third one is the organisation theory perspective which comprised a lot of empirical (and theoretical) analysis of the organisation (Koot 1980), organisational typologies and their interfaces with the environment (Lammers 1983, 1993, 1997), and the subject of interorganisational relationships (Van Gils 1978; Godfroij 1981; Lammers 1993, 1997; Van der Zwaan 1990), i.e. mostly contingency-like studies.

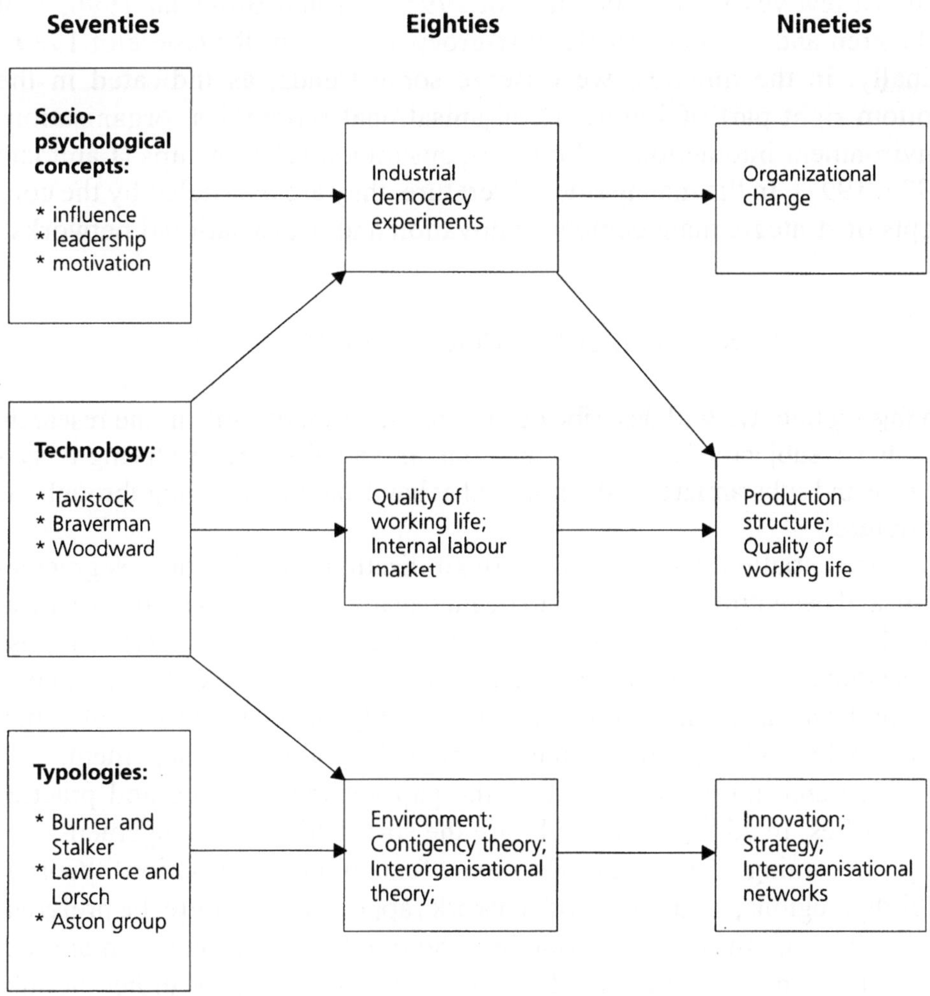

Figure 1. Thirty years of developments in work and organisation theory

Following these paths in Figure 1 over the *nineties* we tend to conclude that the experiments on industrial democracy linked to a double stream of research, viz. a renewed interest in organisational change and organisational development on the one hand (Boonstra et al. 1996; Van Eijnatten 1996; Mastenbroek 1993), and a renewal of sociotechnical thinking, ending up in what is nowadays called Modern Sociotechnical Theory or MST on the other (De Sitter 1994). The latter paid substantial attention to the quality of working life, but in a different way from the labour process vision. We see that the latter has been given continued attention during the last few years (Huijgen and Pot 1995; Vos and Buitelaar 1996; Van Klaveren and Kooistra 1991; Post-groep 1991; Van Ruysseveldt 1989). Finally, in the nineties, we observe some trends, as indicated in the bottom right part of Figure 1: organisational typologies, organisation-environment interaction and interorganisational relationships (Lammers 1993, 1997). In the management literature, they are paralleled by the concepts of strategic management, innovation and organisational networks.

3. SOME ELEMENTARY HYPOTHESES

In this section, we will describe our impressions about shifts in the research. We have, subjectively, put forward some propositions before trying to systemise and substantiate all the material at hand and before going through the literature.

Differentiation, fragmentation, flexibilisation, mobilisation, segmentation, and decentralisation seem to be increasing continually at the organisation level as well as on higher levels of aggregation, so one might suppose these trends to be receiving more and more attention in research. Secondly, research and theorising seem to be increasingly geared towards application and problem solving. Hence, theory enters the realm of management, consultancy and intervention, and so the gap between science and practice diminishes. In addition, not only are the so-called new management concepts becoming popular, but also some 'economic organisation' theories. Thirdly, regions, industries, and networks appear to constitute the preferential unities of study, notwithstanding the trends of fragmentation and decentralisation. Consequently, the units of analysis tend to be either the subsystems or particularly the supra-systems rather than the systems themselves, i.e. the organisations as such.

Our explicit suppositions or 'elementary hypotheses' are eight in number. We expect:

1. A drift towards utilisation, and so to management science, because of a growing need to solve managerial problems;
2. A growing interest in micro-systems and processes, e.g. team work, production lay-out, group dynamics and group performance;
3. An increasing supra-systems orientation, e.g. the importance of markets, interorganisational cooperation;
4. An inclination to apply process approaches (change concepts) rather than structural models, in research as well as in practice;
5. A considerable effort to compare, confront and, if possible, integrate theory;
6. A preference for harmony models rather than using concepts of power, coalition, interest and conflict;
7. A number of new management and new labour concepts instead of the classical Taylor-based high-division-of-labour concept;
8. A lot of empirical research of a qualitative, interpretative nature, mostly within highly preferred in-depth case studies.

In this article we shall check the tenability of these suppositions, and should they turn out to be true, the implication will be that the trends can be supposed to be current.

Hypotheses 5 and 6 are of special importance, at least in the Netherlands: the related contrast pairs are termed the systems versus the parties model (Lammers 1983, 1990, 1993, 1998) or systems versus actor approaches (Godfroy 1995). The parties model appears to be increasingly neglected (coalition and conflict notions included), and also political analyses in organisations. Moreover, we see a tendency to drop systems and structure models in favour of the adoption of actor approaches, preferably in a harmony context.

4. FRAME OF REFERENCE: SOURCES OF INFORMATION

Our next line of action was to delve into recent textbooks, dissertations, conferences and a few representative Dutch journals. In other words, our aim was to draw an adequate sample from the relevant literature on work and organisation published during the last decade. With respect to all of these sources our central question had to be whether they mirror, correct or articulate our suppositions.

In the exploration below, we first consider four journals as our main source. In the field of research and theory on work and organisation, these four journals may be assumed to jointly and adequately reflect the main lines of current thought in the area. The journals concerned are:

1. *Tijdschrift voor Arbeidsvraagstukken*; *TVA* (Journal for Labour studies);
2. *Gedrag & Organisatie*; *GO* (Journal for behaviour and organisation);
3. *M&O, Tijdschrift voor Organisatiekunde en Sociaal Beleid*; *M&O* (Journal for organisation management and social policy);
4. *Bedrijfskunde, Tijdschrift voor Modern Management*; *BK* (Management science journal).

Two of them, *TVA* and *GO* are to be considered key or core journals, since they particularly address items in the area of work and organisation and do so in a genuinely scientific way. *TVA* is highly sociology-oriented, *GO* has a clear affiliation with socio-psychological issues in work and organisation.

M&O and *BK* attempt to serve an 'interface function' between science and practice, we will call them 'management journals'. They translate, on behalf of management, academic insights into 'theory-in-use'. These journals are undeniably interested in scientific research on work and organisation, but particularly from a more practical managerial perspective. *M&O* generally engages in organisation theory, mostly for the benefit of management consultants. *BK* includes a much broader range of management disciplines, such as marketing, production, HRM, business development, etc.

Although the latter two journals with their pragmatic management perspective can be seen as peripheral, they are nonetheless valued by social scientists as well, and are therefore worthwhile studying. We were eager to see, not only how they address management and organisation issues, but also whether labour issues, in particular, penetrate these journals.

In later sections we will also address the contents of dissertations, conferences and recently published books, but first, we will deal with the journals specifically.

5. JOURNALS

From each of the four journals, we arbitrarily chose the three volumes of 1993 to 1995 inclusive, as the objects of our analysis. As far as we could assess, they are not biased by, for instance, special issues, and so might provide a representative picture of (beginning) developments in the nineties. Since all four have very diverging profiles, it proved important to take all four and to consider them together in the end. Unfortunately, it appeared not to be possible to analyse the two management journals according to the conceptual scheme we used for the two core journals.

5.1. *Two management journals*

Consequently, we went through the *M&O* journal and categorised all its 71 articles by main subject, over the three years indicated. In all cases it proved possible to extract one such theme for each article. Book reviews, short comments, editorial prefaces, and the like were not included. The subjects are the following:

- general management, project management, and internal entrepreneurship are the main topics of 14 articles;
- intercultural management and internationalisation are dealt with in 12 articles;
- culture and structure are the themes of 12 articles;
- personnel management is on the agenda 9 times;
- consultancy also appears 9 times;
- organisational learning 4 times;
- organisational change 5 times; and finally
- one article was devoted to each of the following subjects: flexibility, lean production, emancipation, organisational re-design, and quality management.

There seems to be little interest in current items such as flexibility, participation, redesign, information management, quality management, networks and innovation. In general, the concept of labour hardly occurs; just a very small minority of articles deal with labour dimensions such as labour relations, work organisation, employment conditions, labour markets, and working conditions. Interestingly, however, much attention is being paid to culture, change management, consultancy, organisational learning, personnel management, and the methods of organisational change. Moreover, as far as these items are concerned, we observe a trend towards:

1. abstraction, and consequently theoretical generalisation, and nonetheless a
2. pragmatic orientation, i.e. a tendency or drift to application, or utilisation of theory,
3. process approaches instead of expert ones, and theoretical models of harmony rather than conflict.

These have comprised a few of the developments of this particular journal in recent years. These observations, however, clearly contrast with the expectation that the currently popular notions of mobilisation, segmentation, flexibilisation, self-regulation, and de-centralisation should play a conspicuous role. This is not the case, at least not in this journal. A move towards meso-levels of aggregation, i.e. concerning regions, industries, or networks can hardly be observed either. This is noteworthy, as analyses on this level appear to constitute a general trend in the present international-management literature. Furthermore, process thinking seems to prevail over structure-centred approaches, and it is obvious that authors try to avoid talking about conflicts of interests and parties within organisations. Finally, we did not find any micro-systems studies, hardly any confrontation of theories, and very little methodology in the sense that we have defined it.

The journal *BK* largely provides articles of a different content and perspective. This is peculiar, as this journal claims to be a practice-oriented management journal.

As far as the 149 *BK* articles are concerned, it clearly turns out that the well-known functional areas of the firm are being accentuated, and most of them are being covered very well. Among them:

- no less than 39 articles are dedicated to organisational change, communication and coordination;
- the methodology of doing research, of designing organisations, and of developing management theory enjoy substantial popularity, given the 25 articles in this field;
- production and logistics management are the object of 20 articles;
- information management is the topic of 16 articles;
- financial management, 16 articles;
- marketing, 13 articles;
- innovation, 11 (development-marketing-production interfaces);
- even 12 on the so-called new production concepts; and
- only 4 on HRM.

In contrast with *M&O*, network- and industry-level approaches (meso-approaches) appear to be attractive in *BK*. This parallels the general trend of stipulating the role of business environments and networks between companies. Relatedly, information management is given a lot of attention; see e.g. EDI (Electronic Data Interchange). The same holds for new production concepts, the scope of which is usually widened to include the variety of markets surrounding the firm.

Conversely, flexibility and mobilisation are definitely not at the top of the agenda! Neither are segmentation or self-regulation. De-centralisation is sometimes addressed, though not very often. These observations are in accordance with our above observations on *M&O*. Comparably, a growing drive towards pragmatism in theory building can be seen, and no less, a strong emphasis on processes as well (the item of organisational change occurs 39 times). Similarly, conflict models of organisational reality are also missing.

The culture concept, however, raises very little interest, as little as theories on organisational learning do. This strongly deviates from *M&O*. The structure concept is not questioned either. This was also the case in *M&O*. Neither is the participation issue addressed, nor either leadership or motivation. HRM is given a minor position among the competing functional areas of the firm. Communication and coordination, on the contrary, are extremely current themes.

5.2. Conceptual scheme for the analysis of the core journals

When looking for a common frame of reference in order to analyse and compare them, it is worth sketching a rough conceptual distinction first. This is the distinction between the labour relations and the work organisation aspect. In the Netherlands, we have come to term them the contractual and the operational relationship, respectively (Fruytier 1994; Buitelaar and Vos 1996). The first refers to the well-known concept of employment relationship (employment conditions and internal labour relations), the second to the production organisation (work-place set-up, task structure).

In the Netherlands, the former concept partially relates to a generally accepted idea about de-centralisation and differentiation in the field of labour relations. It goes back to Reynaerts (1985) and even much earlier to Ter Hoeven (1972). They concluded that labour relations in our country would increasingly grow into a fragmented, pluralistic transaction model, with as main trends de-centralisation and differentiation, i.e. more and more firm-level transactions and negotiations. Customised elaboration of collective agreements in every enterprise, and also increasing numbers of corporate-level agreements would be the result. Their prediction has proven valid, since we have actually witnessed such developments during recent decades (Faase et al. 1995; Van Hoof 1995). This decomposition of labour relations on the macro- and meso-level consequently resulted in labour and employment relationships becoming more significant at the enterprise level. Therefore these concepts play, at least in the Netherlands, a meaningful role in relation to the very organisation of work in production and service. Rapidly changing production structures, and therefore flexible contracts and employability claims are current practice.

The above distinction between the contractual and operational relationship not only relates to this meso–micro move, but also, and maybe even more, to a couple of scientific main streams that we have known for at least a decade already. Some well-known notions are flexibility, mobility, internal labour market, self-regulation, segmentation, autonomy, re-design, flexible labour relations, production structure, and organisational renewal. They all stem from current theories, particularly on the work organisation. The two main flows that can be distinguished in this respect are a modern and extended version of the old labour process approach, and a fully re-thought variant of the old sociotechnical mode of thinking and revising production situations. The former draws on Piore and Sabel (1984) and Kern and Schumann (1984), and in the Netherlands on e.g. Buitelaar et al. (1988) and Dankbaar (1993); the latter on e.g. Kuipers and Van Amelsvoort (1990) and in particular De Sitter (1987, 1994). The former preferably addresses the employment relationship and its inherent contractual relations, but also employee relations, joint-consultation, co-determination, and, of course, employability (Gaspersz and Ott 1996). The latter is highly dedicated to overhaul, and so to improving the traditional production organisation and to developing adequate theories for that purpose. As a result, new production concepts, flexible specialisation, sociotechnical theory, team-based work, responsible autonomy, and re-design of production set-up are often under discussion (Vaas 1995), even under severe criticism (Vos and Buitelaar 1996).

Recently, several attempts have been made to compare and confront, or even to link or reconcile the two paradigms (Fruytier 1994; Ten Have 1993; Van der Zwaan 1995;

Huijgen and Pot 1995). The well-known Dutch polemic between the labour process proponents and sociotechnical systems' adherents in 1989 and 1990 played a major role in refining the concepts, accentuating the positions, and feeding the debate. An important book in this respect seems to be Buitelaar and Vos (1996), who conducted some intriguing (conceptual) analyses and remarkable conclusions. One of their noteworthy observations is that despite the many sweeping descriptions of so-called new production concepts, the 'lengthened conveyor belt' cannot be overlooked in very many cases. According to these authors, therefore, widespread speculation and even wishful thinking appears to influence what we expect to see in reality.

We stress this dichotomy here, because it clearly reveals a noteworthy threefold Dutch trend in the study of organisations. This is, first, pragmatism, i.e. utilisation and application of theories; second, nevertheless, non-stop theory development; and, third, frequently focusing on work processes and work structures, especially at the shop-floor level. These seem to be significant characteristics of the Dutch scene. That is why we shall use these categories in our subsequent analysis of the two scientific journals.

5.3. TVA and GO

When applying the above dichotomy on the content of the articles of the three volumes of *TVA* we conclude the following. Out of the 76 articles, approximately 30 deal with meso- and macro-issues of labour relations, regional and national labour markets, social security on national and sectoral levels, union membership in certain aspects and areas, and the like. The remaining 46 consist of a minority (13 at most) devoted to the work organisation and related items, such as new production concepts, working conditions, all-round group work, etc. Whereas the far greater part (33) discusses the employment relationship, i.e. employee relations (internal labour relations) and contractual relations (employment conditions: remuneration and training), segregation of women, ethnicity, elderly workers, mobility inside the firm, etc. The frequencies over the years 1993 to 1995 are shown in Table 1. For reasons of comparison, the same data over the period 1987 to 1991 have been added. They seem to indicate a gradual move towards inside-firm items.

Table 1. Content of articles of TVA '87-'91, '93-'95

	1993	*1994*	*1995*	*Total '93 - '95*	*Total '87-'91*
Work organisation (operational relations)	6	2	6	13 (17%)	(20)
Employment relationship (contractual relations)	13	11	8	33 (43%)	(45)
Labour market and labour relations	8	11	11	30 (40%)	(65)
Total	27	24	25	76 (100%)	(130)

We will return to these figures below.

An attempt to mould the contents of *GO* into the category system of *TVA* might look artificial. The subjects and theoretical perspectives seem to diverge to such an extent, that the foregoing categorisation does not seem to fit here. Nevertheless, we have made an attempt. The result can be found in Table 2. In addition, given minimal interpretative freedom, we succeeded in putting 64 out of 92 articles (over the years 1993-1995) into the categories (entries) of 'work organisation' and 'employment relationship'. We consider these two entries, as far as content is concerned, to be rather comparable over the two journals. It does not hold for the third entry—'rest'. The articles under this heading (see Table 2) do not compare with those under the heading 'labour market' and 'labour relations' in the first table.

Table 2. Content of articles of GO, '93-'95

	1993	*1994*	*1995*	*Total '93 - '95*
Work organisation (operational relations)	7	12	5	24 (26%)
Employment relationship (contractual relations)	15	9	16	40 (44%)
Rest (see text concerned)	9	9	10	28 (30%)
Total	31	30	31	92 (100%)

The *GO* articles on work organisation in Table 2 comprise subjects such as job design, job demand control, job motivation, job evaluation, job characteristics, leadership, self-regulation, and empowerment, but also knowledge management and organisational change theory. Therefore, Karasek as well as Hackman and Oldham models occur frequently, as do Argyris and Schön-like organisational development models. On the other hand, the 'employment relations' category (Table 2) contains articles on employee mobility, absenteeism, working conditions and compensation, stereotypes with respect to elderly, female and ethnic workers, output-related pay, health and safety, education and training, multifunctionality, conflict management, gender relations, etc.

Taking into account that theoretical perspectives of *TVA* and *GO* differ, i.e. generally speaking sociological versus (socio)psychological concepts, and taking into consideration, that the *GO* focus is more on small groups and individuals, it is not surprising that at least two thirds of the *GO* articles (64 out of 92) deal with micro-subjects. This compares by and large to *TVA* proportions. Similarly, the proportional distribution of the articles over 'work organisation' and 'employment relationship' is weighted heavily towards the latter, whereas 'work organisation' seems to be a little stronger in *GO*, as might be expected from our earlier explanation. Unfortunately, the relevant data for the period 1987-1991, are not available here, so we cannot illustrate any parallel developments towards with *TVA*, to show an increase in inside-firm interests.

Finally, we would like to restate our observation that the two journals differ essentially in theoretical outlook, as illustrated by the 'rest' category (in Table 2) dealing with e.g. assessment centres, lie detection, social comparison, construct validity of concepts such as conservatism or Rotterian control, stress, and the like. This means that we must not continue our comparative endeavours too far. However, our general conclusion is that the two journals, in principle, and for a significant part, deal with the same subjects in the field of 'employment relationship' and 'work organisation', however complementary they may be, and complementary, we mean: different in theoretical perspective, but nevertheless challenging, inviting integrative efforts.

5.4. Trends in core journals

As we can see in the first table (*TVA*), meso- and macro-issues obtain the reasonably high score of two fifths of all articles. This proportion is 10 per cent lower than the 50 per cent score in the period 1987-1991. We signal a more inward-looking trend, i.e. dealing with problems inside the firm. The macro- and meso-themes are trade union membership and union behaviour, de-centralisation of the labour relations system, differential labour market opportunities of various professions, efficiency of employment agencies, etc. Leaving these subjects aside now, and addressing the company-centred themes, we observe the following, in addition to the above conclusions.

Topics that in *TVA* frequently recur in the domain of contractual relations are: gender, ethnicity and age with a view to job and wage discrimination; and also the subject of vocational and educational training with a view to increasing employment opportunities. Unexpectedly, the items of internal labour market mobility and internal labour market segmentation (dualisation) did not occur very often. They surface no more than participation, absenteeism and co-determination, which seem to be out-of-date issues at present.

With respect to the operational-relations items, the most popular seem to be work load, quality of working life, and poorly paid manual labour, though they only get a relatively moderate score totalling 13 and 20, as opposed to 33 and 45 in the other domain. The same, and even somewhat less, holds for group work, new organisation concepts, and task integration. Meanwhile, technology, automation and surely typologies of production systems hardly come up. They also seem to have disappeared from the present agenda, at least in *TVA*.

Similarly, we can make some general statements about *GO*. Concerning the field of the contractual relations, we can observe that, equally, gender, ethnicity and age are popular items, in contrast to vocational education and training. Internal labour market segmentation and mobility do not enjoy high attention either. On the contrary, in this journal, personnel selection and appraisal, job analysis, work study, and remuneration get all a high score, as well as communication and conflict handling. *TVA* largely neglects these issues.

The quality of working life, stress, work load, and group autonomy also feature in the operational-relations, in addition to, in particular, the classical subjects of work satisfaction and work motivation. Group or team-based work and the so-called new production concepts receive a moderate coverage, mostly appearing under (integrated) organisational development (renewal) or (modern) sociotechnical theory.

We should, however, add three more statements. The first is that cross-national and cross-industry comparisons cover a substantial amount of the *TVA*'s production, whereas they are missing in *GO*. The second is, surprisingly, that personnel or human-resources management is nearly absent in *TVA*, but is given a lot of attention in *GO* (personnel instruments and personnel policy). In *TVA* it seems to be structural, since it was similar in the period 1987-1991, with no more than five such articles. All three of the volumes 1993 to 1995 include only one article comparing personnel management with HRM. The third conclusion is that these volumes of both journals, in contrast to the management journals, comprise few articles on design, development, application, implementation, evaluation, and intervention. This implies that utilisation of research outcomes is not a paramount option and that analysis continues to be the heart in these journals. This particularly applies to *TVA*, whereas it holds less for *GO*. We may conclude that while *TVA* is nearly always involved in analysis, *GO* is much more practice-oriented. The latter demonstrates a clear preference for new production concepts, but also a continued interest in those subjects already preferred by sociologists in the seventies, such as leadership and motivation.

5.5. *Conclusions*

Having analysed and interpreted the data, we will now attempt to check all that we have learned from the four journals, against the eight hypotheses formulated in Section 3. The outcomes, given in Table 4 below, show that a majority of cells of the journals (first four columns) confirm the hypotheses. Only 7 cells show a minus sign, and no more than 6 show a plus minus, so 19 out of 32 are positive. Whatever the significance and meaning of these outcomes, it is certainly too early to draw any further conclusions at this point. First we have to look at the contents of dissertations, conference papers, and books.

6. DISSERTATIONS, CONFERENCE PAPERS AND BOOKS

So far we have dealt with journals only, assuming them to adequately represent what is going on in our field of study. This presumption, however, might result in a biased picture in the end. For instance, it may cause us to overlook all the dissertations, monographs, and textbooks published in recent years, and so that we ignore any special themes dealt with there. Dissertations certainly add value to our inventory, i.e. they provide information regarding what is deemed important nowadays. The WESWA conference papers might also be of interest. All these sources constitute the input of the sections to come.

6.1. Dissertations

In this section, an attempt is made to compose a global overview of all completed Ph.D. research over a certain period, although this does not necessarily mirror the whole area of work and organisation. For example, academic supervisors of Ph.D. projects tend to publish on themes that are different from those of their pupils. This is a special reason to check other publications. Another point that should not be overlooked is the fact that a Ph.D. project has a gestation period of four to five years. In this sense, our sample of dissertations is certainly somewhat biased, as their themes tend to reflect the ideas prevalent at the end of the eighties' decade rather than those of the mid-nineties.

An almost complete overview of dissertations is at our disposal via FACTA, a magazine that periodically provides information on recent publications in the social sciences. Under the category of 'Organisation' we find organisation-oriented dissertations published in sociology, psychology, anthropology, economics, education and spatial sciences, but currently (1993-1995) also in business studies and management science, (where 180 dissertations were classified under this category), see Table 3.

Table 3. Dissertations included under the FACTA category 'Organisation'

High frequencies of occurrence	
25	Information management, DSS, automation, EDI, telematics
18	Production and operations management, OR, performance, quality management
16	Consultancy theory and methodology of organisational diagnosis and re-design
13	External labour markets and labour relations, collective agreements
Moderate frequencies of occurrence	
10	International business, corporate governance, cross-cultural management
9	Organisational strategy
9	Internal labour markets
8	Innovation management
8	Team production
8	Gender relations
6	Business logistics
6	Working conditions
6	Career planning
6	Public administration
5	Knowledge management

Low frequencies of occurrence	
3	Personnel management, Human Resource Management, social policy
2	Co-determination
2	Vocational education and training
2	New production concepts (as such
2	Power
1	Remuneration
15	Varia: social security
180	Total number of dissertations

The first section—high frequencies of occurrence—largely confirms some previously assessed trends. The second shows moderate occurrences, ones that are worth being looked at, one by one. The third shows low occurrences for each item, and therefore indicates areas where further research and explanation are needed.

6.2. WESWA conference papers

The last WESWA conference (1996) constitutes an extra source of information. The conference featured two types of papers, first some state-of-the-art papers on eight well-known themes in the field of labour, and second a large number of mostly empirical research papers in a variety of areas, again concerning a great many aspects of labour.

Going through the papers on work and organisation, we observe that they elaborate on the strategies and processes conditioning and accompanying organisational change, the empirical relationship between quality of working life (independent variable) and innovation (dependent variable), a systems theoretical underpinning of the so-called whole-task group idea, a methodology for comparative evaluations of shop-floor working teams, loyalty and commitment issues in relation to the concept of employability and its consequent employment contracts, the growth and decline of management fads such as 'lean and mean', a comparative assessment of production control models (MRP, Manufacturing Resources Planning) and modern sociotechnical theory, a critical analysis of the sociotechnical premises and assumptions, improvement processes in organisations in relation to operational processes and its problem potential, the introduction of telematics in road transport and the required organisational alignments, and finally the implementation of new production concepts in the banking sector.

We would like to conclude that these descriptions certainly do not contradict our previous observations. On the contrary, little by little they add to the plausibility of most of our hypotheses. Table 4 shows an overview of the scores (see below).

Table 4. Journals and other publications and the 8 hypotheses

	M&O	*BK*	*TVA*	*GO*	*Diss.*	*WESWA*	*Books*
1. Utilisation	+	+	-	+	+	+	+
2. Micro-systems	-		+	+	+	+	+
3. Supra-systems	+	+		-	+		-
4. Process and change	+	+			+	+	+
5. Multiple theory			+	+		+	+
6. Harmony approach	+	+	-	-	-	-	+
7. New concepts	-	+	+	+	+	+	+
8. Qualitative methodology	-	+	+	+	+	+	+

6.3. Books on work and organisation

While referring to our evaluation in Table 4, we will now explain how recent Dutch publications score on each of the eight parameters.

As regards to the utilisation issue, the trend is obvious. Teaching programmes in management education are booming. University faculties and academic chairs of the sociology of work and organisational sociology are dying away, only to be substituted by as many faculties and chairs of management called e.g. HRM, organisation theory, intervention or strategy. As already concluded, the applied nature of most of the dissertations is unmistakable. Equally, in the many books dealing with new organisational concepts, particularly those related to sociotechnics, the drive towards applied and action research appears to be irresistible. The popularity of re-design of work organisation theory is symbolic of this trend (Christis 1998; De Sitter 1994; Huijgen and Pot 1995; Van Eijnatten 1996; Van Hooft 1996; Vos and Buitelaar 1996; Van der Zwaan 1997).

Second, as far as the micro-system label is concerned, the overwhelming interest in self-managing work teams, implying group dynamics, is no less undeniable. We can mention, e.g., Van Amelsvoort (1996), Van Amelsvoort and Scholtes (1995), Boonstra et al. (1996), Van Eijnatten (1996), Haak (1994), Hoogerwerf (1998), Peeters (1994), De Leede (1997), Molleman 1994), Simonse (1995, 1998), and Verkerk et al. (1997). Apart from this development, we may not overlook another theoretical mainstream at micro-system level, which is entirely unrelated. The productive and respected Inter-university Centre of Sociology (Batenburg 1991; Wielers 1991; Van der Meer 1993; Glebbeek 1993; Blumberg 1997; ICS 1995, 1997), which draws strongly on economic organisation theory (rational choice, agency and transaction cost theory), particularly favours the rational actor approach. It seems, however, to be concentrated in this research school and a few business economics departments such as Maastricht (e.g. Wolfs 1992 and Schwan 1993) and a substantial group at Tilburg. This theory, so focused on individual behaviour that it might be 'accused' of far-reaching atomism or reductionism (see Lammers 1997 et al. p: 449), seems to be of limited use as a theory on (specifically) organisations.

With respect to this second point of micro-system orientation, it is important to note that a substantial interest has been shown recently in de-centralisation and autonomy. Lammers et al. (1997) covers many pages in describing the potential, as well as the actual impact of organisational sociology on the theory of design and implementation. Although he admits that its contribution to the very design theory has been limited (p. 631), he clearly observes a trend stipulating the importance of one particular principle of organising, i.e. the 'optimal balance or tension between autonomy and dependency' and stressing the strong interest in the issue of de-centralisation, by referring to such authors as Burger (1992), Kastelein (1990), Mastenbroek (1996), De Sitter (1994). We can consider this trend in relation to the above emphasis on micro-systems. Essentially, the traditional top-down idea of de-centralisation has been replaced by the bottom-up notions of self-regulation. Both concepts, however, remain largely concurrent, and so at least partly identical.

Thirdly, the category of supra-systems is hard to come across in the realm of Dutch books. We saw above that networks, inter-organisational relationships and cooperation enjoy a paramount position in management journals as well as in dissertations. Although the closely related subject of innovation is highly popular (e.g. Dhondt and Vaas 1996), it is not frequently coupled with inter-organisational networks, at least not in books. The explanation is that during the eighties and nineties organisational sociology in the Netherlands lost interest in inter-organisational networks in favour of new perspectives such as 'explanatory' or 'rational choice' sociology, and 'neo-institutionalist' approaches from business economics (Lammers 1997), except for a few studies such as Godfroij (1995), Mijs (1989), and Van der Zwaan (1993). Meanwhile, the ideas of networks, alliances and partnership (Nooteboom 1994) became popular in the managerial fields of innovation, logistics and strategy, rather than in relation to work and organisation.

Certainly, the issues of process and change (fourth item) are nowadays preferred far more highly than structure approaches. Good examples are Boonstra et al. (1996); Doorewaard and De Nijs 1998); Van Eijnatten (1996); Hoogerwerf (1998); De Leeuw (1994); and Schuring (1997). Even complex theoretical ideas by Giddens (1990) are used in an attempt to connect process and structure (Meeus 1994). That organisational 'dynamics' tended to outclass organisational 'statics' then can be read in Lammers et al. (1997: 636-661), where he refers to Boonstra (1991), De Leeuw (1994), Mastenbroek (1996), Ramondt (1996) and Cozijnse and Vrakking (1995), so as to show the shift from expert structure approaches to process models, to change and development approaches and, in particular, to such notions as coaching, negotiation, participatory consultation, organisational learning, and conflict management.

Multiple theory or theory comparison, as the fifth item, can also be given a plus sign in Table 4. Not only did the debate between labour process and sociotechnics proponents take up a remarkable amount of space in the *TVA* journal (1989 and 1990), but the discussion has recently been reopened and repeated in Huijgen and Pot (1995) and Van der Zwaan (1997). As far as the books are concerned, Ten Have (1993) confronted sociotechnical with transaction cost theory, Fruytier (1994) sociotechnical with labour process theory, Meeus (1994) sociotechnical with structuration theory, Van der Zwaan (1995) sociotechnical with labour process theory, Vos and Buitelaar (1997) sociotechnical with transaction cost theory, and, very recently, Hoogerwerf (1998) complemented sociotechnical with organisational learning theory, and finally Christis (1998) critically reviewed and compared a number of theories to gain an understanding of the mechanisms of organisational stress. MST is mostly a part of the analysis. Apparently, it provides 'a common theoretical core ..., that ... can make an important contribution both in explaining problems and in designing better organisations' (Van Hees et al. 1995; De Witte and Van der Zwaan 1998).

Lammers, particularly in his 1990 and 1993 publications and in Lammers et al. (1997) has made some efforts to categorise the myriad of existing theories, and he comes to the conclusion that there is no one grand theory, but two general perspectives, a systems and a parties model. Whereas Lammers claims that these two paradigms can be considered complimentary, and can be utilised in research as such, Kieser (1995) is not convinced that the ongoing process of theoretical diversification will or can be stopped anywhere. Schreuder and Van Witteloostuijn (1992) claim that the 'confrontation of approaches can lead to theoretical progress' (Van Hees 1995), whereas Godfroij (1995) agrees with Kieser (1995) in accepting the inevitability of an ever-increasing diversity, advocating instead in-depth research on so-called 'crystallisation points' such as innovation, organisation of labour, and HRM. Therefore we see a vivid discussion on theory as such, even though the conclusions are as yet ambiguous.

As to the sixth item of harmony models versus parties, coalition, conflict and power approaches, our position is as follows. We would like to follow Lammers et al. (1997) where he describes Mastenbroek's (1993, 1996) notions of organisational parties and their power relationships, their bargaining processes and conflict management (pp. 642, 658). However, we tend to agree more with his next statement (see p. 661) in which he says that Boonstra et al. (1996) use 'a fairly harmonious socio-cultural systems model'. This, after all, is exactly what all the sociotechnical literature is about! It demonstrates peace, consensus, harmony and congruence, rather than portraying parties that are difficult to reconcile. This bias towards harmony seems to characterise all literature focusing on applying theory, even though the presence of all kinds of 'resistance to change' may be acknowledged.

The seventh item of the new labour and organisation concepts can, undoubtedly, be given a plus mark, since all these new concepts appear to feature in some way in the bulk of the applied literature. Empowement, lean production, business process re-design, the mini-company, self-managing teams, sociotechnics, control capacity, organisational learning and knowledge management are referred to and compared rather often (Benders 1993; Dankbaar 1996; Van Hooft 1996; Dhondt and Vaas 1996; Boonstra et al. 1996; Van Eijnatten 1996). The first issue of the *BK* journal in 1998 will be devoted to new production concepts!

Finally, the subject of methodology can be described as a mirror of all the above trends. There is a abundant literature in this area (Den Hertog and Van Sluijs 1995; Hutjes and Van Buuren 1992; Jonker 1990; De Leeuw 1996; Ramondt 1996; Verschuren and Doorewaard 1995; Van der Zwaan 1995).

They all advocate the study of processes, in-depth studies of single or multiple cases, preferably following an interpretative 'qualitative' approach, rather than applying so-called 'quantitative' methods. Good examples are the dissertations by Roberts (1993) and Benschop (1996).

7. CONCLUSIONS

First, we present a summary, Table 5, which is based on the above tables. Thereafter, we provide an interpretation of the main current developments, as we observed so far. This interpretation is displayed in Figure 2. This figure sketches the main themes and the relationships, that we have found between them in this study of trends. Finally, we extend Figure 1 by adding the global trends already mentioned, and this results in Figure 3.

Table 5. Overall assessment of the hypotheses

	+	±	-	*Overall assessment*
1. Utilisation	6	0	1	+
2. Micro-systems	5	1	1	+
3. Supra-systems	3	2	2	-
4. Process and change	5	2	0	+
5. Multiple theory	4	3	0	?
6. Harmony approach	3	0	4	-
7. New concepts	6	0	1	+
8. Qualitative methodology	6	0	1	+

Five propositions can be considered as 'confirmed': the 'hypotheses' on utilisation, micro-systems, process and change, new concepts, and methodology. The few deviant observations in these five issues are mainly due to the nature of the journals, and so appear to be irrelevant to the issue concerned. This reflects the journals' specialisation or differentiation.

As for the three remaining propositions, we would claim that 'multiple theory' is going in the right direction, 'supra-systems', remains however, rather ambiguous, despite three 'correct' scores; and the 'harmony approach' should be definitely rejected, although three cases conform with the 'hypothesis'. Our conclusion is that these three propositions are clearly not underwritten by the findings.

Our task, finally, is to interpret these outcomes. The visualisation in Figure 2 can be of help here.

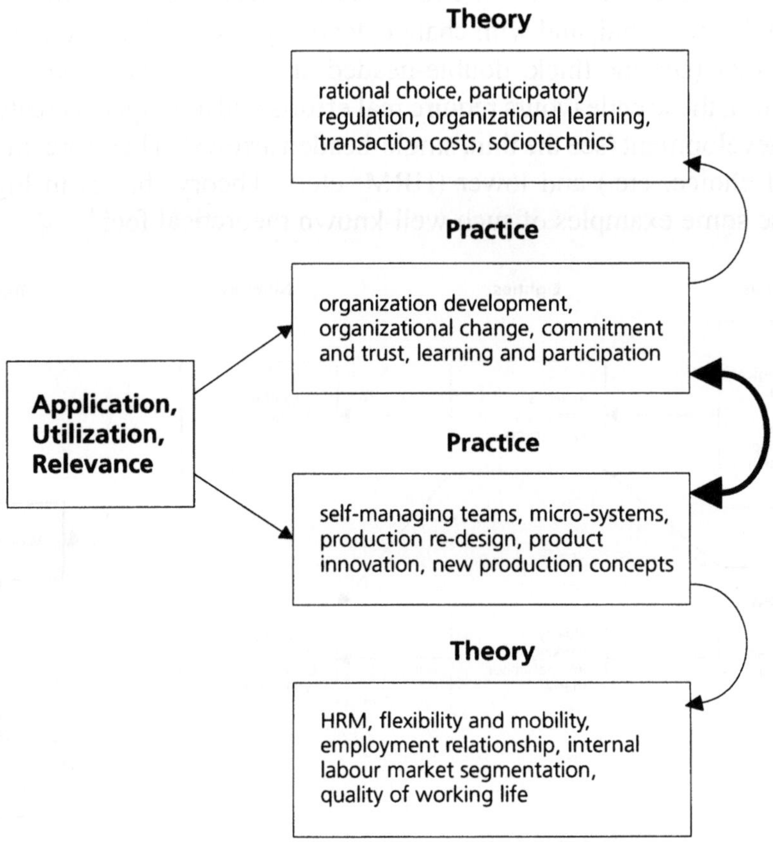

Figure 2. Two practice areas and two theory areas

The first step in explaining this figure can be made by pointing to the plus-scores in the last column of Table 5. They tell us that utilisation at the micro-system level is a crucial endeavour, and that a processual and change orientation is highly valued. See the two boxes in Figure 2 entitled 'Practice'! They contain a number of closely related issues that are highly popular in practice and, therefore frequently appear in the literature. It is for this very reason that we are in need of adequate theory and it explains why so much attention has to be paid to new concepts, multiple theory, methodology, etc. (see Table 5), which, as 'theoretical' endeavours, are represented in the box headed 'Theory' in Figure 2. In other words, practical ambitions or real-life shop-floor issues require theoretical underpinning.

Hence, in Figure 2, firstly we actually claim that application and relevance are linked, in particular, with the two 'Practice' areas of work teams and team work on the one hand, and with change, learning and participation processes on the other (see the thick, double-headed arrow). Secondly, we conclude that, in turn, these endeavours require real efforts and attempts to create (new) theory development (see the thin, single-headed arrows). Therefore, the upper (rational choice, etc.) and lower (HRM, etc.) 'Theory' boxes in Figure 2, comprise some examples of such well-known theoretical foci.

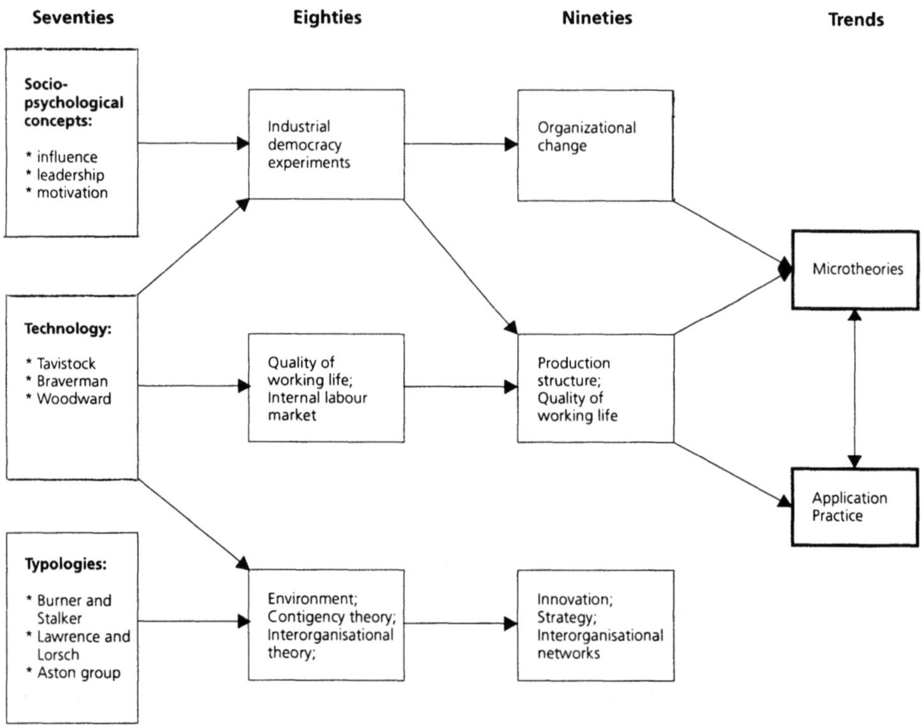

Figure 3. Developments in work and organisation theory and current trends

Another way of visualising what nowadays takes place in the field can be found in Figure 3. It forms a simple extension of Figure 1 in the second section. Figure 1 showed our idea of how work and organisation theory developed over three decades. Figure 3, now, adds in the right-hand column (under 'Trends') what we think the situation will be by the end of the century. We envisage a growing preference for micro-approaches, an intensified search for relevance, and an even closer interaction between the two. This implies that, in line with the foregoing analysis, the nineties' characteristics (Figures 1 and 3) have been further specified and profiled accordingly to the majority of our propositions.

Rejected 'hypotheses' (or propositions), however, are always significant. First, there is our supra-system proposition. This was not underscored, at least not from our 'sources and frames of reference' (see the title of Section 4). We can only explain it by referring to our conclusion about the drift to business economics, reached in Section 6.3.

The subject of supra-systems hardly comes to the fore in the Dutch publications included in our survey. Networks, strategy, inter-organisational relationships and cooperation (e.g. 'partnership') and the related theme of innovation only occupy a central position in a couple of management journals and dissertations, and not in the core journals or in the textbooks. The explanation could be that, during the eighties and nineties, organisational and labour sociology in the Netherlands became disinterested to some extent in inter-organisational networks, favouring, instead, new perspectives such as 'explanatory sociology', 'rational choice' theory, and 'neo-institutionalist' approaches originating from, and flourishing within, business economics (Lammers et al. 1997). The ideas of networks, alliances, partnership, cooperation and competition shifted, therefore, to adjacent management disciplines (industrial organisation, logistics, strategy), and no longer formed a substantial part of the work and organisation perspective.

As far as the harmony approach is concerned, it seems that the application-oriented journals and books indeed tend to be written mainly in terms of the harmony and compatibility of parties, whereas the more academic-analytic literature continues to study competing interests and conflicts. Perhaps the same might be true of what was called 'multiple theory', in that the more academic and less practice oriented colleagues are using a multiplicity and diversity of theories.

Finally, we would like to summarise our findings by making use of an integrated re-design of Lammers' (1993) and Berting's (1992) conceptual schemes (see Figure 4). The top end of the vertical axis represents structuralism and system models, whereas the bottom end displays individualism, process approaches, and party or actor models. The horizontal axis places the concepts of conflict, dissensus and competition (on the left end) in opposition to consensus, harmony and cooperation. What we observed here were rather strong downward forces, accompanied with slight pressures from left to right.

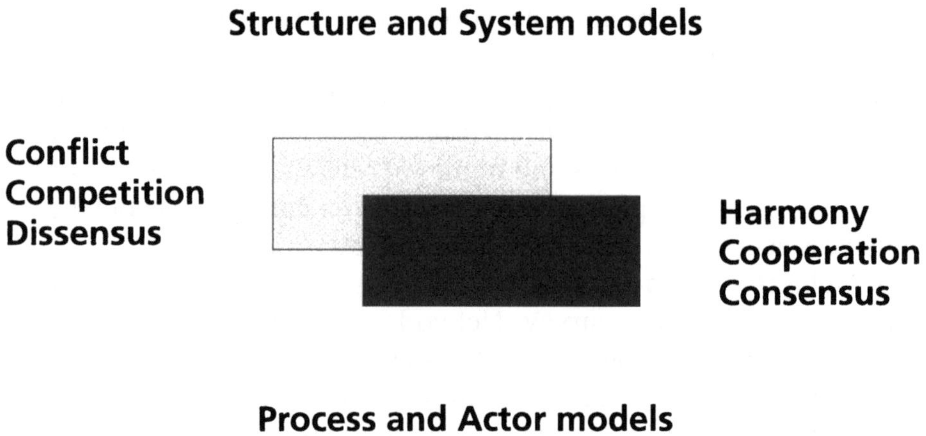

Figure 4. Trends in terms of two well-known dimensions / paradigms

Most importantly, however, we must repeat that our sources, taken together, allow us to draw two clear conclusions. The first is that subjectivist, interpretationist and even constructivist approaches are now being adopted to the same extent as objectivist, rationalist and/or neo-positivist ones. The second conclusion is that the quest for relevance and intervention is growing, and that very soon it might prevail over the search for true insight, based on empirical analysis.

NOTES

[1] This article highly benefitted from the critical comments made by Bert van Hees and Fred Huijgen on an earlier version and for this I am very grateful. Also included in these acknowledgements is the help given by Tom Mijs, Gerard Evers, Joop Schippers and Marco de Witte.

[2] These data (especially from the journals) will be presented in much more detail than is usual in a trend report. This implies that the reader need not necessarily go through the Sections 5.1 to 5.4, which for this reason, are printed in a smaller type.

3 The main chapters in Berting and De Sitter (1971), which deal with the determinants and effects of work satisfaction, such as leadership, motivation, co-determination and related topics, are a good example.

4 See also the 1989 and 1990 volumes of *TVA*.

REFERENCES

Amelsvoort, P. van and G. Scholtes, 1995. *Zelfsturende teams; Ontwerpen, invoeren en begeleiden* (Self-managing teams; design, implementation and Support), Vlijmen, ST-Groep.

Amelsvoort, P. van, 1996. *Het programmeren en regisseren van veranderingsprocessen* (Programming and producing change processes), Vlijmen, ST-Groep.

Batenburg, R.S., 1991. *Automatisering in bedrijf* (Automation in company practice), Amsterdam, Thesis Publishers.

Benders, J., 1993. *Optional options; Work design and manufacturing automation*, Aldershot UK, Avebury.

Benschop, Y., 1996. *De mantel der gelijkheid; Gender in organisaties* (Seeming equality; gender in organisations), diss. 9 december 1996 KUN Nijmegen, Assen, Van Gorcum.

Berting, J. and L.U. de Sitter, 1971. *Arbeidssatisfactie, theorie, methodiek, feiten* (Quality of working life; theory, methods and facts), Assen, Van Gorcum.

Berting, J., 1992. *De technologische factor; Een sociaal-wetenschappelijke analyse* (The factor of technology; a social-science analysis), Rotterdam, Acad. Boekencentrum, RISBO.

Blumberg, B.F., 1997. *Das Management von Technologiekooperationen* (The management of collaboration on technology), Amsterdam, Thesis Publishers.

Boonstra, J.J., 1991. *Integrale organisatie-ontwikkeling* (Integrated organisation development), Utrecht, Lemma.

Boonstra, J.J., H.O. Steensma and M.I. Demeninth (eds.), 1996. *Ontwerpen en ontwikkelen van organisaties; Theorie en praktijk van complexe veranderingsprocessen* (Designing and developing organisations; the theory and practice of complex change processes), Utrecht, De Tijdstroom.

Buitelaar, W.L., (ed.), 1988. *Technology at work; Labour studies in England, Germany and the Netherlands*, Avebury.

Burger, Y., 1992. *Tussen realiteit en retoriek* (Realities and rhetorics), Delft, Eburon.

Burns, T. and G.M. Stalker, 1961. *The management of innovation*, London, Tavistock.

Christis, J., 1998. *Arbeid, organisatie en stress* (Work, organisation and stress), diss. UvA 2 februari 1998, Amsterdam, Het Spinhuis.

Cozijnsen, A.J. and W. Vrakking, 1995. *Ontwerp en invoering; Strategieën voor organisatieverandering* (Design and implementation; strategies of organisational change), Alphen a/d Rijn, Samsom.

Dankbaar, B., 1993. *Economic Crisis and Institutional Change*, Maastricht University Press.

Dankbaar, B., 1996. *Organiseren in een turbulente omgeving* (Organising in turbulent environments), oratie KUN 13 december 1996, Nijmegen.
Dhondt, S. and F. Vaas et al., 1996. *Innovatie en arbeid* (Innovation and labour), Min. van SZW/TNO, Den Haag, VUGA.
Doorewaard, H. and W. de Nijs, 1998. *Organisatieontwikkeling en human resource management* (Organisational development and HRM), Utrecht, Lemma.
Eijnatten, F.M. van, 1995. *Als het maar stroomt* (Let's have production flow!), Assen, Van Gorcum.
Eijnatten, F. M. van, 1996. *Sociotechnisch ontwerpen* (Designing socio-technically), Utrecht, Lemma.
Faase, L. et al., 1995. *Nieuwe breukvlakken in het arbeidsbestel* (New flaws in the labour relations system), Utrecht, De Tijdstroom.
Faase, L., M. Ott and C.J. Vos, 1995. 'Terugblik en voorbeschouwing' (In retrospect as well as prospect), in: L. Faase et al., pp. 11-27.
Fruytier, B., 1994. *Organisatieverandering en het probleem van de Baron von Münchhausen* (Organisational change and the Baron of Münchhausen's problem), Tilburg University Press.
Gaspersz, J. and M. Ott, 1996. *Management of Employability*, Assen, Van Gorcum.
Gils, M.R. van, 1978. 'De organisatie van organisaties', *M&O; Tijdschrift voor Organisatiekunde*: 9-31.
Giddens, A., 1990. *The Consequences of Modernity*, Cambridge Polity Press.
Glebbeek, A., 1993. *Perspectieven op loopbanen* (Career concepts), diss. RUG, Groningen.
Godfroij, A., 1981. *Netwerken van organisaties* (Networks of organisations), VUGA, Den Haag.
Godfroij, A., 1995. 'Crystallisation Points in Organisation Theory', in: G.B. van Hees et al., *Work from the Lowlands*, pp. 135-156.
Haak, A., 1994. *Dutch Sociotechnical Design and Practice*, Assen, Van Gorcum.
Have, K. ten, 1993. *Markt, organisatie en personeel* (Markets, organisation and personnel), Tilburg University Press.
Hees, G.B. van et al., 1995. *Work from the Lowlands; Labour and Organisation Research*, Amsterdam, SISWO publ. 392.
Hees, G.B. et al., 1995. 'Recent Developments in Dutch Labour and Organisation Studies', in: G.B. van Hees et al., *Work from the Lowlands*, pp. i-xiii.
Hertog, F. den and E. van Sluijs, 1995. *Onderzoek in organisaties; Een methodologische reisgids* (Research in organisations; a travel guide in methodology), Assen, Van Gorcum.
Hoeven, P.J.A. ter, (ed.), 1972. *Breukvlakken in het arbeidsbestel* (Flaws in the labour relations system), Alphen a/d Rijn, Samsom.
Hoof, J.J. van, 1995. 'Arbeidsbestel op een keerpunt' (Labour relations at a turning point), in: L. Faase et al., pp. 28-47.
Hoof, J.J. van, 1987. *De arbeidsmarkt als arena* (Labour markets as arenas), Amsterdam, SUA.

Hooft, M. van, 1996. *Synergetisch produceren in de praktijk; Toepassingen van structuurbouw* (The practice of synergistic production; architectural applications, Van Gorcum.

Hoogerwerf, L., 1998. *Opnieuw leren organiseren* (Re-learning how to organise), diss. KUN, Nijmegen, Lemma.

Huijgen, F. and F.D. Pot, 1995. *Verklaren en ontwerpen van produktieprocessen* (Explanation and design of production processes), Amsterdam, SISWO-publ. nr. 387.

Hutjes, J.M. and J.A. van Buuren, 1992. *De gevalstudie; Strategie voor kwalitatief onderzoek* (Case studies; strategies of qualitative research), Meppel/Heerlen, Boom/OU.

ICS, 1995. *Annual Report of the ICS for Social Science Theory and Methodology*, RU, Dept. of Sociology, Utrecht.

Jonker, J., 1990. *Met mate te meten* (Moderately measurable, Assen, Van Gorcum.

Kastelein, J., 1990. *Modulair organiseren doorgelicht* (An examination of modular-organisation theory, Groningen, Wolters-Noordhoff.

Kern, H. and M. Schumann, 1984. *Das Ende der Arbeidsteilung; Rationalisierung in der Industriellen Produktion*, München, C.H. Beck Verlag.

Kieser, A., 1995. 'Recent Trends in Organisation Theory', in: G.B. van Hees et al., *Work from the Lowlands*, pp. 1-20.

Klaveren, M. van, 1994. *Trends en keuzes in het onderzoek naar de kwaliteit van de arbeid* (Trends and choices in research on the quality of working life), Amsterdam, SISWO-publ. nr. 381.

Klaveren, M. van and S. Kooistra (eds.), 1991. *Sociaal ontwerpen; Werknemers beïnvloeden vormgeving en organisatie van hun werk* (Designing social systems; employees influence their work set-up), Utrecht, Jan van Arkel.

Kluytmans, F. and C. Hancké, 1994. *Leerboek personeelsmanagement* (Textbook personnel management), Deventer/Heerlen, Kluwer/OU.

Kluytmans, F. and W. Van der Meeren, (eds.), 1995. *Management van human resources* (The management of HRM), Deventer/Heerlen, Kluwer/OU.

Koot, W.T.M., 1980. *Analyse van organisatiestructuren* (The analysis of organisation structures), Alphen a/d Rijn, Samsom.

Kremer, M., 1996. *Onbetaalde arbeid; onbekende arbeid* (Un-paid labour; un-known labour), WESWA Conference 12/13 November 1996.

Kuipers, H. and P. van Amelsvoort, 1990. *Slagvaardig organiseren; Inleiding in de sociotechniek als integrale ontwerpleer* (Alertness in organising; introduction into sociotechnics as an integrated design theory), Kluwer.

Lammers, C.J., 1990. 'Sociology of Organisations around the Globe', *Organisation Studies* 11: 179-206.

Lammers, C.J., 1993. *Organiseren van bovenaf en van onderop* (Top-down and bottom-up organising), Het Spectrum, Aula.

Lammers, C.J., 1997. *Organisaties vergelijkenderwijs* (Comparative organisations), Aula, Het Spectrum, (orig.: 1983).

Lawrence, P.R. and J.W. Lorsch, 1969. *Developing Organisations: Diagnosis and Action*, Reading, Mass. Addison-Wesley.

Leede, J. de, 1997. *Innoveren van onderop* (Bottom-up innovation), diss. UT, Enschede.

Leeuw, A.C.J. de, 1994. *Besturen van veranderingsprocessen* (Governance of change processes), Assen, Van Gorcum.

Leeuw, A.C.J. de, 1996. *Bedrijfskundige methodologie; Management van onderzoek* (Management methodology and management of research), Assen, Van Gorcum.

Looise, J.C. and Paauwe, J., 1996. *State of the Art: HRM*, paper at the WESWA Conference November 1996, recently published in the brand new Dutch journal *Tijdschrift HRM* 1(1998): 1.

Man, H. de, 1988. *Organisational Change in its Context*, Delft, Eburon.

Mastenbroek, W.F.G., 1993. *Macht, organisatie en communicatie* (Power, organisation and communication), Heemstede, Holland Business Publ.

Mastenbroek, W.F.G., 1996. *Conflicthantering en organisatie-ontwikkeling* (Conflict management and organisation development, Alphen a/d Rijn, Samsom, (4de herz. ed.).

Meer, O. van der, 1993. *Verdringing op de Nederlandse arbeidsmarkt* (Crowding-out in the Dutch labour market), diss. RUG/ICS 6 juli 1993, Groningen.

Meeus, M.T.H., 1994. *Informatietechnologie; plaats en betekenis van arbeid* (Information technology; position and meaning of work., diss. KUB, Tilburg.

Mijs, A.A., 1989. 'Ontstaan en levensvatbaarheid van interorganisationele verbanden' (Emergence and viability of inter-organisational networks), *Sociologische Gids* 36: 48-61.

Mok, A.L., 1990. 'Kwaliteit en kwantiteit van de arbeid' (Quality and quantity of work), *Sociologische Gids* 37 (1990): 141-165.

Mok, A.L., 1994. *Arbeid, bedrijf en maatschappij; in het zweet uws aanschijns* (Work, company and society), Deventer, Stenfert Kroese, (2de druk).

Molleman, E., 1994. *Flexibele inzet van personeel* (Flexible deployment of personnel), Deventer, Kluwer.

Nooteboom, B., 1994. *Management of partnership in toeleveren en uitbesteden* (Partnership management in supplying and sub-contracting), Schoonhoven, Academic Service.

Paauwe, J. and J.H. Huijgen, 1996. *Personeelsmanagement in bedrijf* (The practice of personnel management), Alphen a/d Rijn, Samsom.

Peeters, M., 1995. *Groepswerk in sociotechnisch perspectief* (Group work in a socio-technical perspective), Delft, Eburon.

Piore, M.J. and C. Sabel, 1984. *The Second Industrial Divide*, New York, Basic Books.

Post-groep, 1991. *Onderweg naar nieuwe kantoren en fabrieken* (Towards new offices and new factories), Deventer, Kluwer.

Ramondt, J.J., 1996. *Organisatiediagnostiek* (Diagnosis of organisations), Schoonhoven, Academic Service.

Reynaerts, W.H.J., 1985. 'Kantelende posities, arbeidsverhoudingen in een keertijd', in: *Bespiegelingen over de toekomst van de sociale partners* (Reflections on the social partners future), Den Haag, V5, OSA.

Roberts, H.J., 1993. *Accountability and Responsibility*, diss. RL, 9 juli 1993, Univ. Pers Maastricht.

Ruysseveldt, J. van (ed.), 1989. *Kwaliteit van de arbeid; Hedendaagse stromingen* (Quality of working life; contemporary main-streams), Assen, Van Gorcum.
Ruysseveldt, J. van and J. Visser (eds.), 1996. *Industrial relations in Europe, traditions and transitions*. London.
Schreuder, H. and A. van Witteloostuijn, 1992. 'De Ecologie van Organisaties en de Economie van Bedrijven', *M&O: Tijdschrift vor Organisatiekunde* (Organisational ecology and business economics) 46: 250-278.
Schuring, R.W., 1997. *Procesmodellering van dynamiek in organisaties* (Process models and organisational dynamics), diss. UT, Enschede.
Schwan, R., 1993. *Organisationskonfigurationen und Interne Arbeitsmärkte* (Organisational configurations and internal labour markets), diss. 9 juni 1993 RL, Univ. Pers Maastricht.
Simonse, L., 1995. *Loont het? Beoordelen en belonen van zelfsturende teams* (Performance appraisal and remuneration of self-managing teams), Vlijmen, ST-Groep.
Simonse, L., 1998. *Organisatie-ontwikkeling in productcreatie* (Organisation development in product creation; towards a network organisation of teams paralleled by development teams), diss. TUE 15 mei 1998, Eindhoven.
Sitter, L.U. de, 1987. *Het flexibele bedrijf; Integrale aanpak van flexibiliteit, beheersbaarheid en kwaliteit van de arbeid* (The flexible firm; an integrated approach to flexibility, controllability and quality of working life), Deventer, Kluwer.
Sitter, L.U. de, 1994. *Synergetisch produceren; Human resources mobilisation in de productie* (Synergistic production; HR mobilisation in production), Assen, Van Gorcum.
Stein, B. and M.C. de Witte, 1992. *De Januskop van de industriële samenleving* (The Janus face of industrial society), Alphen a/d Rijn, Samsom.
Vaas, S., 1995. 'Nieuwe produktieconcepten; Nieuwe vormen en gedachten over arbeid' (New production concepts; new forms and notions of labour, in: L. Faase et al., pp. 128-134.
Verkerk, M.J., J. de Leede and H.J. van der Tas, 1997. *Marktgericht productiemanagement; Van taakgroep naar mini-company* (Market-oriented production management; from task group to mini-company), Deventer, Kluwer.
Verschuren, P. and H. Doorewaard, 1995. *Het ontwerpen van een onderzoek* (Research designs), Utrecht, Lemma.
Vos, P. and W. Buitelaar, 1996. *Arbeidsorganisatie en arbeidsverhoudingen in beweging* (Work organisation and labour relations on the move), Amsterdam, Welboom.
WESWA Workbook, 1996. *Werkboek WESWA Congres 1996*, 12-13 November 1996, Utrecht.
Wielers, R., 1991. *Selectie en allocatie op de arbeidsmarkt* (Selection and allocation in the labour market), diss. RUG/ICS, 5 december 1991, Groningen.
Witte, M.C. de and A.H. van der Zwaan, 1998. 'Nieuwe productieconcepten' (New production concepts), *Bedrijfskunde* 70: 2 (special issue), in press.
Wolfs, G.L.M., 1992. *Firm Internal Markets in the Netherlands*, diss, RL 10 juni 1992, Maastricht.

Zwaan, A.H. van der, 1993. 'Netwerken: Samenhang en samenwerking in de gezondheidszorg' (Networks, interdependence and cooperation in health care), in: J.A.M. Maarse and I.M. Mur-Veeman, *Beleid en beheer in de gezondheidszorg*, Assen, Van Gorcum.

Zwaan, A.H. van der, 1995. *Organiseren van arbeid; Balanceren tussen hiërarchie en markt* (Organising labour; balancing hierarchy and market), Assen, Van Gorcum.

Zwaan, A.H. van der, 1997. 'Ontwerpen, ontwikkelen en veranderen' (Design, development and change), *Tijdschrift voor Arbeidsvraagstukken* 13(4): 370-384.

Zwaan, A.H. van der and E. Molleman, 1997. 'Self-organising Groups; Conditions and Constraints', *International Journal of Manpower*, in press.

AUTHOR

Prof.dr. A. van der Zwaan
Groningen University, Fac. Management Sciences
P.O. Box 800, 9700 AV Groningen
tel: 050-3633915, fax: 050-3632330
e-mail: a.h.van.der.zwaan@bdk.rug.nl

FROM INEQUALITY TO PLURIFORMITY
Thinking about gender, work and organisations

Yvonne Benschop, Margo Brouns and Jeanne de Bruijn

1. INTRODUCTION

Since the seventies, a steady flow of publications on gender, work and organisations has appeared in the Netherlands. The boundaries of the domain have been explored enthusiastically in the past 25 years. The result is a broad variety of issues studied: from sexual harassment to affirmative action and from paid labour and unpaid care to female entrepreneurs and feminine management. The asymmetries between the sexes have been substantially documented. The persistency of horizontal and vertical sex segregation, the wage gap that still amounts to 25 per cent and the fact that men spend more time on paid work and women on unpaid care illustrate the inequalities that still exist in labour positions (Hooghiemstra and Niphuis-Nell 1993).

Gender and organisations became a research topic in the seventies, due to developments in the Dutch society. The contribution of work to 'the women's question' (Kool-Smit 1967) found its way into the political agenda in the early days of the second feminist wave. Both in society and in academia, the improvement of women's working positions and economic independence became important issues in a land traditionally characterised by a low participation of women in the labour market. In the eighties, there was a substantial increase in female labour participation. Today, an increasing number of organisations are taking initiatives to make full use of the capacities of male and female employees. Many consider the nineties therefore as emancipated times, with freedom of choice for all, whereas Dutch feminists keep questioning the emancipated quality of Dutch society (De Harde Kern 1996). This results in a debate about the desirability and necessity of preferential treatment for women and decreasing support for affirmative action. The relation between gender, work and organisations has heated the discussion throughout the decades, and new impulses are regularly given.

During the past 10 years, conceptualisations of gender have been shifting in women's studies. Research has been conducted from two major fields: women's labour studies, examining sex differences in paid and unpaid work and women's studies, questioning gendered power processes (Brouns and Schokker 1990). While the first field, where visible differences between men and women in organisations are studied, used to be the most popular, gradually, more attention is being paid to the second field of women's studies, where the meaning of gender distinctions and the organisational (power-) processes (re)producing them are studied. These theoretical frameworks on gender are also making their marks on organisation studies. In this chapter, we present an overview of Dutch research on gender and organisations. We take the different conceptualisations of gender that influence interpretations of work and organisations as our point of departure. What questions appear on the research agenda and what explanations are provided? What are the questions that will be developed in the future?

Before presenting an overview of trends in the Dutch research on gender and organisations, we first discuss the position of women in the Netherlands, thereby explaining the context in which theoretical perspectives on gender, work and organisation are developed.

2. WOMEN AND WORK IN THE NETHERLANDS

From the perspective of gender issues, Dutch society is a remarkable case. Compared to other European countries, the general status of women appears to be weak. All labour market statistics show an extremely low percentage of women involved in paid labour. In 1973, only 29 per cent of all women participated in the labour market. In the European Economic Community (EEC), only Ireland had lower participation rates. Between 1973 and 1989, the Dutch percentage increased to the EEC average of 52 per cent (OECD 1991). Even these low figures are somewhat or even misleading, if one examines the real involvement of Dutch women in paid labour. More than 60 per cent of these women do part-time jobs. There is no other country within the EEC, where the majority of women work in part-time jobs (GB 44 per cent, Italy 11 per cent). The Netherlands has the lowest participation rate of all western countries, if the volume of the female labour force is taken into account. One of the reasons why women are only partly involved in paid labour is the lack of day care centres: in 1988 institutionalised places were available for only 2,5 per cent (!) of all children between the ages of 0 to 4 years (Hooghiemstra and Niphuis-Nell 1993). The organisation of child-care is one of the central problems for Dutch women who want to enter the labour market.

In the field of political participation, the picture is quite different. One out of three members of parliament is a woman (Leijenaar 1996). Compared to other European countries this is a relatively high representation of female citizens in political decision making—France 6 per cent, Italy 8 per cent, Denmark 33 per cent; *Women in Decision-making* 1993. The women's movement is also well organised in different branches (liberal, radical) and to a large extent integrated in social institutions.

These contradictory figures concerning women's position are the result of long-standing traditions of specific gender arrangements in the Netherlands. Pot-Buter (1993) indicates that the labour market participation of Dutch women has been exceptionally low from the seventeenth century onwards. These low participation rates are related to the fact that productivity rates in the Netherlands are among the highest in the world (Plantenga 1993). This relative prosperity has allowed women to stay at home for their children, while their husbands earned the family income. This created opportunities to 'put ideology into practice' institutionalising the gendered structure of the bread-winner–care-taker model (Bussemaker and Van Kersbergen 1993). However, recent historical investigations show the incompleteness of Dutch statistics concerning women's labour. Women very often worked in those branches that were not represented in official statistics: they worked on farms, they did household work, and so on. These women contributed to the family income, combining their productive labour with the care for children and the household. As we can see in the statistics mentioned above, this is still general practice in the Netherlands: part-time work enables women to combine paid labour with raising children. A strong ideology surrounds the tasks of women as mothers. Even in the women's movement, child care services are a controversial issue. Whose interests are served if all women participate in paid labour, leaving their children to day-care centres? (Pessers 1994). Is it in the interest of women, of the state, or of modern capitalism? What about the quality of care in a day-care nursery? Is it good enough for the child? For outsiders, these discussions seem somewhat outdated (Braidotti 1993).

However, it is too simplistic to talk about an outmoded debate. A peculiar phenomenon of Dutch society is its history of 'pillarisation', the division of society along the sectarian lines of different (religious) 'blood' groups. For decades, social life was organised along the different pillars. Opposition was pacified by developing separateness. These socio-political groups permeated public as well as private life: churches, schools, and even neighbourhoods and friendships were mainly constructed within the pillars. Catholics went to a catholic church, voted for a catholic party, were members of catholic unions, spent their leisure time at catholic clubs, etc. The same held true for Protestants and socialists. Women played a very important role in this social division: they had their own organisations within the pillars, but they also guarded the boundaries of the pillars by transmitting these traditions to the next generation, guiding and teaching their children. As a result, women as mothers had (and have) a high cultural status in the Netherlands.

These contradictory features of recent history represent two sides of the same coin: Dutch women stayed at home, having a high cultural status as long as they cared for their children and household, and at the same time, they organised themselves within the different pillars. In the late twentieth century, this results in the paradoxical situation of a weak economic position due to low participation rates in the labour market ànd a strongly developed and heterogeneous women's movement, resulting in a relatively strong political position. No wonder, day care is one of the most precarious topics of feminism.

Women's studies in the Netherlands, especially studies about gender and organisation, is rooted in this field of forces, and it has influenced its development profoundly, as we shall see.

3. RESEARCHING GENDER AND ORGANISATIONS

As we mentioned in the introduction, the field of gender, work and organisations is vast. Our discussion is restricted to the terrain of formal labour, as it is performed in organisations. We mainly discuss research projects developed in contemporary sociological studies of work and organisation, although we also consider studies rooted in other disciplines such as management and organisation studies, economics and psychology. Historical studies, however, influential in both women's studies and in organisation studies, are beyond the scope of this article.

The framework used in our analysis of the research questioning gender in work and organisations distinguishes between four research lines.

These four lines have different research topics, phrase the 'problem' differently, give different accounts for gender inequality and highlight particular organisational issues, while ignoring others (cf. Calás and Smircich 1996).

The first two research lines focus on the unequal positions of men and women in organisations. The first line documents the persistence of sex segregation in organisations. The working of the external and internal labour market is considered the primary explanation for the unequal positions of the sexes. Equal opportunity and affirmative action are seen as important strategies to improve the positions of women. The second line explains the unequal positions rather by factors external to the labour market, such as processes of socialisation and individual choices for children, and for the care of children. Here, altering women's choices is seen as a strategy to reduce gender inequalities in the work place.

The third and fourth line of research focus on the simultaneous construction of gender and work, problematising that constructions of femininity are hierarchically ordered to a masculine norm. The third line studies the contributions organisations make to the (re)production of gender. In this line, representations of gender in organisation structures and cultures are analysed. The agenda for change goes well beyond equal opportunities and calls for the transformation of organisational structures and cultures. Finally, the fourth research line contains studies that address the involvement of gender in the definition, organisation and evaluation of work itself. It questions processes of meaning formation concerning masculinity and femininity. It analyses these processes of meaning formation not only as constructions of thought, but also as actual organisational practices with material effects that bring about power inequalities.

The state of the art we are presenting in this article comes from a particular point of view at a particular point of time. Our own work in this field favours theoretical perspectives and issues addressed in the last two research lines. Here, we are using the deconstructionist analytic technique that is central to those lines. This deconstructionist technique is used to reveal author's strategies to highlight particular organisational issues and practices and cover others, by focusing on particular data and interpretations and suppressing or marginalising alternative data and interpretations (Martin and Frost 1996). We use deconstructionism, therefore, to consider the assertions and explanatory claims of the different approaches to the field of gender, work and organisation.

Before turning to the issues and trends in the Dutch debates, we discuss the conceptualisations of the central notions sex and gender, addressing the meaning and scope of both notions, their relation and the way scholars use them as descriptive and analytical categories in the context of work and organisations.

4. SEX AND GENDER

The first author to make a conceptual distinction between sex and gender was Oakley (1972: 58), who stated '"Sex" is a biological term: "gender" a psychological and cultural one'. While the biological sex principally is a dichotomy, enabling only two positions: man and woman, cultural interpretations of gender are multiple. The distinction between the two notions makes it possible to show that it is not the small biological difference that is so significant, but that it is the importance ascribed to that difference in society, that accounts for its major impact (Schwarzer 1976).

The work of Joan Scott—historian—provided an important impulse to the conceptualisation of gender. She wrote '...gender is a constitutive element of social relationships based on perceived differences between the sexes and gender is the primary way of signifying relationships of power' (Scott 1986: 94). These two elements, gender as a regulation principle in the social relationship between of men and women and the connection of gender with power, have become the central elements influencing the knowledge production on gender issues. Scott and others such as Harding (1986) and Hagemann-White (1989) presented layered conceptualisations of gender. Symbols, institutions, and identity are the important layers constituting gender. This makes it possible to analyse not only the factors that bring about, strengthen or reinforce differences between men's and women's positions and careers, but also the underlying structure of opinions, self-evidences and images characterising work and organisations. Gender interferes with other power relations (e.g. manager/employee, mentor/pupil, etc.) This questions the relative importance of gender for the relations between the sexes in specific contexts and results in a plea for pluriformity.

The layered model of gender has also been specified for organisations. Acker (1992) differentiated between four sets of gendered processes concerning the structure and culture of organisations, interactions between organisation members and the way they perceive themselves and others. This model makes it possible to include the implicit and explicit ways in which gender distinctions are (re)produced in the analyses of organisations. This happens under the label of researching the gender sub-text in organisations. The concept of gender sub-text refers to the opaque, power based processes, that systematically (re)produce the gender distinction via a set of organisational and individual arrangements (Benschop 1996).

The concept of gender is promising, because of the implication that it might avoid or even solve problems concerning the concept of sex, and specifically the reproduction of dichotomy. Masculinity and femininity are not thought of as opposites, but as each others conditions. More than sex, an analysis in terms of gender accentuates the processual character of the production of difference in general, including possible interferences with age, ethnicity and socio-cultural background. Finally, gender is considered a broader concept than sex, because it is not restricted to visible differences between women and men, but can also be linked to apparently gender neutral phenomena and institutions (processes, relations, rules, organisations etc., De Bruijn 1991a). The assumption is that masculinity and femininity are constructed within these presumably neutral phenomena.

In the following overview, we will examine how these different theoretical frameworks of gender have influenced Dutch research in organisation studies.

5. RESEARCH LINES

The overview we present here does not make any claim to be exhaustive, we merely intend to sketch the lines along which different aspects of gender, work and organisations are studied in the Netherlands.

5.1. The functioning of the labour market

In this line of research, authors identify differences between the sexes in labour market participation and seek explanations for the inequalities in the work positions of men and women. Not only the external labour market is studied, but the internal labour market of organisations is also investigated. Both the supply and demand side of labour are examined.

With respect to the *supply side*, the neo-classical human capital theory has been an influential theoretical framework. This economic theory relates people's personal capital (education, experience) to their labour positions. That men generally have better positions than women is explained by the investments they have made in themselves. De Jong (1985) showed that the human capital theory provides insufficient explanation for career differences between men and women. She found in her study at a large bank that, even if women and men have similar starting capital in terms of education and experience, after some time, women held lower-level positions, often outside the core business of the bank. Her findings were supported by Van Doorne-Huiskes and Luijkx (1987), who could not explain pay differences by focusing exclusively on the supply side of human capital. They argued that processes on the demand side of the labour market need to be taken into account to explain the differences between the sexes.

One of the theories regarding this *demand side* has been the double labour market theory, or more general, segmentation theory. In this theoretical vision, the labour market is not a homogeneous whole, but consists of several segments that function more or less separately, and where specific rules hold. Tijdens (1989), in her study of sex segregation and allocation mechanisms, pointed to the interest organisations have in these separate segments. The secondary segment is characterised by less challenging work and poorer working conditions. Because of this segment, the organisation can make use of relatively cheap, flexible and often temporary workers. The primary segment, containing attractive work, is reserved for employees in which the organisation wants to invest: these are mainly men. Because of the relation between flexibilisation and segmentation, the segmentation theory keeps providing a useful framework for understanding sex differences in work positions in the Dutch context, where many women do part-time jobs. Organisations create different jobs for women and for men in response to the images of femininity and masculinity (see also the section on 'reproduction of gender in organisation' for the normative and cultural dimensions of these processes).

Van der Burg (1992) indicated in her research on women in academia, the importance of various allocation processes in the diverse segments of the internal labour market. Women are poorly represented in the universities. Nevertheless, the discrimination thesis was not supported with regard to scientific jobs: women were not directly judged on their sex. In the lower echelons, however, sex was one of the major elements in explaining the differences between men and women. Because of their sex, women were appointed to the lower functions. Veldman and Wittink (1990) found that in the higher segments of the labour market, the allocation processes may differ from the lower segments—that women are not directly discriminated against because of their sex—but the result, nevertheless, is the same: they are assigned to the lower jobs and excluded from the core business jobs. They argued that commitment and the willingness to work long hours are still important elements in the internal selection processes. Many women do not meet these criteria (see also the next section on 'external factors').

There is strong interference in women's careers due to the allocation of domestic tasks. Responsibilities at home influence the willingness to invest much time in paid labour, but the reverse is also true. Low quality of work may have a negative effect on career intentions and careers of women. Jorna and Offers (1994) stated that the quality of work of lower educated young women is related to prevailing gender paradigms in the organisations that employ them. Those gender paradigms seem to service the labour organisation: where flexible, temporary workers are needed for routine jobs, it is considered self-evident for women to leave the labour market when a child is born.

An other example is the work of Hooghiemstra (1995), that described the position of one of the weakest groups on the labour market: minority women. Hooghiemstra distinguished between women from different minority groups (women from Surinam, Turkey and Morocco) and analysed their specific labour market positions in the context of the history of their migration and cultural background. Whereas Jorna and Offers compared the position of men and women in the category 'young lower educated worker', Hooghiemstra researched differences between various groups of migrant women and Dutch women.

Considerable attention has been also paid to the sex ratio of (parts) of organisations and the way this influences the evaluation of male and female workers. Kanter's (1977) token theory about the consequences of numerical relations for work behaviour is often cited in this respect, especially when the positions of women in higher and technical jobs are studied (Demenint and Van Disselen 1992; Vaas 1996). Ott's (1985) results indicated that male tokens in the nursing profession profit from their visibility, whereas female tokens in the police force encounter barriers because of their exceptional position. Recent findings about women in exceptional positions (Benschop 1996; Vaas 1996) subscribed to Ott's conclusions and partly refined them. Women are still confronted with the higher demands that accompany the visibility of a token, and this influences the quality of their work. However, their visibility can also be advantageous, because it is noticed when they perform well.

This line of research allows for a better understanding of the contribution that the organisation of work makes to the continuation of societal relations. The functioning of external and internal labour markets contributes to the inequality of the sexes. In the separate segments of the labour market, the organisation of work differs, demanding full time availability and effort in the primary segment and allowing for part-time performance only in the secondary segment. The division of the sexes over those segments reinforces the dominant societal patterns of the bread-winner–care-taker model. The studies concerning women's positions in the primary segment do not refute this pattern either, for they suggest that women in management ranks are still tokens that have to adjust to majority rules.

The studies discussed here concentrate primarily on the functioning and organisation of the external and internal labour market, but outside the labour market, their theoretical explanations also range to individual choices. This brings us to the next line of research.

5.2. External factors

The second line of research we distinguish explains the differences between the sexes in work and organisation by factors outside the work context. Our discussion of this line addresses two theoretical frameworks: the role theory, historically one of the first theories on women and work, and rational choice theory, one of the most influential approaches in this domain.

The role theory has dominated the research on women and work for a long time. Its starting point is the proposition that there are several societal roles, differently distributed over the sexes. Roughly, women are expected to get married, have children and take care of the household. Men are expected to get married, have children and work full-time to provide a family income (men, their roles and positions are only addressed incidentally in role theory). For women, it holds that their family role would not fit a professional role of employee, for one thing because the professional role is tuned to the situation of many men. Women are expected to give priority to their family role and adjust their professional role accordingly. In 't Veld-Langeveld (1969) was the first, and for a long time the only one, to consider the role conflict that may stem from the combination of motherhood and a paid job, not just with respect to women's individual priorities, but also in matters of an institutional and societal nature. In later studies (Clason 1977; Van Doorne-Huiskes 1979) conducted from a role theory perspective, notions of social psychology have occupied a prominent position. Individual choices and attitudes of women were analysed as central issues against a background of sex socialisation processes and the care of children.

After 1980, the role theory, criticised for different theoretical reasons, was hardly used anymore. Firstly, it was criticised because of its focus on individuals, leaving no room for power relations and the division of labour between the sexes, and secondly, because it suggests a free exchange of roles that does not mirror reality (Outshoorn 1978; Bekker 1983). Finally, the role concept was criticised because it departs from sex differences, overlooking both similarities between the sexes and differences among women and among men. Changes in society also contributed to a more differentiated picture of traditionally uniform roles. The central idea of the relatively fixed differences between men and women appeared in a new shape in the double-life-perspective approach (Sanders 1991).

A more complex theory, bringing in external factors to explain sex differences in the labour market, is the rational choice theory. This has been the primary approach in recent years and is still receiving a lot of scholarly interest. The theory tries to overcome the tension between determinism and voluntarism by linking the influence of social structure on human action to an approach where free will and individual choices regulate action. The rational choice theory considers human behaviour and explains that behaviour is the culmination of the strive to realise goals and preferences to their maximum. Individual choices are subjective, but are made under structural restrictions, such as the normative context. The goals people strive for are considered to be universal: everyone aims at the maximum realisation of physical well-being and social appreciation (Lindenberg 1991; Siegers 1991). Differences in behaviour and positions are explained by the differences in the restrictions that hinder the realisation of these goals.

Sanders (1996) used this theoretical framework to account for the unequal labour market positions of men and women. She examined the choices (young) men and women make regarding their education, school subjects, labour market participation and the combination of paid work and care, considering the circumstances under which choices are made. Sex specific socialisation and the normative baggage of individuals are analysed as the restrictions that influence the choices and labour market behaviour of women and men. Sanders attributed women's unequal position in the labour market to a 'trap': in every choice along the way, girls and women seem to reduce their chances of professional careers in those sectors of the labour market that provide the best opportunities.

Both the rational choice theory and Sanders' use of it to explain sex differences in the labour market have been critiqued from different perspectives. First, the alleged rationality of choices is questioned (Turkenburg 1995). Are rational choices possible? People often have to choose in uncertainty; they have to deal with dissimilar options that are hardly comparable. Either they are not fully informed, or other principles prevail (social norms for instance) over rationality. Fischer (1996), therefore, considered the rationality of choices not to be a useful discriminating basis for predicting the labour market behaviour of men and women. She stated that, according to psychological decision-making theory, it is questionable whether people are capable of making rational, well-considered choices. Furthermore, the rationality of a choice can only be decided within a certain context. Even though girls are told in government and school campaigns to choose 'exact' school subjects, it remains to be seen whether 'fun' school subjects do not imply a rational choice either. Is it rational to keep options open for choosing future education, when someone already knows that she is not interested in those options? Also, the fastest growing sector in the labour market, the one likely to provide the best job opportunities, is the service sector. It may not be the most 'exact' sector, but the one for which, in mass, women are pre-eminently choosing. Secondly, the concept of 'choice' is also problematic. Turkenburg (1996) expressed doubts about the freedom of choice. She claimed that subjective choices are restricted by the influence of the social context and hegemonic power processes and power relations. Finally, the assumption from the rational choice theory that every human strives for physical well-being and social appreciation is questioned. The crucial issues for Fischer (1996) were not the strife for social appreciation, but rather how people think to gain that appreciation and how that influences their decisions. She argued that there is more to the choice of school subjects, an education or a job than the strife for social appreciation. She pointed at a complex range of factors: the identities and expectations of boys and girls, the sex-specific expectations and behaviours in their surroundings and the context in which those decisions have to be made. These criticisms have also been largely developed in the main stream of rational choice theory (Siegers 1991).

Current questions of gender are being influenced more and more by questions of care. The growing labour market participation of women implies that the traditional division of labour into 'bread-winning' and 'care-taking' is loosing influence. For an important part, the welfare state supports this arrangement of care, viewing the breadwinner as a vital function. Now that the big reservoir of cheap female care is decreasing, societal frictions emerge that also effect the organisation of paid work. An increasing number of employees mention their responsibilities for the care of their children, and also more often for their elderly parents. This means that the ideal worker, available for work 40 hours a week, 46 weeks a year for 40 years, is becoming an ever more problematic starting point for the organisation of paid work. Many studies have been conducted on how this ideal worker is used as the norm for wage setting, taxes, pensions and social security (De Bruijn 1991a; Bussemaker and Van Kersbergen 1993; Plantenga 1993). Their implications are that solutions cannot only be found in new government actions, but also in new care arrangements provided by social partners, and, in particular, employers. Then it may be that the acknowledgment of diversity in personnel with regard to paid work and care does not only affect organisations negatively. Organisational contributions to care arrangements also serve the quality of the company, in that human resources management means that human potential is used to the full, extending flexibility and mobility and increasing the involvement and autonomy of employees (Van Doorne-Huiskes 1990). Within this new image, the new worker, male or female, can avoid the potential danger of male or female stigmatisation.

We can conclude that this line of research, in which sex is the primary category, mainly questions the positions and choices of women. Men and their choices often only serve as a contrast: that these choices may constitute restrictions for their female partners often goes unnoticed. The accentuation and problematising of positions and behaviour of women has a number of negative consequences: it activates and stresses sex differences, and therefore is not sensitive enough to similarities or variation. The two following research lines are trying to overcome these drawbacks by using different theoretical perspectives and a different conceptualisation of gender.

5.3. (Re)production of gender in organisational structure and culture

In the following line of research, the layered concept of gender is the primary theoretical framework, although the concept of sex is still used. Sex is used descriptively to point at men and women in organisations, whereas gender is used to analyse constructions of masculinity and femininity. This is one of the most recent lines of Dutch research about the gendered character of work and organisation: the first studies stem from the late eighties. The central issues are the meaning of gender in work and organisation processes and the way certain meanings of masculinity and femininity are related to power inequalities in organisations. The analyses focus on the normative meanings that are attached to gender differences in organisations. Researchers try to get a grip on the complex relationship between processes concerning individual male and female employees and their interactions and processes concerning the structure and culture of organisations.

Several aspects of the organisation have been studied to try and gain an implicit or explicit understanding of the (re)production of gender distinction. It is not so much individual choice that serves as explanation, but the appraisal of femininity and masculinity in the allocation of jobs and in the representation of men and women and the power processes underlying them. The relation of gender and work is considered to be a dual one: gender is an important element in the organisation and division of work, and, at the same time, work is an important element in the construction of gender relations and identities (De Bruijn 1991a). Deconstruction analytical techniques serve to gain a better understanding of this duality of work and gender.

An example of a study regarding the structure of organisations, is Van Oost's (1994) examination of gender processes in the construction of new computer jobs. She found that the formation of jobs depends on how management defines the jobs and the people who fulfil them. Implicit and explicit rules about the meanings of masculinity and femininity are interwoven in the definitions. Jobs have a gender typing: they are often implicitly associated with masculinity or femininity. Jobs such as computer programmer, that acquire a masculine connotation, are characterised by higher wages and better career opportunities than jobs such as a punch-typist, that get a feminine definition, and where high turnover is desirable. Van Oost argued that the gendered definition of jobs is part of hegemonic power regulation, and takes shape through the consent and identification of employees with the given definitions. By depicting hegemonic gender regulation as a process of regulation, consent and identification, women (and men) appear as competent, informed individuals, restricted in their range of action by structural characteristics (Brouns 1993: 137).

Next to the examination of the organisation's structure, the images and representations of masculinity and femininity in organisation culture are getting more attention. Veldman and Wittink (1990) examined the effects of organisation culture on the careers of women and men. They compared the organisation cultures of a multinational and a government organisation, demonstrating that the less coercive culture of the government provides better chances for women. When organisation cultures contain norms about ideal workers, this may pressure employees to arrange things at home the 'proper' way. The careers of women with children may be hindered by these norms, which are organisational translations of societal norms and values. Meanings of masculinity and femininity underlie the problematic connotation of motherhood and the association of masculinity with authority. These meanings are classified hierarchically in the context of organisations: meanings associated with men and masculinity are valued higher. The dominant ideology of equality between men and women, however, lead many organisation members to interpret distinctions between men and women not as having something to do with gendering processes, but rather as being related to mediating factors such as skill, qualifications, care and part-time work. The gender neutral portrayal of such mediating factors veils their gendering effects and depicts them as normal social practice, inherent to organisational routines (Benschop 1996).

Compared to the first two research lines, the research object is shifting here from clear manifestations of gender inequality to the cultural processes producing and reproducing representations of masculinity and femininity. This change of focus corresponds to recent developments in organisation theory, in which cultural processes and processes of meaning formation in organisations are also studied more extensively. The social-constructivist, post-structural and post-modern theoretical frameworks, that facilitate the deconstruction of gendering processes instead of seeking causal explanations for gender inequality, are gaining influence both in organisation studies and in feminist organisation studies. However, power is not only subtle or delicate, it operates along the lines of possession, economic position and division of capital. When it comes to questions of gender, this concrete, visible and quantifiable manifestation of power cannot be ignored (Brouns

1993). The material dimension of the power relations between the sexes is still important, but this is not reflected in the theoretical developments of this third research line.

The last research line we discuss examines the assumptions and effects of gender that are concealed in definitions and assessments of work.

5.4. Definition, organisation and evaluation of work

The representations and meanings of gender in definitions, organisation and assessment of work have recently introduced new research topics. This line of research challenges our prior understanding of what constitutes 'work' and 'organisation' (Calás and Smircich 1996), and focuses on how knowledge about gender, work and organisation is socially constructed.

One terrain in the Netherlands, where such questions have been asked, is job evaluation. In systems of job evaluation, the value of work and of qualifications are explicated: qualitative requirements are translated quantitatively to produce the wage structure (De Bruijn 1991b). This makes job evaluation systems useful, not only for the investigation of the material meaning-formation of work in terms of salary, but also to question possible gender constructions that might be inscribed in those meanings of work (Bajema 1988; Halsema 1996; Brouns et al. 1996). In that respect, more detailed insights into qualifications and the way they are categorised as a dichotomy (hard/soft, schooled/unschooled, brain work/manual work, etc.) can be of help. The categories are often in hierarchical order, and higher qualifications and skills interwoven with classical definitions of men's work, whereas lower qualifications and skills are connected to definitions of women's work (Bervoets and Frielink 1988; Van der Geest, 1993).

Another terrain for questions about definitions of organisations and gender in organisations, is the field of the design and structuring of organisations and jobs. In that field, the conditions for a gendered division of labour and the chances that it will emerge in the architecture of production concepts have been examined (Benschop 1996). A comparison of Tayloristic and socio-technical organisation structures showed that the first type is characterised by a complex structure, simple tasks and a strong division of labour, whereas the second type pre-eminently has a simple structure and strives for a minimum division of labour by creating complex tasks. The Tayloristic emphasis on hierarchical relations and segmentation and the socio-technical emphasis on cooperation, team-based work and integration bring about differences in the structure and culture of organisations. However, both structures (re)produce gender distinctions and it is six of one and half a dozen of the other in what way work is organised. The process may run different tracks, and the manifestations of gender may differ—in Taylorism masculinity is associated with authority and in socio-technical theory with expertise—but the result is still that gender distinctions are being repeatedly made (Benschop and Doorewaard 1996). The importance of taking these gender processes explicitly into account is that by doing so better use can be made of the chances new production concepts may offer women (Vaas 1996).

A third terrain where definitions of gender and work are interwoven is in the construction of identity and subjectivity. Here, we find research on the gender identities of women and men in relation to their professional identities. De Bruijn (1991a) spoke of a tension between gender identity and professional identity; a tension that is particularly visible when men do women's jobs and women do men's jobs. While men tend to make the female profession more masculine, women do not change the content of the job, but may connect it to a specific feminine identity. Aalten (1991) illustrated this for female business women, who compare their profession to being a mother.

This fourth line of research contains questions about the simultaneous construction of gender and work. The studies refer to the level of underlying gendering processes, but research into the meaning of these processes for organisations is still in it's infancy. Often, they are both hard to recognise and to analyse, because they are a self-evident part of daily practice and inherent to organisational routines. Although the attention for differentiation between women and men increases, we still encounter classical, dichotomous categories and meanings of masculinity and femininity in this research line. That traditional and hierarchical sex differences still rule the social practices of organisations, seems to give way to few alternative interpretations of gender distinctions. The relative meaning of gender in a specific context and the interference of gender with other categories of identity, such as race, ethnicity, age and socio-economical background, have not yet been studied much in Dutch organisation studies.

Here we end our short review of the research lines in the Netherlands. We can now try to identify major trends in the research of gender, work and organisations and the challenges that lie ahead.

6. TRENDS AND CHALLENGES

The different lines of research all highlight particular organisational issues pertaining to gender relations. In summary, in the first line, authors identify many empirical manifestations of sex inequalities in the labour market and in the allocation processes constituting the internal and external labour market. In the second line, these inequalities are explained by addressing individual choices of women (and men). In the third line, authors deconstruct organisation processes and the way they (re)produce gender via coherent arrangements of organisation structure, culture, interaction and identity. Finally, in the fourth research line, processes of meaning formation of masculinity and femininity in the very definitions and assessments of 'work' and 'organisation' itself are questioned. Such questioning adds to the other research lines, but does not render the questions asked from other perspectives obsolete. The representation and construction of gender in organisations are relatively new research objects that are studied from theoretical and epistemological perspectives, other than the empirical manifestations of social inequality that have been dominating the research agenda in the Netherlands. Yet, over time, studies monitoring the development of social inequalities in general, and gender discrimination in particular, continue to give important stimuli to the study of gender, work and organisation.

This variation in epistemology, theoretical perspectives, scope and research topics gives a broad overview of the relevant factors and helps to build up a more complete picture of the field of gender in work and organisation. Furthermore, the discrepancies between the different theoretical frameworks used result in strong debates in feminist organisation studies and opens up discussions with other disciplines studying organisations as well, rendering this a lively and dynamic field of study and practice.

The layered reality of gender in organisations can be described in 1998 as follows. Discrimination of women is 'not done', affirmative action is 'outdated' and the idea that women are principally equal to men is accepted in many organisations, and women are treated accordingly. For organisation members, equality serves as an agreeable interpretation of the relations between the sexes, covering unappealing accounts of (power) inequalities (Benschop 1996). However, this interpretation does not hold in practice: women are still discriminated against on the basis of their sex—be it less than some years before. The layered gender concept shows how the alleged equality is an equality on masculine terms. The deconstruction of representations of 'the worker' and 'the organisation' suggests that the norm is associated with attitudes, behaviours and feelings of classic masculinity, that are dominated by rationality and control. Not only women, but also many men are ambivalent to those norms.

With the years, we see a growing attention to differentiation within the categories of women and men. The call for pluriformity is indeed a leading thread in current thinking about gender and organisations. While sex differences are persistent and relatively stable (the wage gap, for instance, continues to be some 20 per cent), analysing the pluriformity of gender is, in our view, a major challenge. A more differentiated conceptualisation of gender, where masculinity and femininity are not thought of as oppositions but as conditional, may shed a new light on work and organisation. Developing new concepts such as 'the new employee' may help to avoid the endless reproduction of the concepts 'masculinity' and 'femininity', with or without the adjectives 'traditional' or 'classical'.

Some new questions are already emerging in this respect. Recent international studies of gender in organisations (especially in Great-Britain and the United States) examine the relations of men, management and masculinities (for an overview see Collinson and Hearn 1996). They highlight the relation between power and gender; studying the masculine image of management and managers and the self-evident association with power and authority. This also allows differences between men and masculinities to come to the fore. To pay attention to multiple masculinities and to the power positions of men as managers and as men, can be an answer to the call for pluriformity in the Dutch context too, where little research has yet been done. We think that interesting questions can be posed about new definitions of organisational masculinity: Will those new definitions reflect demands from young and highly educated employees who want to combine work and care or, instead, will they reflect the requirements of a 24-hour economy, emphasising the need for employees' flexibility, both in working-time and in geographical mobility?

Remarkably, in the field of gender and work there is only a very weak connection to the work of Geert Hofstede (1980) and his model of femininity and masculinity in work-related value structures in different countries. One of the reasons is the difference in approaching femininity and masculinity: the mission of gender studies is to unravel the constructions of femininity and masculinity, whereas Hofstedes departs from stereotypical images of male and female and uses them as un-problematic instruments for interpreting reality. In fact, he reproduces the traditional images, instead of investigating them. Nevertheless, the model can be very helpful in developing new research projects, especially about the relationship between the gendering of a culture and the presence of women in the higher ranks of organisations. According to Hofstede, the Netherlands is one of the most feminine cultures (Hofstede 1996). From this we would expect women to have a substantial share of management jobs. However, Dutch women score on the same level as Japanese women who, again according to Hofstede, are living in a strong masculine culture. How can we explain these phenomena, and how can we relate the gendered organisation processes to the surrounding social-cultural context? Seen from this perspective, integrating gender studies in organisation studies should prove to be very fruitful for both fields of research.

A more differentiated approach to gender also appears in the predominantly American research on the influence of diversity on social relations in organisations (Cox 1993; Kossek and Lobel 1996; Nkomo and Cox 1996; Prasad et al. 1997). This relatively new domain treats the analysis of identity and subjectivity as organisational issues. Diversity focuses attention on the different identities of individuals: people are not just Americans, Europeans, or Africans, but man, woman, manager, worker, old or young, etc. Gender is one identity category, but not the only one, and is not always the most important. Studying the complex interactions between diverse identities helps to gain a better insight into the dynamic (re)production of social inequalities in organisations.

Finally, we expect that social-constructivist or post-modern theories of work and subjectivity, that have so far received relatively little attention in the Dutch context, will also contribute to the research agenda. Social-constructivist perspectives of gender in organisations render organisations and organisation theories themselves central issues of research. Organisations can be considered complex constructs, with dominant texts and discourses, but also with underlying racial, ethnic and gender sub-texts (Smith 1990). In analyses of organisation cultures (Gherardi 1995) and organisation theory (Wilson 1996), it is the processes producing and reproducing gender relations that are the focus of attention. They examine how gender is 'practised' on a daily basis, by questioning how people experience and construct reality, how meaning is formed and how certain meanings are privileged and others marginalised. How to 'practise' masculinity and femininity differently, and more diversely, is explicitly part of the constructivist strategy. Providing more local, fine grained analyses and situated constructions (Bordo 1994) of gender and work is a major challenge for the Dutch field of organisation studies.

REFERENCES

Aalten, A., 1991. *Zakenvrouwen. Over de grenzen van vrouwelijkheid in Nederland sinds 1945* (Businesswomen. On the boundaries of femininity in the Netherlands since 1945), Amsterdam, Sara/Van Gennep.

Acker, J., 1992. 'Gendering organisational theory', in: A.J. Mills and P. Tancred (eds.), *Gendering organisational analysis* Newbury Park, Sage, pp. 248-260.

Bajema, C., 1988. *De onvolledigheid van functiebeschrijvingen van vrouwenfuncties* (The incompleteness of job descriptions of women's jobs), Projectgroep Vrouwenarbeid, Groningen, RUG.

Bekker, M., 1983. 'Socialisatie' (Socialisation), in: S. Poldervaart (ed.), *Vrouwenstudies: een inleiding* (Women's studies: an introduction), Nijmegen, SUN.

Benschop, Y., 1996. *De mantel der gelijkheid. Gender in organisaties* (Covered by equality. Gender in organisations). Assen, Van Gorcum.

Benschop, Y. and H. Doorewaard, 1996. 'Lood om oud ijzer. De gendersubtekst van Tayloristische en sociotechnische organisaties' (Six of one and half a dozen of the other. The gender sub-text of Tayloristic and sociotechnical organisations) *Tijdschrift voor Arbeidsvraagstukken* 12: 238-250.

Bervoets, L. T. and Frielink, 1988. 'Over kwalificatieverschillen tussen mannen en vrouwen' (On differences in qualifications between men and women) *Te Elfder Ure* 41: 145-159.

Bordo, S., 1994. 'Feminism, postmodernism and gender skepticism', in: A. Hermann and A.J. Stewart (eds.), *Theorising feminism: parallel trends in the humanities and social sciences*, Boulder, Westview Press, pp. 458-481.

Braidotti, R., 1993. 'Women's studies at the University of Utrecht, an editorial introduction', *Women's Studies International Forum* 16: 311-324.

Brouns, M. and A. Schokker, 1990. *Arbeidsvraagstukken en sekse* (Questions about work and sex), STEO-trendrapport 2, Den Haag, STEO.

Brouns, M. 1993. *De homo economicus als winkeldochter. Theorieën over arbeid, macht en sekse* (The 'homo economicus' remaining in store. Theories about work, power and sex), Amsterdam, SUA.

Brouns, M., L. Halsema and J. De Bruijn (eds.), 1996. *Waardering van werk. Opstellen over functiewaardering* (Valuation of work. Essays about job evaluation), Amsterdam, VU Uitgeverij.

Bruijn, J. de, 1991a. *Omstreden kwaliteit: omtrent vrouwenarbeid en beleid* (Disputed quality: about women's work and policy), Oratie. Amsterdam, Vrije Universiteit.

Bruijn, J. de, 1991b. 'Functiewaardering en de beloning van vrouwenwerk' (Job evaluation and the compensation of women's work), *Tijdschrift voor vrouwenstudies* 45: 19-31.

Burg, B.I. van der, 1992. *Loopbaanverschillen tussen mannen en vrouwen binnen arbeidsorganisaties* (Career differences between men and women in work organisations), Groningen, Wolters-Noordhoff.

Bussemaker, J. and K. van Kersbergen, 1993. 'Gender and welfare states: some theoretical reflections', in: D. Sainsbury *Gendering welfare states* London, Sage, pp. 8-25.

Calás, M.B. L. and Smircich, 1996. 'From "The Woman's" point of view: feminist approaches to organisation studies', in: S. Clegg, C. Hardy and W. Nord (eds.), *Handbook of organisation studies* London, Sage, 218-257.

Clason, C., 1977. *Beroepsarbeid door gehuwde vrouwen: de betekenis van het verrichten van beroepsarbeid door gehuwde vrouwen in de rolverdeling tussen man en vrouw* (Professional work by married women: the meaning of doing professional work by married women in the division of roles between man and woman), Groningen, Rijksuniversiteit Groningen.

Collinson, D.L. and J. Hearn, 1996. *Men as managers, managers as men. Critical perspectives on men, masculinities and managements*, London, Sage.

Cox, T., 1993. *Cultural diversity in organisations. Theory, research and practice*, San Francisco, Berrett Koehler.

De Harde Kern, 1996. *Wel feministisch, niet geëmancipeerd: feminisme als nieuwe uitdaging* (Feminist, not emancipated: feminism as a new challenge) Amsterdam, Contact.

Demenint, M.I. and C.E. Disselen, (eds.), 1992. *Vrouwen, leiderschap en management (Women, leadership and management*) Utrecht, Lemma.

Doorne-Huiskes, A. van, 1979. *Vrouwen en beroepsparticipatie. Een onderzoek onder gehuwde vrouwelijke academici* (Women and professional participation. A study among married female academics), Utrecht, Rijksuniverseit Utrecht.

Doorne-Huiskes, A. van and R. Luijkx, 1987. 'Beloningsverschillen tussen mannen en vrouwen in een universitaire organisatie' (Pay differences between men and women in an academic organisation), *Mens en Maatschappij* 62.

Doorne-Huiskes, A. van, 1990. *Positieve actie en culturele transformaties: over de lotgevallen van vrouwen in arbeidsorganisaties* (Affirmative action and cultural transformations: on the experiences of women in work organisations), Wageningen, Landbouwuniversiteit.

Fischer, A.H., 1996. 'Hoe rationeel zijn sekse-stereotiepe keuzes? Een reactie op Karin Sanders': "De rational-choice-benadering voor het verklaren van sekseverschillen op de arbeidsmarkt"' (How rational are sex stereotypical choices? A reaction to Karin Sanders': 'The rational-choice approach to explain sex differences in the labour market'), *Tijdschrift voor Vrouwenstudies* 67: 296-304.

Geest, L. van der, 1993. *Hele taakgroepen en seksesegregatie* (Team based work and sex segregation), Minisymposium Nieuwe Productieconcepten, nieuwe kansen voor vrouwen? (Seminar New production concepts, new chances for women?) Amsterdam, 30-9-1993.

Gherardi, S., 1995. *Gender, symbolism and organisational culture*, London, Sage.
Hagemann-White, C., 1989. 'Geslacht en gedrag' (Gender and behaviour), in: S. Sevenhuijsen (ed.), *Socialisties-Feministiese Teksten*, Baarn, Ambo. pp. 33-48.
Halsema, L., 1996. *'Wij zijn wijkagenten, geen wijkzusters'. Functiewaardering bij de politie* ('We are policemen, not care takers'. Job evaluation in the police force). Paper presented at the SISWO-conference 'Van de hoed en de rand'.
Harding, S., 1986. *The science question in feminism*, Ithaca and London, Cornell University Press.
Hofstede, G., 1980. *Cultures's consequences: International differences in work-related values*, Beverly Hills, CA, Sage.
Hofstede, G., 1996. 'De Nederlandse samenleving is extreem feminien' (The Dutch society is extremely feminine), *Elsevier* 38.
Hooghiemstra, B.T.J. and M. Niphuis-Nell, 1993. *Sociale atlas van de vrouw, Deel 2* (Social map of the woman), Rijswijk, Sociaal Cultureel Planbureau.
Hooghiemstra, E., 1995. 'De arbeidsmarktpositie van allochtone vrouwen in Nederland' (The labour market position of minority women in the Netherlands), *Tijdschrift voor Arbeidsvraagstukken* 11: 129-142.
Jong, A. de, 1985. *De positie van vrouwen bij een grote bank, onderzoek naar de achtergronden van het verschil in positie tussen mannen en vrouwen* (The position of women in a big bank: studying the backgrounds of the differences in position between men and women), Rotterdam, Erasmus Universiteit.
Jong, A. de and A. van Doorne-Huiskes, 1989. *Stijl van leidinggeven van vrouwen en mannen* (Leadership styles of women and men) Den Haag, Ministerie van Sociale Zaken en Werkgelegenheid.
Jorna, A. and E. Offers, 1994. *Jonge vrouwen werken aan hun toekomst* (Young women working on their future), Amsterdam, SUA.
Kanter, R.M., 1977. *Men and women of the corporation*, New York, Basic Books.
Kool-Smit, J., 1967. 'Het onbehagen bij de vrouw' (The concern of the woman), *De Gids* 130: 9-10.
Kossek, E.E. and S.A. Lobel (eds.), 1996. *Managing Diversity, Human Resource Strategies for transforming the workplace* Cambridge, Blackwell.
Leijenaar, M., 1996. 'Deelname van vrouwen aan politieke besluitvorming. Een onderzoek naar strategieën in Europa' (Participation of women in political decision making. A study about strategies in Europe), *Tijdschrift voor Vrouwenstudies* 17(2): 144-159.
Lindenberg, S., 1991. 'Social approval, fertility and female labour market behaviour', in: J. Siegers, J. de Jong-Gierveld and E. van Imhoff (eds.), *Female labour market behaviour and fertility: a rational-choice approach*, Berlin, Springer, pp. 32-58.
Martin, J. and P. Frost, 1996. 'The organisational culture war games: a struggle for intellectual dominance', in: S. Clegg, C. Hardy and W.R. Nord (eds.), *Handbook of Organisation Studies*, London, Sage, pp. 599-622.
Nkomo, S.M. and T. Cox, 1996. 'Diverse identities in organisations', in: S. Clegg, C. Hardy and W.R. Nord (eds.), *Handbook of Organisation Studies*, London, Sage, pp. 338-356.

Oakley, A., 1972. *Sex, gender and society*. London, Temple Smith.

OECD, 1991. *Shaping cultural change. The role of women*, Paris, OECD.

Oost, E. van, 1994. *Nieuwe functies, nieuwe verschillen, Genderprocessen in de constructie van de nieuwe automatiseringsfuncties 1955-1970* (New jobs, new differences. Gender processes in the construction of new automation jobs 1955-1970), Delft, Eburon.

Ott, M., 1985. *Assepoesters en kroonprinsen: een onderzoek naar de minderheidspositie van agentes en verplegers* (Cinderella's and crown princes : a study to the minority position of female police officers and male nurses), Amsterdam, SUA.

Outshoorn, J., 1978. 'Zo vader, zo zoon en van moeder op dochter' (Like father, like son and from mother to daughter), in: *Socialisties-Feministiese teksten 1*, Amsterdam, Sara. pp. 67-96.

Pessers, D., 1994. *De weg van het hart* (The way of the heart), Laren, Balans.

Plantenga, J., 1993. *Een afwijkend patroon, honderd jaar vrouwenarbeid in Nederland en (West) Duitsland* (A different pattern: hundred years of women's work in the Netherlands and (West) Germany), Amsterdam, SUA.

Pott-Buter, H., 1993. *Facts and fairytales about female labour, family and fertility*, Amsterdam, Amsterdam University Press.

Prasad, P., A. Mills, M. Elmes and A. Prasad (eds.), 1997. *Managing the organisational melting pot, dilemmas of workplace diversity*, London, Sage.

Rojahn, K., 1996. *Gender in the context of leadership*, Amsterdam, University of Amsterdam.

Sanders, K., 1991. *Vrouwelijke pioniers. Vrouwen en mannen met een 'mannelijke hogere beroepsopleiding aan het begin van hun loopbaan* (Female pioneers. Women and men with a 'male' higher professional education at the start of their careers), Groningen, Thesis.

Sanders, K., 1996. 'The rational-choice-benadering voor het verklaren van sekseverschillen op de arbeidsmarkt: de operationalisering van de normatieve context' (The rational-choice approach for the explanation of sex differences in the labour market: the operationalisation of the normative context), *Tijdschrift voor Vrouwenstudies* 67: 286-295.

Schwarzer, A., 1976. *Der Kleine Unterschied und seine grossen Folgen: Frauen über sich, Beginn einer Befreiung* (The small difference with the big consequences), Frankfurt am Main, Fischer.

Scott, J., 1986. 'Gender: a useful category of historical analysis', *American Historical Review* 1053-1075.

Siegers, J.J., 1991. *Interdisciplinaire economie* (Interdisciplinary economics), Groningen, Wolters-Noordhoff.

Smith, D.E., 1990. *The conceptual practices of power, a feminist sociology of knowledge*, Boston, Northeastern University Press.

Tijdens, K., 1989. *Automatisering en vrouwenarbeid* (Automation and women's work), Utrecht/Amsterdam, Jan van Arkel/Stichting Informaticacongressen.

Turkenburg, M., 1995. *Een baan & een kind; aspiraties en strategieën van laag opgeleide vrouwen* (A job & a child; aspirations and strategies of lower educated women), Tilburg, Tilburg University Press.

Turkenburg, M., 1996. 'Flirten met een spierballentheorie. Reactie op Karin Sanders': "Zin en onzin van de rational-choice-benadering; de operationalisering van de normatieve context". (Flirting with a muscular theory. A reaction to Karin Sanders': 'Sense and nonsense of a rational-choice approach: the operationalisation of the normative context'), *Tijdschrift voor Vrouwenstudies* 67: 305-313.

Vaas, F., 1996. *Vrouwen in technische beroepen* (Women in technical professions), Delft, Eburon.

Veld-Langeveld, H., in 't, 1969. *Vrouw-beroep-maatschappij* (Woman-profession-society), Utrecht, Bijleveld.

Veldman, A. and R. Wittink, 1990. *De kans van slagen, de invloed van culturen en regels op de loopbanen van vrouwen* (The chance to succeed: the influence of cultures and rules on the careers of women), Leiden/Antwerpen, Stenfert Kroese.

Wilson, F., 1996. 'Research note: organisational theory: blind and deaf to gender?'. *Organisation Studies* 17: 825-842.

Women in Decision-making, 1993. European network of experts 'Women in decision-making', Brussels, European Council.

AUTHORS

Dr. Y. Benschop
University of Nijmegen
P.O. Box 9108, 6500 HK Nijmegen
tel: +3124 3613007, fax: 3611933
e-mail: Y.Benschop@bw.kun.nl

Dr. M. Brouns
Groningen University, UCG
Grote Rozenstraat 38, 9712 TJ Groningen
tel: 050-3636244, fax: 050-3637165
e-mail: m.l.m.brouns@ppsw.rug.nl or: debleek@bart.nl

Prof.dr. J. de Bruijn
Free University of Amsterdam
De Boelelaan 1081 c, 1081 HV Amsterdam
tel: 020-4446846 (6805), fax: 020-4446820
e-mail: jgm.d_bruijn@scw.vu.nl

SUBJECT INDEX

S

T

U

V

W

MIX
Papier aus verantwortungsvollen Quellen
Paper from responsible sources
FSC® C105338

If you have any concerns about our products,
you can contact us on
ProductSafety@springernature.com

In case Publisher is established outside the EU,
the EU authorized representative is:
Springer Nature Customer Service Center GmbH
Europaplatz 3, 69115 Heidelberg, Germany

Printed by Libri Plureos GmbH
in Hamburg, Germany